SELF-EMPLOYMENT FOR LOW-INCOME PEOPLE

SELF-EMPLOYMENT
FOR LOW-INCOME PEOPLE

Steven Balkin

FOREWORD BY *Robert E. Friedman*

PRAEGER

New York
Westport, Connecticut
London

Library of Congress Cataloging-in-Publication Data

Balkin, Steven.
  Self-employment for low-income people.

  Bibliography: p.
1. Self-employed. 2. Self-employed—Europe.
3. Self-employed—Developing countries. 4. Self-
employed—United States. I. Title.
HD8036.B35   1989   331.25   88–35735
ISBN 0–275–92807–1 (alk. paper)

Library of Congress Catalog Card Number: 88–35735
ISBN: 0–275–92807–1

First published in 1989

Praeger Publishers, One Madison Avenue, New York, NY 10010
A division of Greenwood Press, Inc.

Printed in the United States of America

∞™

The paper used in this book complies with the
Permanent Paper Standard issued by the National
Information Standards Organization (Z39.48–1984).

10 9 8 7 6 5 4 3 2 1

To the Peddlers of Maxwell Street

Contents

Tables and Figures

TABLES

FIGURES

Foreword

I first encountered Steven Balkin in 1980 when he was conducting a preliminary survey of entrepreneurial training programs run under the Comprehensive Employment and Training Act (CETA). Having studied economic development strategies in general, and economic development-training linkages specifically, for some years even then, I was aware of only two that were CETA-sponsored: the Hawaii Entrepreneurship Training and Development Institute (HETADI) and Florida's Be Your Own Boss (BYOB) programs. And the number of people interested in such exotica was only marginally larger. But in his typically methodical and intrepid manner, Balkin proceeded to uncover 30 more, and then extend the search, beyond the ill-fated CETA, throughout the decade. The field of microenterprise development for the disadvantaged and the interest in it exploded during that time.

Now that experimentation with and interest in self-employment has broken the surface of public attention, it invites political and academic scrutiny. It therefore becomes essential for all who would develop self-employment practice and policy to understand what we know and the dimensions of the field. This book provides the essential reference tool.

In *Self-Employment for Low-Income People,* Balkin brings together for the first time anywhere most of what is known about microenterprises for the disadvantaged, tapping an extraordinarily diverse set of databases that are rarely integrated. For the first time we can discern the dimensions of the field as it ranges from economic theory to demographic fact, from Bangladesh to Minneapolis, from immigrant experience to public policy. Here in one place is a wealth of information. And, to Balkin's credit, he gives as much weight to the experience of program practitioners—where the real expertise in this rapidly developing field resides—as to economic theories.

I come away from reading this book impressed by the potential possibilities microenterprise development offers for personal and economic development, and how much practitioner wisdom remains yet to be captured. What is possible simply can't be known from what exists. Take for example the varying rates of self-employment among ethnic groups. We know that as business formation rates increase, so do rates of business success, levels of income, and intergenerational entrepreneurship; what we do not know is whether all groups can be brought up to the business ownership levels of the most successful, or how. Or take program designs and outcomes. Not only are we unable to tell from current program performance what design is best, but adequate data on the impacts of current programs are hardly satisfying.

Or, perhaps most importantly, we know little about the relationship between self-employment and economic growth. This is crucial. We now know that entrepreneurship is a major determinant of long-term economic health and growth of nations; what we do not know is whether self-employment is fairly classified as a form of entrepreneurship that provides the foundation—institutional, behavioral and cultural—for longer-term and larger growth. I do believe this fundamentally is the case, but the fact is it remains to be demonstrated to the satisfaction of more skeptical observers.

Balkin invites scrutiny. Throughout the book, during the discussions of programs or data, he offers his opinions on the implications of the findings. Initially, some reviewers suggested separating the reporting from the analysis. But on reflection, by interspersing his judgments—often controversial—Balkin requires the reader to think for him/herself.

But even as Balkin displays the limits of our understanding of microenterprise development, he suggests the possibilities. He estimates that opening a realistic self-employment option to all Americans might create 400,000 to 7,000,000 jobs at a cost of $3,000 to $10,000 per job—well below the per job cost of most economic development programs, and a fraction of public works program costs. Even if one chooses the most conservative of assumptions, his calculations reveal potential benefits sufficient to justify extensive efforts to promote self-employment. And even if one questions his conclusions that such programs should be targeted for the most severely disadvantaged, his documentation of business success by the poorest of the poor must be taken as proof not only of the untapped potential of the poor, but of the economy as a whole. If we can find ways to ensure that the most disadvantaged have a reasonable chance to bring their skills to the marketplace, we may expand the opportunity for all people to produce and contribute to the growth of the economy.

In the end, *Self-Employment for Low-Income People* not only tells us where we are, but motions us forward.

Robert E. Friedman
The Corporation for Enterprise Development

Preface

This book is essentially a literature review and policy essay that tries to gather diverse literature from various disciplines to provide practical suggestions. I have tried to be a sponge, soaking up information wherever it was and reporting on it keeping jargon to a minimum. I hope I have not misinterpreted the literature from the wide variety of fields covered. There were many avenues I wanted to explore or explore further, but time and space did not permit. There is much work to be done in this relatively unexplored field. I would like to see cross-disciplinary micro-enterprise or self-employment studies programs emerge at universities to encourage the exploration of this fascinating policy-important, but undeveloped field. There is a need for collaboration among academics, entrepreneurs, helping professionals, and low-income people.

This book is directed, in particular, to those who operate self-employment programs, fund self-employment programs, consider policy about self-employment, and look for alternative strategies to alleviate poverty, create jobs, and improve economic development. While I do make policy and program design recommendations, they should be taken as just one view. A main theme of this book is that the literature and views that can be brought to bear on this topic are diverse. There are good ideas and programs out there but no conclusive proof of what model works or works best. So, I hope this book will widen horizons and encourage experimentation. I hope that readers will contact me to suggest overlooked programs, submit rigorous program evaluation results, and provide different points of view.

Acknowledgments

I had many conversations with wise people both supportive and skeptical. I would like to thank the following who contributed comments and criticisms. Larry Babbits, Elizabeth Balanoff, Jeffrey Balkin, Kurt Bauman, Winnifred Brown, Kathleen Burton-Snell, Kathleen Christensen, Allen Cohen, Sari Cohen, Carolyn Eastwood, George Hemmons, David S. Evans, Rona Feit, Robert Friedman, Ed Gross, Gerald Hills, Mary Houghton, John Hughes, Meriwether Jones, George Kaladonis, Coralee Kern, Gary Langer, Dolores Lavelle, Sheila Leahy, Fred Lee, Jing Lyman, Lois Mitchell, Frank Morn, James Moseby, Judy Nye, Frances Oxley, Aldo Palmas, Waino Pihl, Joseph Persky, Fred Raines, Chris Reed, Cilla Reesman, Sam Rosenberg, Sam Sains, Matt Salo, Leon Segal, June Sekera, Art Smith, Jack Sol, Alvin Starr, Howard Stein, Bernard Strubris, Richard Taub, Jean Thorne, Sheldon Wagner, Richard Weisbrot, Wim Wievel, and Bismark Williams. My apologies to those people whose names I missed at this writing.

I also want to thank the following organizations for financial support: The Coleman–Fannie May Candies Foundation, The Joyce Foundation, Roosevelt University, the Office of Social Science Research–University of Illinois at Chicago, and the German Marshall Fund of the United States. I'd like to thank the National Commission on Jobs and Small Business for selecting me to write the report on which this book is based. The views expressed are my own and do not necessarily reflect those of my grantors. I alone bear the full responsibility for any mistakes or mistaken views expressed in this book.

I would, in particular, like to thank John Hughes and Jean Thorne of the Coleman-Fannie May Candies Foundation, who early on encouraged my work, and call attention to their pioneering efforts in entrepreneurship education. Their Chairholder conferences, Campus Entrepreneurial Learning Programs, Entrepreneurial Awareness Programs, along with other efforts have provided entrepreneurial encouragement for all in society.

I most assuredly want to thank my wife Barbara who provided ideas, emotional support, editing assistance, and typing expertise.

I.

Background

Introduction

CRIME AND SELF-EMPLOYMENT

The idea for this book came from conducting evaluation research on ex-offender rehabilitation programs. I was amazed to find that even though these programs put forth sincere efforts at training clients and obtaining job interviews for them, the rate at which actual job placements occurred was very low. The idea then struck me that perhaps self-employment activity might be an appropriate job source for this group. Economic models of participation in criminal activity view the decision to engage in criminal activities in the same framework as one views a businessperson's decision to choose between risky payoff alternatives. Crime is treated essentially as entrepreneurial activity.[1] Therefore, a person who previously engaged in crime might find entrepreneurial activities more suitable than wage employment. This might be especially true if one's wage work opportunities were in the secondary labor market.[2] There is no authoritarian boss; one can set work rules, and there is risk. If one desires to work less than a 40-hour week, come to work drunk, or use inappropriate language, self-employed persons can do these things and not get fired. They may lose customers and hence income, but they can still retain their self-created job. Big mistakes are not necessarily job fatal in self-employment. Presumably, inefficient behavior will lessen over time as self-employed persons feel the immediate economic consequences of their misbehavior. Furthermore, it can be expected that the experience of greater control and independence associated with direct participation in the market will have a humanizing influence. Customer satisfaction may enhance self-esteem.

It is incorrect to think that a self-employed person does not have a boss. The market is the boss. It is very exacting, but it is diffuse. Supervision, via the market, is diffuse. If a self-employed person behaves in a nasty or sloppy way to a customer, the customer may be lost. But he or she won't lose all customers for one or a few incidents of misconduct, and the self-employed person may be able to do something in the future to regain customers. Most of all, self-employment does not depend on being acceptable to a personnel administrator guided by excessive credentialism and irrelevant rule-of-thumb selection criteria. One does not have to conform to the strictures that unnecessarily constrain most wage workers.

If decent wage jobs aren't obtainable, one creates work (or moves) rather than waiting for a General Motors Saturn plant to drop from the sky. One could argue that if this approach makes so much sense, why haven't ex-offenders or other disadvantaged groups already done this to a larger extent. My response is they do participate in self-employment, and some disadvantaged groups participate in self-employment more than the average. Some of it is in officially recorded self-employment but much is in the irregular (unrecorded) sector.[3] Furthermore, there appear to be impediments and disincentives that limit participation in this earning mode. If they were removed, more low-income people would participate in self-employment.

Discussing these ideas with me, a colleague remarked that encouraging savvy ex-offenders to become self-employed might be feasible, but this approach would not likely work for very many of the disadvantaged. That became a central question for this research. Could a policy assisting low-income people to become self-employed make sense and be applicable to a large portion of low-income or even underclass people?[4] The trick would be to devise policies and programs that remove impediments and disincentives for low-income people to engage in self-employment activities. I hope to shed light on the following three questions: (1) Can low income/disadvantaged people create their own jobs through self- employment? (2) Can they be assisted to do it on a large scale? and (3) Should they be encouraged to do it?

TARGET GROUPS

The idea of assisting people to become self-employed is not to be applied generally. I am not advocating it as an economic development or job generation policy in general, but I do think it offers an opportunity that low-income people should be in a position to consider.[5] I use the term "low income" to refer to those at the bottom of the income distribution who have disadvantages besides just low income, such ashaving low levels of education, facing age, sex, or race discrimination, being a single parent, or having physical or social handicaps.[6] There are a good number of low-income people who are poor temporarily because they are just starting their careers or have had a bit of bad luck. Too often, programs are directed at people who officially meet the eligibility criteria of being poor but who would succeed on their own at something. The laid-off Ph.D. waiter is not a target I have in mind for subsidized assistance into self-employment. I am most concerned about those who might be called the hard-core unemployed or the underclass. Of those, the following is a list of at least six low-income sub-groups who I think could use self-employment assistance: (1) those naturally possessing an entrepreneurial bent but not the resources or the polish, (2) those without a job who want to enhance their survival, (3) those unable or unwilling to labor under conventional work rules, (4) those who seek flexibility to better mesh personal life-style with work, (5) those who want to work in a particular industry or occupation that would generate higher earnings in self-employment than in wage employment, and (6) those who have had some self-employment experience and want to expand upon it.

INTEREST IN SELF-EMPLOYMENT

Little is known about how interested low-income people are in pursuing self-employment. My impression is that owning your own business is still part of the American dream for most Americans. For the *Wall Street Journal*, the Roper Organization conducted a national telephone interview survey of adults to determine their views on the "American Dream." One question asked them to evaluate opportunities to get ahead in various types of employment.[7] The highest rating was given to business ownership: 58 percent replied that it was an excellent or good way to get ahead. The response of blacks did not differ from whites. Non–high school graduates and blue-collar workers rated business ownership as a way to get ahead only slightly less than the average (48% and 54% respectively, as opposed to 58%. Though dated, Lipset and Bendix's (1954) study of labor markets found that the desire for business ownership was greater among blue-collar workers than among white-collar workers.[8] Mayer and Goldstein (1961, p. 22) comment on the finding that business ownership is a working-class goal: "It is one of the few positions of higher status attainable to manual workers today whose educational limitations preclude an executive or professional career."

SELF-EMPLOYMENT AND ECONOMIC MOBILITY

I do not want to suggest that the route of self-employment is or should be the preferred route for personal economic advancement. The traditional route of advancement through obtaining higher levels of formal education culminating with a good job in a corporate or government environment seems preferable. It is likely, on the average, to generate higher incomes and be less risky. A good blue-collar job in manufacturing with a strong union is also a worthwhile goal. However, if people cannot make use of more formal education because the formal education system failed them, or if good blue-collar union jobs don't exist in the community anymore, then self-employment activity can be encouraged, at least as a stopgap. It can be a stopgap until better wage jobs appear in the community, or one moves to a community where there are better wage jobs, or the formal education system can better serve low-income people, or life circumstances change (a child grows up or a drug habit is kicked), or human capital is built-up through the self-employment experience such that one can now get that better wage job. Some low level self-employment activities may evolve into substantial business firms. However, self-employment does not have to be a career, it can be a stepping stone to someplace, just as most jobs are.[9] Self-employment can also be a desirable alternative to a stifling wage job that ignores talent or potential.

ASSURING SUCCESS

There are instances when I try to explain these ideas and get a hostile response: "How can you suggest that low skilled, low educated, low income people can succeed in a small business when the failure rate is so high and there are many instances of highly educated, high income people with large amounts of available capital who fail at small business?" Businesses fail, generally, either because of lack of sufficient capital or inadequate management. For low-income, low-skilled people, the types of businesses that they could start would, of necessity, be very small and very simple. They would be labor intensive rather than capital intensive. Capital would not be the big constraint. Sophisticated management skills are required to run a larger or growing business. Knowledge of principles of economics, accounting, finance, marketing, and organization seem essential. But running a very simple one-person, owner-manager business is not going to require such sophistication. Many low-income people, while not possessing good academic skills, do have very good intuitive business reasoning skills, picked up from the streets.[10] To the extent that the low-income target group does not fully possess the requisite skills, reality-based business advice and services can be made available free or at a nominal charge by a yet to be developed institution. A theme of this book is that it is *not* through solely independent efforts that we can expect a large portion of low-income people to start their own businesses and succeed. Linking up with a mentor, a relative, or supportive institutions, can fill the gaps to generate the gambit of components sufficient for a successful small enterprise. I have been to conferences where successful entrepreneurs spoke about how they became so rich. All these speakers like to brag about how they started with nothing and then rose to money and power. When I listen carefully between the phrases, a theme clearly emerges: *Nobody does it on their own.* They might not have started with a million dollars, but they had an influential relative or friend, a good education, and a bit of good luck. Somewhere along the line, someone helped to open doors. Individual effort does count, but it takes more than motivation to become successful in business. That "more" is what much of this book is about.

One of this book's omissions is that I have not specifically covered community-owned or worker-owned cooperative ventures as a means for generating jobs and equity capital for low-income people. I think these enterprises are, for the most part, too sophisticated and complex to implement on a large scale as start-up businesses for poverty clients. This seems a good alternative for persons with close ties to the labor market, in particular for workers facing plant closings. This approach may prove more widely implementable in the future for underclass people. I leave it to other researchers to show that. In my quest for simplicity, I emphasize individualistic business ownership. However, I do support the notion that business success often comes from cooperation combined with competition.[11]

A major reason for business discontinuances is that while a business may technically be generating money profits, the profits may be too low. If the money profits are expected to remain low compared to what someone could earn elsewhere with their labor and capital, a switch to that better alternative, holding psychic rewards the same, is likely. Low-income people have low opportunity costs. A business that yields a low amount of money profit may be deemed a failure for a middle-income or rich person. That same business may be considered adequate (and hence successful) to a low-income person. It is adequate if it enhances survival, yields an income greater than other activities, supplements income from other sources, meshes better with one's life-style than other activities, or acts as a temporary source of income until something better comes along. Low-income people are, perhaps, more likely to succeed at a small enterprise because their criteria for success are likely to be more modest.

SUPPORTIVE MACROECONOMIC AND INDUSTRIAL POLICIES

In addition to supportive institutions and removal of innocuous but inhibiting regulations, supportive macroeconomic policy is required to create a demand environment where these very small businesses (sometimes called "micro-enterprises") are more likely to survive. It is important to consider, though, that a strong expansionary macroeconomic policy may be enough by itself to provide jobs and increased incomes for low-income people, perhaps even better jobs than can be achieved through micro-enterprise development policy and programs. However, until that golden era of macroeconomic policy arrives, especially in this era of high government deficits, a micro-enterprise development approach can be considered useful, especially for the urban underclass, and structurally unemployed.

Industrial policy concerns favoring certain industries which have the potential for growth and the provision of good jobs. If industrial policy can bring stable low skill–high pay wage jobs back, that is preferable to favoring self-employment. But one could do both. Certain types of self-employment may pay better than those good factory jobs, and some structural unemployment problem is still likely to remain that self-employment can address. I am not arguing that self-employment be relied upon solely or mainly to alleviate poverty, only that it be seriously considered as one option in the mix of strategies to improve incomes.

COMING ATTRACTIONS

The first part of this book provides background information. Topics include self-employment theories, empirical analyses of self-employment, and a description of immigrant and ethnic group experiences with self-employment, and a description of black business movements. In thinking about self-employment, it is useful to incorporate elements from the various disciplines that have developed theories of how and why people become business owners. Doing this provides ideas for what a balanced self-employment training program might look like. Looking at the empirical evidence of the characteristics of business owners compared to wage workers helps in the identification of situations conducive to successful self-employment. Ethnic and immigrant experiences with self-employment are described because people often point to them as evidence of the use of self-employment for upward mobility. Some characteristics of those experiences may translate to useful policies and programs. Black or minority self-employment is often used as a proxy for self-employed persons who are poor. The use of self-employment as a way to uplift poor blacks is not a new idea. We may learn something from seeing how it worked in the past.

The second part provides descriptions of self-employment training programs from the Third World, Europe, and the United States. Micro-enterprise development has been frequently implemented around the world. We should be better able to think about encouraging self-employment in the United States after seeing what has been done in other countries. There are self-employment programs currently operating in the United States. A review of what exists now may help us know what is possible in the future.

The third part proposes and discusses policies to encourage self-employment for low-income people. A theme here is that low-income people might be able to pull themselves up by their bootstraps if clutter is removed from the way and they are assisted in obtaining a decent pair of boots. Self-employment training programs are not the only way to augment self-employment activity on the part of low-income people. Various strategies and techniques are considered, including program (re)design. A model for estimating the job creation impact of self-employment programs is presented along with an exhortation about the importance of evaluation.

NOTES

1. The inclusion of criminal activity as a form of entrepreneurship has often been noted by social scientists. For example, see: Casson (1982) and Gould (1969).

2. The concepts of primary and secondary sectors are often used in this book. Referred to as the dual labor market theory, the economy can be segmented into two sectors (Piore 1971; Rosenberg 1981). The primary sector is generally associated with oligopolistic industries. Its traits are jobs with high wages, good working conditions, employment stability, due process in the administration of work rules, and chances for advancement. The secondary sector is associated with industries that are highly competitive. Jobs in this sector tend to have low wages, poor working conditions, instability, harsh and arbitrary discipline, and little opportunity for advancement. There is some (in fact, little) mobility between the sectors. An explanation for poverty is that people acquire bad work habits when confined to the secondary sector.

3. I specifically have in mind here the "extra legal" sector—activities that are the same as those of mainstream businesses but that are partially or totally unrecorded. This is sometimes referred to as the informal sector. This is to be distinguished from the criminal sector of the underground economy.

My impression is that most businesses start from activities that are loosely organized where rule compliance is weak. When firms are able to sustain themselves with stabilized cash flows, they then can afford to become compliant with business regulations. If one defines the "aboveground" economy as firms that are fully compliant with regulations, then I would conclude *most* firms originate in the underground economy.

4. I use the term *underclass* to refer to those at the very bottom of the income distribution. These are low-income people with weak ties to the labor market, many of whom experience welfare dependency and exhibit forms of social pathology such as teenage pregnancy, criminal behavior, and substance abuse. The Urban Institute defined an underclass neighborhood as a census

tract with high concentrations of people in each of the four categories: female-headed households, high school dropouts, families on welfare, and working-age men who do not regularly work. For definitions of the underclass see: Wilson (1987), Bane and Jargowsky (1987), Wilkerson (1987), and Ricketts and Sawhill (1986).

5. I do not want to suggest that self-employment ought to be the central medium for an entire community's, minority's, or women's economic development program. An economic development strategy should be based on a mix of economic activities which heavily emphasizes high-income high-growth occupations.

6. For a poverty alleviation strategy, I do not think programs should have as their first priority those with just a disadvantage (e.g., women or minorities) but not also low income and low skilled. Too often business development programs aimed at minorities or women are used only by middle-class people.

7. The other types were wage employment in large corporations, small business, government, and non-profit organizations.

8. The Roper Organization (1987) found different results: 61 percent of white-collar workers rated business ownership as an excellent or good way to get ahead compared to 54 percent for blue-collar workers.

9. It is hoped that the self-employed will earn above the minimum wage rate and generate above-poverty incomes. They are not, however, expected to generate middle-class incomes immediately. This may just have the effect of helping the welfare poor become the working poor. That, in my opinion, is an improvement. Strategies can then be developed to assist the working poor to become nonpoor. This last task is easier than the first. Taggart (1982) suggests that low hourly earnings and limited hours of employment rather than joblessness are the major causes of economic hardship. Self-employment activity may be able to address those labor market inadequacies.

10. Sowell (1975, p. 236) comments that starting and operating a business is not intellectually complicated but is based upon small bits of information acquired by actual experience, a trial-and-error endeavor. He, therefore, feels that the process of producing business owners is a gradual one and can't be taught in schools. I think he is right, but nonclassroom based self-employment training programs that emulate what real business owners do and build upon actual experience may speed up the process.

11. The forms of cooperation that are most complementary to simple individualistic enterprises are trade associations and producer cooperatives. Producer cooperatives are organized by individuals who produce a similar product and then band together for some common purpose. Usually it is for marketing or purchasing. Worker cooperatives, on the other hand, are businesses owned and managed by workers on the principle of one member, one vote. If worker cooperatives are small, for example, five or less members, that is essentially a form of partnership and seems do-able for people with very modest educational backgrounds. It is when worker cooperatives become large that the organization seems too complex for the target group in mind. These may be made more practical by extensive provision of outside technical assistance.

Mier and Wiewel (1983) are cautiously optimistic about the job generation and career development potential of community-based businesses. They do admit, "involvement in business activities requires community organizations to become increasingly sophisticated." Michaelson (1979) studied 136 profit ventures owned by Community Development Corporations. He concluded that these enterprises may have been a relatively cheap way of creating jobs.

2

Self-Employment Theories

INTRODUCTION

Twentieth century theoretical notions of self-employment include: economic theories of the function of the entrepreneur, economic human capital theory of self-employment, psychological theories of entrepreneurial personality, sociological notions of the importance of social networks in entrepreneurial events, and eclectic social science models of why people start businesses. These various theoretical approaches to self-employment and entrepreneurship are overlapping and can often be viewed as complementary, each providing a piece of understanding. As background, the differences between the self-employed and entrepreneurs follows.

SELF-EMPLOYMENT VERSUS ENTREPRENEURSHIP

According to economic theory, the hallmark of entrepreneurs is that they receive economic profit. This is a return above the wages and interest that they could receive elsewhere. Entrepreneurs are popularly considered bold and imaginative, capturing opportunities missed by others. In contrast, the self-employed merely work directly for the market rather than for an employer. The firm intermediates between labor and consumers: it acts as a go-between. Self-employment is disintermediation: Purchasers of the goods and services buy directly from self-employed persons rather than through firms which hire labor and function as middlemen. People oriented to the self-employment mode of work often do it to provide themselves with a job, not primarily to earn economic profits or to enhance the growth of a firm.[1] A self-employed person need not be an entrepreneur. But being more entrepreneurial, through program efforts or policy supports, may enhance their earnings and viability. While the focus of this book is with self-employment rather than with entrepreneurship, it is useful to consider some of the existing literature on entrepreneurship.

ECONOMIC THEORIES OF THE FUNCTION OF THE ENTREPRENEUR

Economic theory acknowledges the existence of entrepreneurs as the factor of production that receives pure profits for organizing the other factors of production as a firm unit and for bearing risk.[2] The term *entrepreneur* was coined by the French speaking economist R. Cantillon (1755). The literal meaning is "undertaker [of a project]."

However, there is no established single theory to explain the existence and behavior of entrepreneurs.[3] In the twentieth century, some of the principle economists who have commented on the function of the entrepreneur have been Knight (1921), Schumpeter (1934), Kirzner (1973), Leibenstein (1978), Lucas (1978), and Casson (1982).

Knight's (1921) view is that entrepreneurs receive pure profit as the reward for bearing the costs of uncertainty of production and hiring decisions. The most important characteristic of an entrepreneur is self-confidence. When self-confidence is combined with low risk aversion and capital, an effective entrepreneurial decision can take place.

According to Schumpeter (1934), the function of the entrepreneur is to innovate in at least one of five ways: introducing a new good, introducing a new method of production, opening a new market, finding a new source of materials, or creating a new type of business organization. People who perform at least one of these functions are entrepreneurs regardless if they are owners or employees. Motivations for the entrepreneur include the dream to achieve medieval lordship, the will to conquer (as in a sport), and the joy of creating.

Kirzner (1973) considered awareness to disequilibrium as the most important trait of an entrepreneur. The entrepreneur looks for opportunities for profit when wrong prices exist in the market. According to Leibenstein (1978), entrepreneurship is the creative response to organizational inefficiency. This reponse takes two forms: providing factors that improve production methods, and actions that combine resources where good information is lacking.

Lucas (1978) used a notion that individuals have different amounts of "entrepreneurial" ability.[4] Individuals who have the most entrepreneurial ability become entrepreneurs first. People become entrepreneurs until the marginal entrepreneur is equally likely to choose business ownership or wage work. Those with more ability than the marginal entrepreneur operate firms, while those with less become wage workers.

Casson (1982) asserts that the essence of entrepreneurship is being different. Entrepreneurs hope to profit from their difference in perception by coordinating scarce resources in a different way. Further, limited personal wealth is a major constraint, and entrepreneurial strategies are developed to minimize this. Casson developed a list of entrepreneurial success principles which concern information, skills, and strategies. Information about opportunities can be obtained from several sources, which include the family, feedback from past activities, and clubs. Formal education (particularly for those without wealth), negotiating tactics, and organizational skills are important for an entrepreneur to have or acquire.

It is not realistic to expect many low-income people to become entrepreneurs in the full sense of that term as described in this section. The motivation for many low-income people to engage in self-employment is to survive. It is unlikely that they primarily seek pure economic profit, dream of medieval lordship, engage in self-employment as a creative activity, or try to capitalize on being different. Nonetheless, by helping to provide the missing links, it may be possible to assist low-income people to form businesses of their own. Program efforts or policies supplying the missing ingredients, together with the diligent and persistent participation of the low-income candidate, may be able to emulate the entrepreneurial condition. Programs themselves may have to be entrepreneurial.

HUMAN CAPITAL THEORY OF SELF-EMPLOYMENT

This is the basic conceptual framework used in most of the statistical studies of self-employment presented in the next chapter. People rationally choose among alternatives so as to maximize their earnings.

According to Long (1982), the individual selects a type of employment by weighing potential money and nonmoney returns. Holding constant nonmoney benefits and costs, "the individual selects the type of work providing the highest present value of expected after-tax income" (Long 1982, p. 33). There are tax benefits to self-employment and, therefore, a person is more likely to choose self-employment, the higher the expected taxes as an employee.[5]

In Bearse (1984), the self-employed differ from wage workers because employees usually work under a contract, while the self-employed bear risk for not receiving payment for work on a regular basis. Bearse applied the framework for analyzing occupational choice to self-employment. In deciding whether or not to become self-employed, one considers the opportunity cost: the wage income foregone by engaging in entrepreneurial activity. Borjas (1985), in his study of immigrants, used a similar hypothesis. A person compares the market wage as a salaried worker with the expected net income from self-employment and then chooses the activity which, ceteris paribus, generates the greatest payoff.

Fredland and Little (1985) used the approach that earnings are the result of innate and acquired skills. Given the same risk, skills, and occupation, a self-employed person should earn the same as a salaried worker. However, returns should be higher for self-employed individuals if their activities have higher risk and they have the same degree of risk aversion as salaried workers. In addition, one needs to obtain an appropriate job to fully exploit one's skills. Since, in a world of imperfect information, it is hard to screen for all characteristics relevant to job performance (e.g., innovation), "self-employment is an alternative for those who have or believe they have human capital which employers discount" (Fredland & Little 1985, p. 121). Casson (1982, p. 300) subscribes to the view, similar to the above, that the most important reason for becoming self-employed is that wage employment provides insufficient scope to exploit one's talents. He also suggests three other reasons for choosing to become self-employed: it may be the only alternative to unemployment; wage employment may be too demeaning in that someone else controls your labor; and an individual may require part-time convenient work.

Lazear and Moore (1984) have the view that a major difference between self-employment and wage employment is that in self-employment the worker and owner are the same person, and this eliminates any disharmony of interests. This could make self-employment earnings pay better. The disadvantages of being a one-person firm include having to undertake many tasks at which one may not have a comparative advantage, and difficulty raising capital implying that the scale of plant will be less than optimal (Lezear & Moore 1984, p. 283).

PSYCHOLOGICAL THEORIES OF THE ENTREPRENEUR

The contribution of psychology mainly concerns personality characteristics that entrepreneurs are thought to have more of. McClelland (1961) ascribes entrepreneurial behavior to a high need for achievement formed in childhood.[6] Individuals with a high need for achievement set moderately difficult goals to maximize the likelihood of achievement satisfaction, are interested in concrete feedback, like assuming personal responsibility, show initiative, and have a high level of exploratory behavior. For a business person with a high need for achievement, profit is considered to be of secondary importance to expansion and growth.[7] McClelland developed tests to measure "need for achievement" and created classroom-based entrepreneurial training programs in India to increase it.[8]

Entrepreneurs are also thought to have a strong belief that they control their own lives rather than feeling manipulated by the external environment. This is the concept of locus of control. Rotter (1966) developed an internal-external scale to measure locus of control. This has been used to predict who is likely to become an entrepreneur.[9]

Collins and Moore (1970) provided a Freudian framework for viewing entrepreneurial control needs. They used Thematic Appreciation Tests to uncover personality characteristics. They concluded that because of unresolved fears of the father, the entrepreneur establishes a business as a means of working through the oedipal impasse. "The business is his own mistress . . ." (Collins & Moore 1970, p. 47).

Sexton and Bowman (1985, p. 131) indicate, in addition, other personality characteristics of the entrepreneur: moderate risk-taking propensity, ability to tolerate ambiguity, high need for autonomy, dominance, independence, self-esteem, and a low need for conformity. Trinia et al. (1984), in addition, consider the personality characteristics of Machiavellianism, openness to innovation, and rigidity. The empirical literature is mixed, however, about whether so-called entrepreneurial characteristics distinguish the entrepreneur from managers or other high-achieving individuals.[10]

SOCIOLOGICAL THEORIES OF SOCIAL NETWORKING AND BUSINESS OWNERSHIP

Sociological theories of how people become business owners often use the work of Granovetter as a foundation. Economic activity is "embedded in concrete, ongoing systems of social relations" (Granovetter 1985).[11] According to Aldrich and Zimmer (1986), social relations provide linkages between entrepreneurs, resources, and opportunities. Social relations involve transmission of information, exchange of goods and services, and expectations of behavior. An individual has both strong and weak ties in a social network. Strong social ties are formed from past interactions whereby individuals acquire a reputation of trustworthiness, which minimizes risk. Because of the large number of ways that persons in business can take advantage of one another, trustworthiness becomes a valuable attribute for one seeking assistance and cooperation from others. However, strong ties often provide redundant information (you get similar information from members of your clique). Therefore, weak ties are also important to substantially expand one's network and knowledge (Aldrich & Zimmer 1986, pp. 18-20).

Most business owners acquire their initial capital from family and friends rather than from formal financial institutions. Casson (1982, p. 199) provides four reasons why the family is a good source of capital: the borrower's idea probably won't be stolen by family members; family members have known the borrower long enough that they can assess his or her trustworthiness to repay the loan; the family can easily monitor how the capital is being used; and the family can exert pressure if things go wrong.

Social networks not only can provide monetary resources but, more importantly, are an important source for acquiring business information. In a study of Indiana new firms, Birley (1985) found that "the main sources of help in assembling the resources of raw materials, supplies, equipment, space, employees and orders, were the informal contacts of family, friends, and colleagues." From a mail survey of successful entrepreneurs, Kent et al. (1981) discovered the following: (1) the decision to become an entrepreneur was related to having an association with another person who had started a business; the strength of this effect increases when that other person was a parent, and (2) entrepreneurs are likely to discover their innovative product, service, or technology while an employee in another business. Gibb and Ritchie (1982) found similar results in their study of 50 British would-be entrepreneurs. Goldschieder and Kobrin (1980), Shapero and Sokol (1982), and Laban and Lentz (1985) all found strong evidence that the likelihood of being self-employed is strongly influenced by having a parent who was self-employed. There is also fairly extensive literature on the importance of mentors in training and acquiring promotion within an organization (Zey 1984; Lunding et al. 1978).

Because business owners like to claim they did it on their own, one must be cautious about making inferences from asking people how they started their businesses.[12] The act of starting a business seems to be a combination of both individualistic effort and obtainng help from social networks. I conceive of four types of nascent self-employed people, defined by cross-classifying low/high amounts of individualistic effort with low/high amounts of social networking. The four self-employed types that emerge are *wage workers, classic entrepreneurs, business inheritors,* and *resourceful opportunists.* See Figure 2.1.

Wage workers are not very motivated to do it on their own and have relatively few skills for exploiting social networks. The term *wage worker* is only a tag and does not mean actual wage workers are not motivated or skilled at social networking. Most business owners were at one time wage workers. It rather refers to a mindset or an intention. This type is the least likely to become a business owner. However,

Figure 2.1
Four Types of Business Owners

Individualistic Effort

	Low	High
Low	1) <u>wage worker</u>. lowest likelihood of business ownership. Ownership through circumstance.	2) <u>classic entrepreneur</u>. modest likelihood of business ownership. Lacks supports.
High	3) <u>business inheritor</u>. high likelihood of business ownership, but low likelihood of keeping it profitable.	4) <u>resourceful opportunist</u>. high likelihood of business ownership, but unlikely to acknowledge the help of others.

Social

Networking

The four cells are ranked in ascending order with people in cell (4) having the highest likelihood of business ownership.

wage workers do become business owners through circumstances, both good and bad.

  Classic entrepreneurs, who do it all on their own, are the second least likely to start a business. They try to will themselves into a business but are only partially successful because information and supports are lacking. The *Business inheritors* use their well developed social networks to obtain their businesses through family or friends. They have a high probability of starting a business but only a modest probability of keeping it profitable. The most likely to start a business and succeed are the *Resourceful opportunists*. They are high on having and using social networks and on applying individualistic effort. However, because *Resourceful opportunists* apply large amounts of individualistic effort, they are unlikely to acknowledge the help of others. Therefore, in researching them, the importance of social networking may be missed.

Is it more important *who* you know or *what* you know? The answer, from the social network approach, seems to be: It is more important who you know because who you know determines what you know. Conducting business in a competitive environment involves withholding information from other businesses, institutions, and potential entrants. This provides a competitive edge. Business owners are very reluctant to provide sales, earnings, and ingredient information to outsiders. Either one develops "insider" information analytically from textbooks and research, stumbles upon it by chance, or acquires it from (or through) family, friends, fellow employees, or employers. One can not depend upon the first two methods. In the course of day-to-day life, I have interviewed business owners and asked about their personal background and the circumstances that led to the founding of their businesses. Practically all either had parents who operated a business, had wage work experience in the industry in which they started their business, or had a friend who was instrumental in providing information about the opportunity. Without these jump-off points, I think it is very difficult to start a business.

AN ECLECTIC SOCIAL SCIENCE MODEL OF ENTREPRENEURSHIP

Shapero (1979; 1981) provides an insightful review of social science literature on entrepreneurship. Company formation occurs when four conditions are present: displacement of the nascent entrepreneur, a disposition to act, perception of credibility, and availability of resources. Displacement refers to some personal circumstance that drastically changes or disrupts one's life. Displacement can be positive, such as perceived new market opportunities or encouragement by peers, customers, or bankers; or negative, for example, being fired. Displacement can be externally imposed, such as being a political refugee, or it can be internally perceived, such as reaching a traumatic birthday. Most displacement influences are believed to be of a negative nature.

Many people are displaced but few react by forming a company. That requires a *disposition to act.* This concerns one's psychological propensity for entrepreneurship, as described in a previous section.[13]

The third factor, *perception of credibility,* concerns envisioning oneself starting and operating a company. According to Shapero, a person cannot begin to think about forming a new business unless he/she believes it possible. In psychology, this would be referred to as self-efficacy. Sources that impart credibility come from observing examples of similar persons forming a company, such as one's family, colleagues, or classmates. He further notes that many entrepreneurs have experienced previous business failure, implying failures impart credibility.

The last factor, *availability of resources,* when combined with the occurrence of the aforementioned three conditions, is sufficient for a business to be formed. Business formations are related to the availability of venture capital. In hard times, despite the displacement caused by job loss, the lack of capital inhibits company formation.

Overall, Shapero's eclectic approach provides a view of entrepreneurship different from most economic models that have people rationally and deliberately jumping to opportunities based on differential money earnings. He notes that, "of the many company formations studied, seldom are any found that resulted from a rational, calculated, carefully planned succession of decisions and actions" (Shapero 1979, p. 15).[14]

Some of Shapero's entrepreneurial conditions apply to U.S. low-income people. They are "displaced" in the sense that they are not in the economic mainstream of society, and there are blockages to their obtaining status. There may be a "disposition to act" in the sense of having difficulty accepting authority imposed by others. What seems to be lacking is "perception of credibility" in the form of peer role model business persons and "availability of resources." These are gaps that programs can fill.

THEORETICAL FRAMEWORKS AND PROGRAM PRINCIPLES

As a way to integrate these different theoretical frameworks, I will use them to design a hypothetical self-employment training program. The topic of program design is more fully discussed in chapters 8 and 9. I introduce the topic of training program design here to demonstrate the usefulness of these disparate theoretical frameworks.

Human capital theory from economics says one chooses activities based on relative earnings in alternative opportunities; psychology says the alternative opportunities one considers are based on dimensions related to motivation; sociology says social networks provide the

Figure 2.2
Theories of How People Become Business Owners and
Corresponding Implied Programs

Theory	Origin	Implied Program
1. Entrepreneurial Personality	Psychology	Enhance Motivation: build confidence, self-esteem, and positive attitudes
2. Relative Opportunities	Economics	Make Self-employment Pay Better: obtain market research, learn business skills, improve access to capital, and advocate for selective regulation
3. Social Networks	Sociology	Expand Social Contacts: provide access to mentors, use family resources, and join associations

opportunities to begin with. These three approaches to the study of self-employment seem complementary. One could, therefore, judiciously use principles from each of these approaches to design a self-employment training program. While there is overlap in function, techniques derived from principles of the three disciplines provide mutually reinforcing ways to encourage self-employment. Figure 2.2 is an outline of examples of what such a program could offer.

From psychology, one can incorporate program elements that enhance motivation by building self-confidence, self-esteem, and positive attitudes. Techniques to achieve this can include pep talks, role playing, peer support, awareness exercises, hypnosis, observation and discussions with successful business owners, operant conditioning, and methods of cognitive-behavioral modification.

From economics one can incorporate program elements that make self-employment pay better by obtaining market research, teaching business skills, improving access to capital, and advocating for selective deregulation. Techniques to do this include collective professional market analyses, classroom instruction, internships, field exercises, attaching a micro loan fund to the program, and obtaining waivers from government regulatory and welfare officials.

From social network theory in sociology, program elements can be incorporated that expand and better utilize social contacts by providing access to mentors, teaching how to use family resources, and associating with business persons in one's industry of choice. Techniques to do this include matching clients with local businessperson advisors, obtaining internships, delaying entry into self-employment by increasing work experience in one's chosen industry, doing an inventory of all friends and family, and joining associations.

If the implied techniques from all three approaches were utilized, they might provide a balanced and effective program to increase the likelihood of a client starting a business, and once started, reduce the probability of failure.[15] However, big issues remain that include what proportions the elements should be in, how best to integrate them, who should provide them, and how best to modify them for persons with low levels of formal education. These are discussed in Part III of this book.

SUMMARY

Various theories on entrepreneurship and self-employment were described. These included economic theories of the function of the entrepreneur, economic human capital theories of self-employment, psychological theories of entrepreneurial personality, sociological theories of the importance of social networks in entrepreneurial events, and eclectic social science models of why people start businesses.

Theories that focus on the entrepreneur may not be totally relevant to the issue of self-employment for low-income people. However, they are still worthwhile to consider because they may suggest the types of services that self-employment programs should offer.

Using the various theories, a hypothetical self-employment training program was constructed which had elements derivable from each. From psychology, it was derived that programs ought to enhance motivation; from economics, programs should develop ways to make self-employment pay better; from sociology, programs should help clients expand and better utilize their social networks. Since self-employent programs seldom consider the importance of social networks in their training, there should be greater effort to incorporate or expand elements of it into programs.

NOTES

1. Carland et al. (1984) tried to distinguish the entrepreneur from the small business owner. Differences focused on purposes (profit and growth vs. personal goals) and management (innovative behavior and strategic practices vs. the lack of it). Mayer and Goldstein (1961), and Scase and Goffee (1980), both conclude that the majority of small business owners (at least in their samples) do not conform to the classic image of the entrepreneur. Casson (1982, p. 303) suggests that a business owner with a low standard of living who works long hours may appear to be an entrepreneur acquiring capital for expansion, but "it is perfectly consistent with non-entrepreneurial behavior by people with little ability, a strong aversion to conventional employment, and little preference for leisure."

2. Two good fairly recent reviews of the literature on the economics of the entrepreneur can be found in Casson (1982) and Evans and Leighton (1987).

3. Economists who follow the Austrian school of thought take the view that no predictive theory of the entrepreneur is possible. If one knows how entrepreneurs act to reap returns greater than elsewhere, one is likely to stop theorizing and become an entrepreneur.

4. Evans and Leighton (1987) describe the work of Lucas and list a number of subsequent articles based on his theory of entrepreneurship.

5. The tax benefits of self-employment include the possibility of not reporting some income and the ability to count some consumer expenditures as business costs.

6. Boys who have a high need for achievement were more likely to live in a nuclear family as opposed to an extended family; to have had parents who set moderately high standards, were warm and encouraging, and had fathers who were not dominating, allowing their sons to try things on their own. Further, a parent's sense of superiority was hypothesized to be a factor in raising children in achievement-oriented ways (McClelland & Winter 1969, pp. 33, 34).

7. A high need for achievement seems similar to the Protestant work ethic, by which individuals are expected to labor diligently for the intrinsic reward of fulfilling one's calling.

8. The program used games, paper and pencil exercises, outside reading, and tests to increase one's need for achievement. Training elements included the following: recognizing and producing achievement fantasies, self-study, formulating goals, and providing a setting with interpersonal supports (McClelland & Winter 1969, pp. 39-78). Harper (1984) provides a description of programs in developing countries which utilize Achievement Motivation Training as a component.

9. See Gartner (1988), Brockhaus and Horowtiz (1985), and Sexton and Bowman (1985) for a review of these studies.

10. Ibid.

11. Granovetter takes the position that most theories of economics, whether by economists or other social scientists, either ignore social relations or assume individuals are totally bound by them. However, economists have for a long

time been aware of personal contacts as an important source of job information in local labor markets. See Wial (1988) for a review of this literature.

Allied with the contributions of sociologists is the research of anthropologists, which provides ethnographies of occupational groups and business operators in less developed countries. Ideas about the interrelationship between culture and work are provided by these studies. This field has been expanding into studying participants in the informal sector of developed countries. See, for example, *Anthropology of Work Review*.

12. Carsrud et al. (1987) provided an exploratory study of the importance of networks and mentors in starting businesses and concluded that doubt is cast on the notion that networks and mentors are important. Given the methodological weakness of the study, I, instead, interpret their findings as supportive of the importance of mentors and networks.

13. To emphasize the desire for independence on the part of entrepreneurs, Shapero (1979) cites empirical studies that found entrepreneurs would not readily switch to wage work even if it paid better. Economists would call this the psychic income of owning a business.

14. Scase and Goffee (1980, p. 33) found, from interviews with small business owners in Britain, that business formation was often a function of personal discontent and a random occurrence. Further, one should distinguish between the providers of capital, who are more likely to be rational maximizers, and the users of capital, who are trying to implement some personal plan.

15. Of the three realms of techniques that self-employment training programs use, the least considered and the least developed are from social network theory. I feel the effectiveness of self-employment training programs could be greatly improved by greater consideration of the importance of social networks and the development of compensatory social networking techniques.

3

Empirical Analyses of Self-Employment

INTRODUCTION

The focus of this book is on very small businesses with few employees, usually family members, or none at all. The term self-employment includes this sector, but it also includes large businesses. Many think self-employment means only employment of the individual, that is, a sole proprietorship business with no employees, but that is not correct. The hyphenated word, self-employment, is just another term for business ownership, implicit or explicit.[1]

Operational definitions of self-employment will be examined here. Then, the underreporting problem will be discussed, followed by a review of results of empirical studies that investigated characteristics of the self-employed, including whether they earn more than wage workers.[2]

OPERATIONAL DEFINITIONS OF SELF-EMPLOYMENT

Current Population Survey Definition

Self-employment is defined by the U.S. Department of Labor Bureau of Labor Statistics Current Population Survey (CPS) as "those who work for profit or fees in their own business, profession, trade or operate a farm" (Becker 1984, p. 18). Several groups who closely fit this description are, however, excluded by the CPS definition. These include owners of incorporated businesses (they draw a salary from their businesses), unpaid family workers, and holders of two (or more) jobs en-

Table 3.1
Dimensions of Self-Employment Important for Determining Inclusion
into a Sample

    I.   Legal Form
        a. Proprietorship
           1. Single Proprietorship
           2. Partnership
        b. Incorporated

    II. Work Week
        a. Full Time
        b. Part Time

    III. Sales Size
        a. Casual
        b. Non-casual

    IV. Employee Size
        a. Owner-manager & No Employees
        b. Few Employees
        c. Many Employees

    V.   Multiple Job Holding
        a. Only Owns Business
        b. Owns a Business and Works in Wage Job
           but Business is Primary
        c. Owns a Business and Works in Wage Job
           but Wage Job is Primary

    VI. Multiple Business Holdings
        a. Owns One Business
        b. Owns More Than One Business

    VII. Career Status
        a. Careerist: self-employed in the current period
           and a previous time period
        b. Entrant: self-employed in the current period
           but wage employed or unemployed in a previous period

    VIII. Industries
        a. All
        b. Nonagricultural

gaged in self-employment but whose primary job is wage employment (side businesses).[3] This definition of self-employment, therefore, refers essentially to sole proprietors and partners of unincorporated businesses. These people may be working at their businesses either full-time or part-time.[4] It seems the CPS definition tries to capture those individuals who are self-employed as a primary, renumerative, and substantive activity.[5]

Most researchers have concentrated on the nonagricultural self-employed. Some also restrict the sample to full-time workers. Table 3.1

describes the important dimensions of self-employment that are considered when operationally defining it for statistical research purposes.

Size of Business of the Self-Employed

The legal form of a business can be used as a proxy for size or substance. Analysis of 1983 data from the Survey of Income and Program Participation (SIPP), using the CPS definition, reveals that 82 percent of the nonagricultural self-employed were sole proprietors and 18 percent were partnerships (Haber et al. 1986). Further, 78 percent of sole proprietorships employed only one employee, 9 percent employed two employees, and only 13 percent employed three or more.[6] In contrast, of partnerships and incorporated business arrangements, only 13 percent had only one employee; 21 percent had two employees, and 67 percent had three or more employees (Haber et al. 1986, p. 21). Self-employment, using the CPS definition, includes predominantly, but not solely, very small businesses. Of course, when owners of incorporated businesses are included among the self-employed, the proportion of larger businesses in the mix increases.

Self-employed businesses can be described by the following additional dimensions that also can be used to capture business size and substance: whether the business is noncasual (having expected yearly gross receipts greater than $1,000), and whether a self-employed individual works full-time at the business. Of the total nonagricultural self-employed in 1983, 61 percent (or 4.6 million people) worked full-time at noncasual businesses, and 39 percent (or 3 million people) either operate a casual business or operate a business part-time.[7] The majority of the self-employed engage in business activity of some substance, but a substantial proportion do not.[8]

CHARACTERISTICS OF BUSINESS OWNERS USING A BROAD DEFINITION

The characteristics of the self-employed, using the narrower CPS and similar definitions, will be described in a following section of this chapter. First, characteristics of the self-employed using a broad definition will be portrayed. This would include the full-time self-employed, the part-time self-employed, people working in casual businesses, and dual job holders. This broad definition would include a lot more of very small businesses.

The following statistics were obtained from a special survey conducted by the U.S. Census for 1982. A random sample of 25,000 businesses were sampled from five groups: Hispanic, black, other minorities, women, and nonminority males. The universe was Internal

Revenue Service tax forms: those who filed forms 1040 Schedule C (individual proprietorships), 1065 (partnerships), or 1120S (subchapter S corporations).[9]

Using this broad definition of business owner, Table 3.2 describes four characteristics: business size, education and experience of owners, family background of owners, and business finance. Most businesses are home based, and between a third and a half are less than full time operations. Almost half of all business owners have a high school education or less.[10] Business ownership does not seem to require a college education. However, over 75 percent of business owners have had substantial wage work experience, and a third to a half have had managerial experience. Approximately 10 to 20 percent have previously owned a business. Approximately 70 to 80 percent are married, and between 20 and 40 percent have close relatives who owned a business. However, only between 7 and 20 percent worked for their business-oriented relatives. Most businesses did not start with "big bucks." A quarter to a third of business owners started with *no* capital.[11] Including these, between 60 and 70 percent started with less than $5,000 capital. Business ownership, in general, does not seem to require a great deal of capital. Only a quarter to a third of business owners borrowed some of their initial capital. Capital can still be a constraint for a low-income person, but it does not seem to be an insurmountable barrier to business ownership. In summary, becoming a business owner does not require a great deal of education or money capital. It does however, seem to require wage work experience and a supportive family background.[12]

Why Nonminority Males Do Better

Nonminority males have higher rates of self-employment than do women, blacks, or Hispanics, and their businesses are larger. Table 3.2 may reveal why this is so. Nonminority males and women have had almost twice the advantage of having business-oriented relatives compared to blacks and Hispanics. Nonminority business owners have less formal education than black and Hispanic business owners. However, nonminority males have had more wage work experience, previous ownership experience, and most strikingly, have had substantially more experience working in a managerial capacity. Prior managerial experience furnishes both a relevant business background as well as higher wage earnings to accumulate capital. Slightly more nonminority males are married, had more relatives who owned a business (compared to blacks and Hispanics), and had more experience working with close relatives who owned a business. In short, nonmi-

Table 3.2
Selected Characteristics of Business Owners

	Non-Minority Male Owners	Women Owners	Black Owners	Hispanic Owners
BUSINESS SIZE				
1. % business operated from residence	51%	56%	54%	47%
2. % work at business 29 hours or less per week	34%	49%	48%	37%
EDUCATION AND EXPERIENCE				
3. % highest education is high school grad or below	44%	45%	51%	58%
4. % previously owned a business	22%	14%	11%	15%
5. % worked more than two years as a paid employee	85%	80%	78%	77%
6. % worked in a managerial capacity	52%	37%	36%	39%
FAMILY BACKGROUND				
7. % married	82%	71%	70%	80%
8. % had close relatives who owned a business	39%	41%	21%	28%
9. % worked for close relatives who owned a business	19%	14%	7%	10%

Table 3.2 (continued)

	Non-Minority Male Owners	Women Owners	Black Owners	Hispanic Owners
BUSINESS FINANCE				
10. % started with no capital	26%	36%	31%	27%
11. % started with $5,000 or less capital	59%	72%	70%	64%
12. % started with some borrowed capital	34%	25%	31%	33%

The data in this table was generated from samples.
Source: U.S. Bureau of the Census, *1982 Characteristics of Business Owners* (1987), compiled from various tables.

nority males seem to have a richer background in family and work experiences that provide a business advantage.[13]

REPORTING PROBLEMS

In discussing self-employment as a statistical phenomenon, the word *reported* should be used to modify self-employment because this better describes the type of information generally available in studies of this sector. The basic sources of information are data from mail surveys, interviews, or form filing with either Dun and Bradstreet or the Internal Revenue Service. There are several reasons to expect respondent underreporting of being engaged in self-employment. These include attempts at hiding the activity from taxing, welfare, or regulatory authorities, lack of respondent awareness at the time of the interview that he/she is engaged in self-employment (e.g., having a casual business such as baby sitting), not having a permanent address, and lack of formal records which might affect recall.[14]

There may also be misreporting of earnings. Studies by Kahn (1964), the Internal Revenue Service (1979), Park (1981), and Haber et al. (1986) all found significantly greater underreporting of income by the self-employed compared to wage and salary workers.[15] An important use of information on self-employment earnings is to compare it to the earnings of similarly situated wage workers. In considering training options, it is useful to know if individuals are likely to earn more in self-employment or wage work, everything else held constant. In analyzing such comparisons, one should keep in mind the various elements of earnings whose inclusion in or exclusion from the data can lead to relative overstatement or understatement of earnings for a particular mode of work. Both self-employment and salary employment include money wages for one's own labor. However, the self-employed tend to work longer hours and more weeks in a year (Becker 1984). Therefore, annual earnings for the self-employed may be a relative overstatement of earnings per time. Self-employment earnings also include implicitly a return to capital. A wage worker may also be earning some return to financial capital (e.g., in a certificate of deposit) but it is not embedded in his/her wage earnings data. This relatively overstates earnings for the self-employed. A self-employed worker has to pay fringe benefits out of his/her earnings while a wage worker receives these as part of earnings, but they are not added into the earnings data of the wage worker. This again relatively overstates earnings for the self-employed. There are implicit income perks that are associated with operating a business but are unavailable to wage workers. These include such things as using the business car for personal travel or the home as a place of work, and obtaining goods for personal consumption from inventory (Becker 1984).[16] This relatively understates earnings data for the self-employed.

In summary, then, there are three elements which lead to overstatement of self-employment earnings, one element that leads to understatement, and in addition there is an element of reporting understatement. I am not sure what the net effect is. Possibly the overstatements and understatements cancel each other out, leaving the observed earnings differentials as a good measure of the true earnings differentials between self-employed and wage workers.

EMPIRICAL STUDIES

The recent empirical literature on self-employment consists of empirical studies using different U.S. data bases and having various purposes. Some described the growth in self-employment and the characteristics of the self-employed; others determined the significant variables that explain participation in self-employment versus wage employment, compared the earnings of the self-employed with wage workers, compared rates of business ownership using different data bases, and explained immigrant and minority participation in self-employment. Eighteen self-employment empirical studies were used for this review.

Growth of U.S. Self-Employment

Becker (1984), using CPS data, found nonagricultural self-employment increased each year since 1970, growing 46 percent from 1970 to 1983.[17] In 1970, 5.2 million nonagricultural workers were self-employed, increasing to 7.6 million in 1983 or 7.8 percent of nonagricultural employment. In contrast, nonagricultural wage employment increased by 29 percent during that same 13-year period from 69.5 million to 89.5 million workers. This increase in self-employment since 1970 is a reversal of a trend that has shown a steady decline in self-employment since 1830 when 80 percent of free white Americans were self-employed (Corey 1966). Social scientists have, for a long time, thought that self-employment is an economic anachronism (Myrdal 1944; Mills 1951; Light 1984). Their framework was that since a greater share of economic activity would be conducted by large corporations, small businesses would be competing among themselves for an increasingly smaller share of the market.

Long (1982) suggested that this trend reversal is partly a function of inflationary creep in income tax rates in addition to the growth of the service sector and rising unemployment. Balkin (1986) suggested the explanation lies in a movement to a more service-oriented economy where economies of scale are less important. Further, increasing foreign competition has been forcing large firms to contract work to smaller firms where cost savings can be obtained by using nonunion labor, loose work rules, and lax regulatory compliance.[18] At the same time, women and baby boom adults were entering the labor force in greater numbers and required greater flexibility in work rules so they could better mesh life-styles with work. Blau (1987), in addition to explanations mentioned above, suggested rising real retirement benefit levels which increased the degree that wage workers sought self-employment partial retirement, and wage rigidity. His time series regression analysis found the following six effects could explain most of the increase from 1973 to 1982 in the proportion of male workers that were self-employed (in order of importance): an increase in a self-employment factor productivity index, a decrease in the marginal tax rate at $7000 real income, an increase in the marginal tax rate at $17,000 real income, an increase in the social security benefit level, a decrease in the real minimum wage, and a decrease in the age of the male labor force (Blau 1984, p. 461). Evans and Leighton (1987), using a logit regression model, found that recent changes in self-employment rates were closely associated with increases in the proportion of older workers who had done graduate work; increases in employment in service, construction, and retail industries relative to manufacturing and mining; and increases in federal income tax rates. They also speculate on changes in self-employment in the coming decade: the aging of the baby boom generation is likely to increase participation in self-employment, while the decline in the dollar (improving the manufacturing sector) and the lowering of federal income tax rates are likely to lower participation.

Unemployment and Self-Employment

The counter-cyclical nature of self-employment (increases in self-employment during recessions) is suggested by the observation that during the four recessions since 1969, nonagricultural self-employment increased moderately. According to Becker (1984), nonagricultural self-employment came out each cyclical downturn earlier than its wage and salary counterparts. He suggests that when dual job holders, whose secondary job is self-employment, lose their primary wage job, self-employment becomes their primary job. In addition, people may *newly* enter self-employment upon the loss of a wage and salary job.

Evans and Leighton (1987), using individual level longitudinal data, analyzed entry into self-employment from either unemployment or wage work.[19] The percent of unemployed male workers in their sample that switched into self-employment ranged from a low of 3.89 percent in 1973, continually increasing to 9.02 percent in 1980, and the rate of switch into self-employment was much greater for the unemployed than for wage workers, being almost three times as high, 9.02 percent as opposed to 2.84 percent, in 1980. They also found evidence that individuals who earned low wages were more likely to switch to self-employment, as were individuals who changed jobs frequently. From their regression analysis, they also found switching into self-employment to be significantly related to having engaged in jobs that required independent thought and negatively related to living in areas of high unemployment. This last result implies that one is more likely to switch to self-employment if one is unemployed but living in an area where the general unemployment rate is low.

Poverty and Self-Employment Participation

Bauman calculated the rate of full-time self-employment for the poverty population in the Great Lakes states. The poverty population is defined as anyone earning less than the poverty income standard. His startling finding is that the self-employment rate for persons in poverty who worked full-time is twice that of the self-employment rate for the total full-time working population (13% versus 6%) (Bauman 1988, p. 340).

This refutes the conventional wisdom that low-income people are unlikely to become small business owners because they lack skills and resources. It is unclear, however, whether this supports the policy of encouraging this group to enter self-employment. A key interpretive issue can be raised: Are the poor more resourceful than we thought, or are people poor because they participate more in self-employment? An important finding from the above two sections is that self-employment is, in part, a refuge for unemployed and low wage workers. That disadvantaged workers regularly switched to self-employment, without program assistance, suggests that research is needed to uncover the processes they use, and perhaps base policies or programs on ways to emulate their methods of transition, particularly for those able to earn high self-employment income.

DEMOGRAPHIC CHARACTERISTICS OF THE SELF-EMPLOYED

Age

The self-employed tend to be older than wage workers. In 1983, 45 percent of the self-employed were 45 and older, whereas only 28 percent of wage workers were 45 and over (Becker 1984). Becker posits that younger workers rarely have financial resources and skills to start their own business. A common and sound route to starting a business that I have observed is to work for someone else to acquire skills and know-how for a particular type of business and then start one yourself. Since it takes time to learn-by-doing and to realize you may be smarter than the boss, serious self-employment seems more likely to occur later in life. A further impetus for the older self-employed is that wage workers often become self-employed to supplement retirement income (Becker 1966, p. 16).

The research of Fuchs (1982) and Quinn (1980) found that the probability of older male involvement in self-employment increases with age. Due to the flexibility attached to self-employment, older workers may increase their participation in self-employment as they age as a form of partial retirement (Quinn 1980). Part of the reason for increased participation in self-employment is because of the greater ability to reduce the workweek to less than 35 hours compared to wage workers. Wage and salary workers are more likely to drop out of the labor force, that is, fully retire, or switch to self-employment as retirement approaches (Fuchs 1982).

Bearse (1984) and Evans and Leighton (1987) found that the rate of self-employment participation increases with age and then remains fairly constant.[20] Evans and Leighton (1987, p. 64) discovered, paradoxically, that the probability a man will *start* a business is roughly the same for all age groups. The two results are reconciled when it is considered that the older a person is, the more opportunities he or she will have had to start a business to become self-employed in.

Race and Ethnicity

Caution: Underreporting Is Likely Present

While researchers have consistently found the statistical incidence of self-employment lower among blacks, they may be using invalid data. It is suspected that the underreporting problem is especially severe for blacks. The usual sources of data tend to measure self-employment only in the regular economic sector. This leaves out self-employment in the irregular or underground economy. Information does not exist on how many firms are in this sector or their racial distribution.[21] Light (1984) contends that ethnographic research has stressed the importance of "hustling" as a black underclass economic activity. Hustling involves a variety of activities, many of which are mainstream business activities. The incidence of self-employment among blacks and other minorities would be higher if one could estimate self-employment incidence in unreported businesses in addition to reported businesses.

Minority Participation in Self-Employment

According to CPS data, blacks were less likely than the population at large to be self-employed in both 1979 and 1983, and this proportion dropped from 5.5 to 3.8 percent (Becker 1984, p. 16). Black self-employed workers were likely to be in different occupations than white self-employed workers. Blacks, operating their own businesses, were likely to be in the occupations of sales, service, farming, operator, fabricator, and laborer. White self-employed workers were more likely to be in managerial, professional, and technical areas (Becker 1984).

Bearse (1984) concluded why blacks participate less often in self-employment activity. Blacks are more likely to have only one earner per family, more likely to be unmarried and not heads of households, less likely to have assets or sources of interest and dividend income, have a higher proportion of females who are self-employed than other groups, have attained less education than other groups, and are concentrated in blue-collar industries and occupations (Bearse 1984, p. 131).

Long (1982), Brock and Evans (1986), and Evans and Leighton (1987) also found being nonwhite or black significantly reduced the probability of being self-employed.[22]

Minority Business Participation and Formation

Chen et al. (1982) reported that nonminorities have a higher business participation rate than minorities. Chen hypothesized that a lower minority business participation rate was due to a lower business formation rate and a higher failure rate. Stevens (1984) devised an analysis with a new data base to test this hypothesis. The highest formation rate was for Asians, followed by Hispanics and then blacks. The surprising result was that the failure rates were almost identical for the three minority groups. This suggests that differences in business participation are due to the variation in business formation. Once formed, businesses fail at about the same rate for all minority-ethnic groups.[23]

Immigrant Self-Employment

Borjas (1986) estimated the effects of various immigrant socioeconomic characteristics on the probability of being self-employed. His findings were that self-employed probabilities are larger for immigrants than for native born, and the greatest propensity for self-employment for immigrants (compared to native born) occurs five to ten years after immigration.[24] He noted that the rapid increase in self-employment rates experienced by recent immigrants may be caused by the relative decline in opportunities in the salaried sector over the last decade. Further, a reason immigrants are more likely to be self-employed than similarly skilled native workers is that "geographic enclaves of immigrants increase self-employment opportunities" (Borjas 1986, p. 505).

Sex

Female Versus Male Participation in Self-Employment

Most researchers have found that the self-employment rate is much higher for males compared to females. According to CPS data, a much greater proportion of the self-employed in 1983 were men (71%) compared to wage workers (55%) (Becker 1984). However, self-employed women increased five times faster than self-employed men and more than three times as fast as women wage workers between 1979 and 1983.[25] Bearse (1984) found similar results.

Possible explanations for this male bias in self-employment participation include discrimination in capital markets, lack of role models, discrimination in business social networks, and sex typing of occupations.[26] Institutions may be reluctant to loan money to a prospective business owner if the owner is a woman. Either she is perceived to lack the know-how of the rough and tumble world of business or she is perceived to be more concerned with home life than business life.

Girls have been traditionally nurtured and rewarded to be docile, dependent, and uncompetitive; this is seen to be counterproductive in a male-dominated world of competition (Sekera 1983, p. 8). Women have also not been encouraged to gain knowledge of basic business subjects such as accounting, finance, and computer analysis (Sekera 1983, p. 13). Further, it may be more difficult for a woman to believe she can credibly start and manage a business because women lack sufficient businesswomen for role models. Access to information is another key to successful business starts. Women have been denied access to many informal "old boy" business networks.

Another problem may concern the sex typing of occupations and their ease of operation in self-employment. Female-typed occupations may be more difficult to conduct in the self-employment mode (e.g., teachers and seamstresses) than male-typed occupations (e.g., accountants and truckdrivers).

Sex and Self-Employed Earnings

Self-employed men earn more than self-employed women.

Becker (1984) found the median earnings of self-employed men ($14,360) were substantially above those of self-employed women ($6,644). This also occurred across occupational categories. This was due to the higher professional skill component in the occupational distribution of self-employed men. Aronson (1985) observed that the differential in earnings between self-employed women and self-employed men and the differential in earnings between self-employed women and wage worker women appear to be growing wider. Self-employed women have become relatively worse-off in earnings.

Marital Status

Most reseachers found being married increased the probability of being self-employed. Long (1982) explained his finding on the basis that being married is likely to assist self-employment for three reasons: capital can be obtained from the income or assets of the spouse; the spouse can subsidize the business by working for below-market wages in the business; and if the spouse has an outside job, that can act as insurance against the risk of fluctuating self-employment income (Long 1982, p. 34).

Casson (1982) suggests the family is a valuable source of information. Being married, in a sense, doubles family size, the information pool, and the capital pool. A common route to business ownership that I have observed is for a person to start a business while the spouse continues to hold a wage job. If the business appears to be successful, the spouse then works part-time in a wage job and part-time in the family business. Eventually, if the business continues to be successful, the spouse works full-time in the family business. This allows for a steady stream of income for living expenses while the business gets off the ground. It is difficult for a single person to save up a year or two of living expenses prior to starting a business to maintain the prior standard of living until the business earns a profit.

Borjas (1986) explained his finding that married males were more likely to be self-employed than unmarried males on the basis that marriage solves the business problem that employees may shirk. A spouse working in the business is likely to be an excellent partner or employee since the couple share the identical goal—maximizing the family income.

Bearse (1984) found "being married" to be significantly related to being self-employed when all minority groups were included in his sample.[27] Brock and Evans (1986), however, found marital and family status *not* to be significantly related to being self-employed, when other variables were used for control.

Education

Education and Self-Employment Participation

Most researchers have found higher levels of education increase the probability of being self-employed. Both Borjas (1986), and Bearse (1984) found "years of completed education" to be positively related to the probability of being self-employed. Borjas' explanation was that a higher education level increases one's ability to provide a service that others may want or increases managerial skill (Borjas 1986, p. 494).[28] Brock and Evans (1986), however, did not find a significant relationship between educational attainment and being self-employed, though they did find a positive relationship between education (being a college graduate) and self-employment earnings.

Education and Self-Employment Earnings

Most researchers found higher education levels associated with higher self-employment earnings. Bates (1985), Brock and Evans (1986), and Lazear and Moore (1984) all found evidence consistent with this. Bauman (1988), and Evans and Leighton (1987) explored a related issue and found that the impact of education on self-employed earnings was generally greater than the impact of education on wage earnings.[29]

Evans and Leighton (1987) estimated the returns (per year) from education, training, and wage experience for both male self-employed and male wage workers.[30] Business experience, wage experience, formal education, management training, professional training, and skilled training all increase earnings of both groups. While not all results are statistically significant, they found that formal education, management training, and skilled training increase earnings for self-employed workers *more* than for wage workers. Further, business experience, wage experience, and professional training increase earnings for self-employed workers *less* than for wage workers. It is particularly interesting that wage workers earn a substantial return from self-employment experience. This suggests that self-employment can serve as a training ground for wage work.

High School Dropouts, Self-Employment Participation, and Earnings

Many policymakers and academicians are skeptical about the ability of individuals with a low level of education to engage in self-employment activity. However, persons with a low level of education already significantly participate in self-employment and in some industries they earn more than wage workers with the same education. Statistics on this were obtained by myself from a Current Population Survey special tabulation to derive the industrial distribution of full-time self-employed male dropouts.[31] A dropout is one who had less than 12 years of formal education. There were about 800,000 male dropouts who were self-employed in 1986. They were operating their businesses mostly (84%) in the industries of agriculture-forestry-fisheries, construction, services, and retail trade.

Table 3.3 expresses the industrial distribution of male dropout workers in another way—using self-employment rates, the number of self-employed male dropouts, as a percent of all male dropout workers. This rate provides a measure of the activity of male dropout workers in self-employment relative to their size, and can be used for comparison with other groups. 11.8 percent of all male dropout full time workers were engaged in self-employment. For male dropout workers, the industry category with the highest concentration engaged in self-employment was in agriculture–forestry–fisheries. 44.4 percent of the male dropout workers in that industry grouping were self-employed. Manufacturing had the least concentration in self-employment. Only 1.3 percent of the male dropout workers in manufacturing were self-employed.

Referent group self-employment rates are also provided in Table 3.3.[32] 10.9 percent of all full time workers (across all educational groups—males plus females) were self-employed. The self-employment rate for all male dropouts (11.8%) was higher than this. The self-employment "advantage" of being male outweighs the educational disadvantage of being a high school dropout. Education does have an effect

Table 3.3
Self-Employment Rates of Male Dropouts by Industry

Industry	Self-employment Rate*
All Industries	11.8%
Agriculture, forestry, fisheries	44.4%
Mining**	7.2%
Construction**	16.9%
Manufacturing**	1.3%
Transportation, communications, and public utilities	7.6%
Wholesale trade	8.3%
Retail trade**	15.6%
Finance, insurance, and real estate	11.1%
Services**	16.8%

SELF-EMPLOYMENT RATES FOR REFERENCE GROUPS (ALL INDUSTRIES)

All Workers	10.9%
All Males	14.3%
Males with just high school completion	13.5%

$$\text{SE Rate} = \frac{\text{\# of self-employed male dropouts in the Industry}}{\text{\# of male dropout workers in the Industry}}$$

* Data is for full-time workers and self-employment includes the incorporated self-employed.

** Median earnings are greater in self-employment.

Source: Special tabulation from March 1987 Current Population Survey.

though. The self-employment rate of males, whose highest level of education was completion of high school, was higher (14% greater) than that of dropout males. Finishing high school does increase the likelihood of entering into self-employment. Further, the self-employment rate of all males was considerably higher (21% greater) than the self-employment rate of male dropouts.

Of particular interest is a comparison of the median earnings between male dropouts who were self-employed and male dropouts who were wage workers. For five of the nine industrial categories, self-employed male dropouts had higher median earnings.[33] These five industries are mining, construction, manufacturing, retail trade, and service.[34] They are indicated by a double asterisk in Table 3.3. This finding suggests that, in general, a male dropout who is working (or planning to work) in one of those five industries would earn more income if self-employed in that same industry.[35] This result is tentative, however, pending further statistical refinement.[36]

I also considered the situation whereby educational disadvantage is exacerbated by adding a racial disadvantage. The industrial distribution for full-time self-employed black male dropouts was similar but not identical to full-time self-employed male dropouts. There were about 50,000 black male dropouts who were self-employed full-time in 1986.[37]

Labor Market Experience

Labor market experience is thought to increase the ease of starting a business by providing knowledge of business operations, an expanded social network, market opportunities, and sources of finance. Borjas (1986) found increases in labor market experience increased the probability of being self-employed for five out of his six immigrant ethnic groups. The exception was for blacks. He also found the effect diminishes with the amount of labor market experience. An extra year of labor market experience has a greater impact on the probability of being self-employed when one has fewer years of labor market experience.

Hours and Earnings

According to Becker (1984), the self-employed work longer hours than wage workers. The average length of the work week for the self-employed was 40 hours in 1983, while the average work week of wage workers was 38 hours. Approximately a third of the self-employed worked at least 49 hours each week.

Do the self-employed earn more than wage workers?[38] Empirical results do not provide conclusive answers. Becker (1984), Fredland and Little (1985), Haber et al. (1986), Evans and Leighton (1987), Bauman (1987; 1988), and Aronson (1987) generally found either the self-employed earned less or their earnings were not significantly different from those of wage workers.[39] In contrast, Long (1982), Borjas (1986), and Bates (1986) found that the self-employed earned *more* than wage and salary workers. The outcome partly depends on how self-employment and the self-employed sample are defined. For example, the full-time incorporated self-employed generally earn more than wage workers. Studies that include them as part of the self-employment group are more likely to find the self-employed earn more. Further, the answer of who earns more depends on such things as industry, occupation, education, sex, and race. Therefore, for purposes of advising individuals or targeting populations, the general question of "do the self-employed earn more than wage workers?", may not be relevant. What does seem important is to know the characteristics of those who do earn more in self-employment compared to wage work. This information, however, will be in the form of an average. A group that is likely to do better in wage work on average will contain many individuals who can do better in self-employment because of some special circumstance not accounted for by the general statistical models. It is useful to know what the existing statistical research says, but we shouldn't be bound by it when it comes to helping individuals.

Upward Occupational Mobility, Race, and Self-Employment

Pomer (1985) investigated black and white male advancement out of low-paying occupations between 1962 and 1973. He hypothesized that self-employment is an unlikely means of upward mobility for blacks, especially in comparison to whites. He argued that blacks are impeded by difficulty in obtaining capital, the lack of entrepreneurial tradition, and prejudice on the part of consumers (identifying blacks and their products with lower-class status).

His tables of movement between 1962 and 1973 "show the important role of self-employment in white advancement to managerial positions" (Pomer 1986, p. 11). Twenty percent of white self-employed workers became managers, all without change of industry. In contrast, none of the initially self-employed black workers became managers.[40] Further, of white private sector employees who became managers, about half became self-employed managers. Thus, for whites, self-employment does provide a channel for upward occupational mobility. If the attributes of the process which fosters white upward mobility through self-employment can be translated to black self-employment, an additional upward mobility channel may be opened up to blacks.

Self-Employment Sectors Suitable for Low-Income People

Some sectors in the economy seem to be more suited than others for low-income people to start businesses. Characteristics of good sectors include low money capital requirements, low skill requirements or skill requirements that can easily be learned, markets not saturated, the possibility for gradual entry, potential for finding a protected market niche, government regulations that are not severe, the possibility of linkage to a more established business, expectation of a low failure rate, and the potential for earnings greater than in wage work.[41] Two sectors which may fit many of these requirements are home-based businesses and franchises. A preliminary examination of these two sectors uncovered good potential and is reported in Balkin (1988c; 1988d).

SUMMARY

The following characteristics of reported self-employment are consistently shown in the studies reported here. The self-employed have greater variance in work hours, are more likely to be male, are more likely to be older, are more likely to have additional years of formal education, have been in the labor market longer, are more likely to be married, are more likely to be of a nonminority, have greater participation by immigrants (especially for those who have been in this country a few years), have a variance in participation rates due to differences in formation rates rather than failure rates, have been increasing as a part of the work force since 1970, may not be entrepreneurial in character in the classic economic sense, and have greater participation by low-income and unemployed people than the population in general. This last finding is very important in that it provides evidence that starting small businesses is not an unusual activity for poor people. Perhaps what is needed is assistance for them to do what they already do but with an eye to doing it better.

The answer to the question of whether workers earn more in self-employment activity compared to wage work was not conclusive. The answer is not a general one, but depends on definitions and on such things as industry, occupation, education, sex, and race.

Knowing the characteristics of people most likely to become self-employed can allow a program manager to select those clients with the most likely prospects for becoming self-employed. This practice is questionable. A major purpose of self-employment assistance is to help those into self-employment who would not be able to do so otherwise. In particular, people who have little education and are women, minorities, or youth need that assistance.

Rather than using the results of these studies for screening, one could develop useful programmatic principles by thinking about the processes behind a finding. For example, if the reason women are engaged in self-employment less often than men is that they lack access to business social networks, child care, and credit, a program can be developed to help women become self-employed by linking them to established networks, providing access to child care, and developing a micro-loan fund. Examples of some programmatic principles derived from these studies include not encouraging clients to expect more income just because they are self-employed rather than wage workers; informing clients that relative earnings will depend on the industry and occupation one is in; pointing out the advantage of greater flexibility in work hours for the self-employed; encouraging clients to obtain more formal education—if that is feasible; encouraging a client to obtain more wage work experience before starting a business, and if that is feasible, encouraging a working client first to try self-employment as a part-time activity; and suggesting that there are economic advantages to being married.

NOTES

1. By "implicit" I mean an individual is working for fees but does not have a separate business location and name. For example, someone doing free-lance writing is implicitly a business owner even though he or she may not be formally organized as one. However, there still is a gray area. The difference between self-employment and wage and salary employment status is not completely clear. There are situations where payment is in some form of results-based compensation that could be categorized as either a wage job (employer-employee relationship) or self-employment. Examples are piece rate work and commission sales.

2. Most of the empirical studies in the chapter are by economists and focus on testing some aspect of human capital theory. Some empirical evidence on social network theory and personality psychology was presented in the previous chapter. I purposely tried *not* to concentrate on portraying theories as competing and then analyzing the empirical studies on the question of who is right. That can be done elsewhere.

3. The Current Population Survey reports that the incorporated self-employed accounted for 2.8 million workers in 1982; unpaid family workers accounted for slightly more than 600,000 workers, and 1.6 million wage workers holding dual jobs were self-employed as their minor second job (Becker 1984, p. 14).

4. In 1983, about 67 percent of the self-employed, defined this way, worked full-time (Haber et al. 1986, p. 5).

5. It is unclear why the CPS should necessarily exclude incorporated business owners from "self-employment." Many empirical studies run their analyses both including and then excluding the incorporated self-employed. Including the incorporated self-employed will increase the amount of large-sized and sophisticated businesses in the mix of owners considered self-employed.

6. Data on number of employees was not broken down just for partnerships. In 1983, of all the private sector for-profit business owners, approximately 63

percent were sole proprietors, 14 percent were partnerships, and 23 percent were owners of incorporated businesses (Haber et al. 1986, p. 9).

7. Eighty-four percent of the self-employed (CPS definition) own noncasual businesses, and 67 percent work at their business full-time. Seventy-two percent of the self-employed who own noncasual businesses work full-time (Haber, et al. 1986, p. 5).

8. This does not include wage workers (1.6 million) who own side businesses, that is, they work full-time at a wage job and also own a business. This is the fastest growing sector of business owners (Haber et al. 1986, p. 1). They would be counted as wage workers according to the CPS definition.

9. This is a very broad definition of self-employed in that it is more inclusive on the lower end of the self-employed distribution. This definition, using IRS tax returns, probably includes quasi-businesses (Star 1981). These are superficial business creations used to obtain tax advantages (e.g., classifying a hobby as a business). This definition, though, still excludes owners of large corporate firms. Excluded from the universe were firms filing a regular 1120 S corporation tax return, or firms with ten or more partners or shareholders. This part of the universe was relatively small.

10. This is consistent with the notion that many employers use a college degree as a screening tool. If you are smarter than the typical employee but still get screened out, this provides an incentive to start a business.

11. Starting with "no capital" probably means no incremental outlays, out of pocket expenses, or borrowing. For example, a musician could have invested in education, equipment, and clothes. Then he/she decides to start playing for income. Substantial capital was accumulated from the past but was not an incremental outlay to currently start playing for fees.

12. It would be useful to obtain the same statistics but for full-time operations where the owner has at most a high school education.

13. This is the strongest compared to blacks and Hispanics but less strong compared to women. Part of the reason for this is that comparing nonminority males to these groups compounds two effects—sex and race.

14. If unreported self-employment activities are a stable proportion to reported self-employment activities, then this problem is not too severe. We then only have underestimates of *levels* of self-employment activity but can accurately trace *changes* over time and between groups.

15. A different way to measure self-employment activity could utilize the participant observation ethnographic approach of living or working in the informants' environment to first develop trust. Then, field notes are taken and interviews performed. Another technique could use records from different sources to cross-check for underreporting. This could be done infrequently with a random sample of the population to determine the degree that self-employment underreporting occurs so that self-employment figures can be appropriately adjusted upward. Self-report surveys have been developed by researchers in the field of criminal justice to measure participation in illegal activity. Information is sought in different ways and specific questions are added just to determine the degree which the respondent is telling the truth, in general.

16. Some of those implicit income perks also have tax benefits. Further, the

self-employed have a positive side benefit of having more discretion over their work time to better mesh work and leisure.

17. The Organization for Economic Cooperation and Development (OECD) is comprised of the countries of Europe, Australia, New Zealand, Japan, Canada, and the United States. In the last 15 years, about a third of OECD countries experienced an increase in the proportion of self-employment in total civilian employment and about a third of OECD countries experienced a decline in that proportion (OECD 1986).

18. It is important for a firm to consider the advantages of producing a product or service internally over contracting it out. The more advantageous it is to contract, the greater will be the growth in small firms. Among the factors that keep labor inside the firm are control over quality, maintenance of a stable core work force, and tasks requiring integrative teamwork.

19. The years used for their analysis were 1971, 1973, 1975, 1976, 1978, and 1980.

20. However, Long (1982) found the variable age had mixed results.

21. There are several studies that attempt to measure how large the underground economy is in terms of billions of dollars and percent of GNP. Estimates range from 5 to 33 percent of GNP. See Carson (1984) and Ferman, Henry, and Hotman (1987).

22. Though not statistically significant, Brock and Evans (1987, p. 165) found that "blacks earn 20% *more* in self-employment earnings than do otherwise comparable nonblacks."

23. Bates (1986) observed that minority entrepreneurs have improved in terms of being better educated and operating in more sophisticated lines of business; yet, many of the minority entrants into self-employment are poorly educated and operate in traditional lines of business. His explanation for this anomaly is that the upgrading of minority entrepreneurs comes from the part-time self-employed who enter more systematically into self-employment and have lower failure rates. The lower educated minority entrant, with no immediately prior self-employment experience, tends to enter self-employment in traditional lines of business and have high failure rates.

24. Long (1982) and Brock and Evans (1987) also tested for the effect of immigrant status on self-employment. Their results were not as unambiguous as Borjas'.

25. For more on this phenomenon, see U.S. Small Business Administration (1985).

26. For an annotated bibliography on the problems of women becoming business owners and operating businesses, see U.S. Department of Commerce (1986). For a narrative on this topic, see Gould and Lyman (1986).

27. However, for the blacks only SMSA sample, "being married" was not significant. Bearse (1984, p. 122) notes a possible explanation why marital status may not be conducive to starting a business: "facets of family status mean increased responsibilities that can make one reluctant to assume entrepreneurial risks."

28. Contrary to the evidence presented here, Casson (1982) takes a view that education may disadvantage an entrepreneur. Formal education entails an opportunity cost of foregone on-the-job training "learning the trade" and

delays the start of an entrepreneurial career. This may have the following three consequences: (1) It can make the entrepreneur a poor supervisor because tasks are delegated which he/she has never had to perform; (2) formal education may inculcate uniform views which destroy individuality and diversity which are crucial to discovering gaps in the market; and (3) formal education may encourage one to ask questions where precise solutions can be obtained, avoiding issues where no definite answer can be given (Casson 1982, pp. 356-357).

29. Lezear and Moore (1984) explored this issue and found this effect reversed for about half of the occupations used in their analysis.

30. Evans and Leighton (1987) and Brock and Evans (1986) utilized a technique to correct for selection bias in some of their regression analyses for earnings. This technique, developed by Heckman (1979), is used to estimate the impact of explanatory variables on earnings for a *typical* individual, rather than what would happen to earnings for those who *self-select* themselves into a particular mode of employment. When the technique was used here, it reduced the size and significance of the regression coefficients. An important conclusion they make from their use of this technique is, "it is the unusually poor wage workers who sort themselves into self-employment" (Evans and Leighton 1987, p. 58).

31. A similar analysis was performed for female self-employed dropouts, but since the self-employment rate for females is much lower than for males, there were too many empty cells to derive a comparable analysis.

32. These comparisons should be interpreted with some caution since standard errors were unavailable to perform significance tests.

33. Median earning comparisons for male dropouts were also performed by six aggregate occupation categories. Only in the occupation "service" did self-employed male dropouts earn more than wage workers. In contrast, several industrial categories did show that the self-employed earned more. This suggests that the self-employed, in general, work in different jobs than wage workers.

34. I can only speculate as to why some of these industries pay better for male dropout self-employed workers. Retail and low-level service industries tend to pay low wages, so it is not too hard for a self-employed worker to beat that.

35. It is likely that those who newly switch to self-employment will earn *less* than the average, for that industry. It takes time initially to generate profits. I was informed by an operator of a self-employment program that clients generally don't begin to match their previous wage earnings until their business is between six months and a year old.

36. Some of the cell sizes were very small, and standard errors were not available to do tests of significance. It is likely that some of the differences are not significant. Further, other control variables should be used besides education, sex, race, and full-time status, and correction should be made for selection bias if the data is to be used to infer what happens to a typical person who switches to self-employment.

37. This is only 6 percent of the total number of full-time self-employed male dropouts.

38. An area of inquiry that is important, but I did not find addressed, is

whether experience in self-employment is related to employment stability. Do workers who have had experience, or more experience in self-employment, have less unemployment in their lifetime? The self-employment experience may be providing skills and information that enhance worker resourcefulness.

39. An interesting side finding from Fredland and Little (1985) was that the typical self-employed person did not decide to become self-employed, quit his job, and start a business. The average self-employed person in their sample became partially self-employed at first as moonlighting. As the business grew, self-employment became a greater part of total economic activity.

40. Pomer (1985) observes that the majority (55.6%) of upwardly mobile blacks obtained mainstream positions in either the manufacturing or public sector. These are sectors that have experienced decline and therefore limited upward mobility for blacks.

41. There are conflicts among these attributes. For example, easy entry without restrictions is likely to drive down business earnings. There may be ways to permit easy but limited entry into certain lines of business for low-income people but entirely restrict entry for others. This would be the reverse of what is customarily done.

4

Immigrant and Ethnic Group Experience with Self-Employment

INTRODUCTION

Studies in Chapter 3 have suggested significant variation in ethnic and immigration experience with self-employment. This chapter explores how immigrant/ethnic groups use social networking to enhance prospects for self-employment and the practices of particular ethnic/immigrant groups that heavily use self-employment as avenues for economic attainment. Special attention is given to Gypsies, the Amish, and the Hmong as examples relevant to the underclass. Because it merits special attention, a separate chapter will concentrate on describing prominent black business movements.

RELEVANCE OF IMMIGRANT MODELS FOR THE UNDERCLASS

Immigrant participation in self-employment can be seen as a relevant model for U.S. underclass persons because immigrants have handicaps also. Immigrants have difficulty with the English language, have different customs from mainstream society, often have meager capital endowments when they reach the United States, and face discrimination in labor markets.

There are differences also. While immigrants may appear to possess modest capital endowments, many come with substantial human capital (skills, formal education) from middle-class backgrounds in their own native lands, and have had prior entrepreneurial experience. Opening up a shop in the United States is natural if one owned a shop back home. Further, the act of immigration itself is a type of entrepreneurial event—taking a risk, striking out in a different direction, and uncovering new opportunities. Immigration may be self-selecting those with more entrepreneurial ability.

In terms of the black underclass, differences may be more striking. Lieberson (1981) argued that the use of occupational niches used by immigrant groups to generate economic activity and mobility were and are unavailable to U.S. blacks because blacks as a group are too large. Intrusion by blacks in a particular occupational or business area deemed desirable by whites would be threatening to whites. Whites then engage in segregation practices to shut them out.

Sowell (1975) takes the view that the small size of Asians and Jews and the discrimination against them worked to assist their economic mobility. These circumstances discouraged their search for success through the political process. Instead they developed self-sufficiency, relying on education and community organizations. Blacks and Irish, more politically active ethnic groups, have achieved slower economic advances than Asians and Jews.

In any case, those considering advocating self-employment for low-income people can look to immigrant/ethnic group business formation strategies, translating what works into programs for low-income, even nonethnic, groups.

ANCESTRY GROUPS AND SELF-EMPLOYMENT PARTICIPATION

Fratoe (1986) estimated self-employment rates for the 50 largest ancestry groups in the United States, using 1980 Census data.[1] Ancestry here refers to the country of origin of one's ancestors upon coming to the United States, regardless of the number of generations back. The ancestry groups with the five highest and five lowest rates of self-employment are presented in Table 4.1.

It should not be too surprising that Russians rank at the top when one considers that this ancestry category is likely a proxy for Eastern European Jews.[2] The Lebanese, ranking second, are also known historically to have been prominently engaged in mercantile activities. Puerto Ricans, considered to be the most disadvantaged of the Hispanic groups, rank at the bottom. Next to the very lowest are sub-Saharan Africans. This group mainly contains native American blacks. Both blacks and Puerto Ricans are large minority groups. Also ranking in the bottom five are the Vietnamese, very recent immigrants to the United States in 1980. I suspect that their rate of self-employment has risen substantially since 1980.

Of the intermediate-ranked groups, we can observe that the Koreans have the highest participation in self-employment among Asians and

Table 4.1
Self-Employment Rates and Rankings of Some Ancestry Groups among the 50 Largest Ancestry Groups in the United States

Ancestry Group

Five Highest	Self-employment Rate
1. Russian	11.7%
2. Lebanese	10.7%
3. Rumanian	10.4%
4. Swiss	10.4%
5. Greek	9.5%

Some Intermediate Rankings

18. Korean	6.9%
23. Japanese	6.5%
24. Chinese	6.0%
25. Italian	6.0%
30. Polish	5.2%
32. Irish	5.0%
NATIONAL AVERAGE	4.9%
34. Cuban	4.8%
35. Asian Indian	4.7%
39. American Indian	3.3%
43. Jamaican	2.2%
45. Mexican	1.9%

Five Lowest

46. Vietnamese	1.7%
47. Haitian	1.6%
48. Dominican	1.5%
49. Subsaharan African	1.4%
50. Puerto Rican	1.1%

Source: 1980 Census: calculated from Fratoe (1986).

that Cubans have the highest rate of self-employment among Hispanics. It is surprising that American Indians had a much higher ranking (39) than one would have suspected based on their disadvantaged status. Jamaicans, an ancestry group that is primarily black, have a low self-employment rate, but it is 60 percent greater than that of sub-Saharan Africans. Fratoe (1986) also reports that groups with higher rates of self-employment also have higher self-employment earnings.[3]

It would seem useful to probe into the characteristics of particular ancestry groups that ranked high in self-employment to uncover their secrets of success. Some prominent literature in this area includes coverage on Jews (Sarachek 1980, Rosentraub and Taebel 1980, Weisser 1986), Greeks (Lovell-Troy 1980, Chock 1981); Koreans (Kim and Hurh 1983, 1985; Young and Stontz 1985; Light and Bonacich 1988), Japanese (Bonacich and Modell 1980), Chinese (Wong 1977, Kwong 1987), and Cubans (Wilson and Martin 1982, Portes 1987).

Caution must be used in *simply* translating practices from the ethnic groups above to low-income groups of today or to another ethnic group. For example, the Jews are often considered a "model" ethnic group. Their heavy participation in self-employment stems from centuries-old discrimination that prevented them from participating in other forms of employment. Jews responded to this by developing internal mechanisms to provide for their own.[4] This development strategy was complemented by a high degree of resourcefulness derived from an emphasis on literacy that was an important by-product of religious learning. However, they may not be an appropriate group for low-income people to emulate today. The current economic approach taken by a large percentage of Jews seems to be based on the goals of obtaining a college education, entering the professions, and assimilating into all sectors of the economy. To the extent that Jews still enter self-employment, it is likely to be more individualistic in a classic capitalist mode, rather than collectivist.[5] It is still, though, generally based on long-term preparation drawing on both cultural and class resources developed over centuries. At present, I don't think there are any short-cut, short-term approaches to emulate the Jews. For a long-run approach, there is a lot that low-income groups can learn from the Jews to assist their own economic development, but I don't think there is any "Jewish business strategy" out there to be copied for quick results.[6]

Further, there is a problem of overgeneralization. Asian Americans are considered to be another "model" success group.[7] Hurh and Kim (1986) express their view of the consequences of this stereotyping:

Since the Asian Americans' "success" may be considered by the dominant group as a proof of openness in the American opportunity structure, there is constant danger that other less successful minorities may be blamed for their own failure and become victims of scapegoating ("Japanese have made it. Why can't they?").... The probable effects may be summarized as follows: (1) incorrect perception of Asian Americans' upward mobility (2) an increased sense of relative deprivation, and (3) a feeling of resentment against Asian Americans (Hurh and Kim 1986, p. 25).

These arguments suggest that one should be cautious in translating self-employment approaches used by one ethnic group to another group.

With this caution in mind, the "success" principles of ethnic groups will be discussed in the following section.

SOCIAL NETWORKING AND SELF-EMPLOYMENT

Miriam Rozen (1984) reported on recent immigrant entrepreneurs and found that family ties and intra-ethnic networking were prominent mechanisms that fostered formation of immigrant enterprises. Immigrant groups tend to develop particular industry niches. In New York vegetable stands tend to be owned by Koreans; business district newsstands tend to be owned by Indians and Pakistanis; Chinese are heavily involved in the garment district; and Israelis are active in electronics, auto parts, and clothing stores.

The inclusion of new immigrants into established networks occurs sometimes even before the immigrant arrives. Because immigration priorities are given to relatives of naturalized citizens, many start out already knowing someone in the United States. Knowing someone and speaking their language provides information and assists entry into an industry. Rozen quoted an Israeli jeans manufacturer, "If you know the guy's cousin or a cousin of his cousin, you feel safer about giving him the first $500 worth of merchandise" (Rozen 1984, Sec. F, p. 15).

Immigrant entrepreneurs also can make better use of immigrant labor. They speak the same language, and there are greater social ties between labor and management. Immigrant entrepreneurs can pay their labor less for the privilege of working with and for fellow countrymen. This may be a price immigrant workers are willing to pay to avoid the strange, foreign, and socially discriminating practices of mainstream employers. This exploitation of labor may be providing immigrant entrepreneurs with a cost advantage that fosters business success while at the same time providing entrepreneurial models for the immigrant workers to emulate when they obtain the capital and language facility to leave their boss.[8]

Light (1984) provides four reasons for the relatively higher rates of self-employment among certain U.S. minorities: "Jews, Chinese, Japanese, Greeks, Macedonians, West Indians, Dominicans, Gypsies, Koreans, and Arabs" (Light 1984, p. 199). These four reasons are transplanted cultural endowments, relative satisfaction, communal solidarity upon becoming a minority group, and prevalence of sojourning.

According to Light, transplanted cultural endowment refers to group values and motivations that are favorable to business formation. These are displayed in characteristics such as diligence, thriftiness, profit seeking, and individualism. These are often augmented by class resources: human capital, physical capital, and money capital. The established upper and middle classes equip their young to prosper, regardless of the country.

Relative satisfaction refers to the well-being arising from immigration to a high-wage country from a low-wage country. Immigrants have been willing to accept low rates of return, long work hours, danger, and poverty to maintain their businesses. Relative to the country of origin, these situations look good and therefore encourage continued participation in marginal businesses that native-born owners would be unwilling to accept.

Communal solidarity refers to well developed social networks that are generated by co-ethnics' need to stick together when they become minorities in a foreign country. These networks result in cooperation and information sharing in the business sphere. One such prominent institution arising from an immigrant social network is the rotating credit association. This is a type of credit union arrangement in which a group of people will each contribute a sum of money for one or a few people to use to invest in a business or some other important purpose. When these loans are paid back, another set of persons can invest to start businesses.

Sojourning refers to immigrants' intentions to repatriate. In the temporary journey in the host country, the sojourning immigrant intends to amass as much money as possible as quickly as possible. This, Light and others think, provides motivation that translates into a competitive advantage in small business enterprise activity.

Light contends that the business success of particular immigrant groups was not solely due to class resources. He cites the examples of Cubans in Miami, and Koreans in Los Angeles to show the importance of ethnic resources. Cubans use language and cultural barriers to provide privileged access to markets and sources of labor (Wilson and Portes 1980).[9]

Koreans, while highly educated (70% of Korean immigrant men in Los Angeles had college degrees) and endowed with substantial money capital, still supplement these class resources with ethnic resources (Light 1984, p. 204).[10] "Koreans made use of rotating credit associations, nationalistic appeals for labor peace, vertical and horizontal integration of firm, internal and formal restraints of trade and political connections with City Hall developed by leading Korean business organizations" (Light 1984, p. 204). Light further argues that immigrant business success has a lot to do with their balanced mixing of individualistic competitive behavior with collective efforts at cooperation among business co-ethnics. He cites Useem (1980) who has studied two generations of the American business elite. Useem found upper-class institutions in abundance (clubs, resorts, prep schools) that foster upper-class consciousness and internal cohesion.

Black self-employment fits into Light's framework. First, he views the incidence of black self-employment as not necessarily lower than other ethnic groups. Blacks may just be overrepresented in the irregular economy. They have the circumstances that lead one to resort to self-employment—labor force discrimination and high unemployment—but blacks are low in ethnic resources and class resources. Light (1984, p. 209) suggests they are low in ethnic resources because they have developed highly individualistic, heavily illegal styles of coping with poverty. They also are low in class resources that have persisted for generations. Greater resources for blacks would have enhanced the mobility of marginal irregular businesses into the regular measured small business sector.

GROUPS HEAVILY INVOLVED IN SELF-EMPLOYMENT AND THAT DEVALUE FORMAL EDUCATION: GYPSIES AND THE AMISH

Gypsies and the Amish can be viewed as examples relevant to low-income groups such as the United States underclass because they are groups that predominantly engage in self-employment activity, and yet they devalue formal education. This is not to argue that formal education should be devalued. It is to provide examples of how groups with very low levels of formal education can still heavily engage in self-employment activity.

Gypsies and the Amish share some remarkable similarities besides devaluing formal education. These similarities include European origin, strong nuclear families that heavily rely on extended kin networks, use of low technology, use of child labor, respect for the elderly, using the elderly in economic activities, a hard work ethic, small size compared to the general population, internal mechanisms for dispute resolution, use of excommunication to maintain cultural rules, and avoidance of noncoethnics. Both groups are adept at using ethnic resources through cultural endowments and communal solidarity.

Gypsies

Gypsies are a particular ethnic group, active in self-employment, that stands out as having handicaps similar to those of the underclass. Sway (1984) notes that unlike other middleman minorities, Gypsies are, in general, illiterate. This handicap denies them access to better occupations and prevents the establishment of highly developed formal social and economic institutions (newspapers, banks). Despite this handicap, they have exploited various middleman niches to remain a commercially viable ethnic group. Gypsies have developed highly flexible and adaptive business practices which rely on family labor, intraethnic cooperation, a dual ethic, and a hard work ethos.

Sway identifies five strategies Gypsies use to assist the development of their self-employment mode of economic activity. These are nomadism, exploiting available resources deemed worthless by society, avoiding age barriers in the distribution of labor, and becoming multioccupational. One reason Gypsies choose self-employment rather than wage labor for economic activity is that most employers would be "Gajos," non-Gypsies. Non-Gypsies are considered unclean and morally inferior. Taking orders from a non-Gypsy is undesirable and even humiliating. However, outwitting a non-Gypsy in the competitive arena of business and trading is a source of ethnic pride.

Gypsies use nomadism to find and exploit new markets after markets have been depleted. Rather than limit one's market to a fixed location, often with a high overhead to maintain a permanent place of business, Gypsies continually find customers by moving about. Gypsies often provide specialized services to smaller towns that don't have a threshold population to support a permanent business in that activity. Gypsies also often engage in different activities depending on the season. There are winter and summer economies. One Los Angeles extended Gypsy family described by Sway spends the fall and winter showing old cowboy movies in rural areas of Mexico. In summer they concentrate on fortune-telling, renting air-conditioned hotel rooms, and promoting Madame Ludmilia the clairvoyant.

Gypsies have been willing to do work no one else has wanted and exploit the availability of free resources. Gypsies have an ability to "make something out of nothing." Home production with the use of family labor and vertical control of the production process are attributes of Gypsy business which keep costs down. These allow Gypsies to obtain income from a business that has been deemed unprofitable by others. Gypsies from Washington State and South Carolina "haul odd pieces of uncut lumber from logging camps for a fee and make furniture for sale.... Both British and Swedish Gypsies have found extremely lucrative niches by collecting and selling waste scrap" (Sway 1984, pp. 88-89). British Gypsy women go door-to-door asking for rags. The better pieces are sold to secondhand clothing stores. The leftovers are sold to rag dealers. Gypsy women are also heavily involved in fortune-telling, which they have been trained to do since childhood.

Gypsies have occupations that are sex typed. For example, fortune-telling is almost always a woman's job, and buying and selling horses or used cars is almost always men's work. Yet, the family will rearrange its division of labor to accommodate the most profitable income earner. Men will care for the children, cook, and clean if the wife is engaged in a lucrative fortune-telling business.

Every member of a Gypsy family is expected to contribute to its economic success regardless of age. Children learn shrewd business practices early in life. They spend most of their time with the family, and the family spends much of its time engaged in business activities. Children are also used to perform lower-skilled tasks in family businesses. Children learn an occupation while being trained "to avoid being cheated, how to bargain, and how to handle themselves in a market place situation" (Sway 1984, p. 93).

The elderly contribute to family income even if infirm. Elderly Gypsies who obtain disability or welfare payments are considered contributors to family income through "passive employment." Those able to work are used in Gypsy businesses to perform less strenuous tasks. The concept of formal retirement is unknown among Gypsies.

The fifth strategy, described by Sway, is not to depend solely on one occupation. The practice of being multioccupational is a form of job security. If one market closes, one can quickly turn to others. In Los Angeles Gypsy families, it is common for men to engage in body and fender work, used car dealing, blacktopping of driveways, roof repair, and promoting the wife's fortune-telling business.

I posed a question to Dr. Matt Salo, a researcher on economic activities of Gypsies (Salo 1985). My question was "Can underclass U.S. Blacks use these economic strategies developed by Gypsies?" In a personal letter he responded:

Of course Blacks like anybody else could learn to live like Gypsies and be successful—although their color may be an extra obstacle. But, this would entail changes in attitudes, social organization and an acquisition of skills the Gypsies have spent centuries in perfecting. It is unlikely any of this could occur with normal means of socialization. Gypsies are successful for cultural reasons. Their whole lifestyle is geared toward an effective hustling type economy. Although individuals can be and have been adopted by Gypsies and taught their survival strategies, entire groups can't be similarly accommodated.... The Gypsy model is too different. However, I'm not saying that there might not be aspects of Gypsy economic strategies that could be transferred.... Probably any realistic program would have to be introduced piecemeal.[11]

My view is that there seem to be economic strategic lessons from Gypsies applicable for the underclass. The ability to find demand for a service as ethereal as fortune-telling is a tribute to the cunning of Gypsies. This suggests that persons, to eke out a living, do not need to be involved in producing something tangible or a service that is conventionally useful. Economists know this: There are many persons in that profession who participate in a type of fortune-telling called economic forecasting. They, too, are often wrong about the future. The success of the pet rock and edible panties offer proof that one can earn a living producing and selling something quite insubstantial.

The strategies of nomadism can be applied in a more circumscribed sense. Self-employed persons should be encouraged to be flexible in picking their business locations: Locate at a point of strong demand and move when demand falls off. Don't necessarily locate in a place because it is familiar and involves small transportation costs. Fixed permanent business locations are more expensive and decrease spatial mobility to serve different market areas.

Perhaps the most important lesson to be had from Gypsies and from other economically successful ethnic groups is the use of the family as an economic resource. Two parent families are more effective than one parent families, and an extended family is more effective than a nuclear family alone. Strategies that strengthen underclass families are likely to be reinforced by economic rewards, particularly if a self-employment Gypsy-type economic strategy is employed. The family also seems to be a key transmission mechanism by which attitudes toward economic achievement are transmitted to children. Underclass families may need help to effectively encourage their children to attain economic success.

The Amish

The Amish work mainly as independent farmers and craftsmen in rural North America. Their high participation in self-employment stems from their attachment to farming, rural life, and avoidance of a mainstream worldly existence. The rural focus for their economic life makes their success principles difficult to apply to the urban poor. Still, I feel there are important lessons to be obtained from observing how they conduct their economic activities. In the past they were viewed by non-Amish as an obscure sect who resisted education and exploited their children. Today they are objects of a thriving tourist industry and: "are revered as hard-working, thrifty people with enormous agrarian stamina, and by some, as islands of sanity in a culture gripped by commercialism and technology run wild" (Hostetler 1980, p. 4). First a little of their history will be presented and then their economic organization will be discussed.

The Amish first came to the United States in the eighteenth century primarily from Switzerland, Germany, and Holland to settle in Pennsylvania on the invitation of William Penn. They are related to the Mennonites but separated from them around 1700 on the insistence of Jacob Ammann. Ammann, from whom the name "Amish" derives, held fast to the doctrine of shunning (social avoidance), excommunicated members, and also favored more conservative ways of dress.

The Amish (and Mennonites) were considered heretics in Europe by both established Catholic and Protestant churches for advocating the principles of adult baptism, separation of church and state, and pacifism. They were hunted down and many were burned at the stake. To survive they retreated to remote regions where they were forced to become self-sufficient and develop innovative labor-intensive farming methods. When the opportunity arose to come to America, the Amish flocked there seeking religious freedom and farmland.

A striking characteristic of the Amish is their adherence to tradition generally defined by the eighteenth and nineteenth centuries. The Amish are an evolving society, and they do bring new ways of doing things into their culture. They are just deliberately very slow about it, at least 50 years behind the times. They resist being controlled by the outside world and want to choose to adapt at their own pace taking into account nature, cultural continuity, religion, and respect for elders. Being old fashioned also maintains their distinctiveness from the non-Amish and reinforces the notion that they are a chosen people. Besides their plain and old looking clothes, they do not use automobiles, motor driven tractors, or electricity. No electricity precludes television, radios, record players, telephones, and computers. It necessitates using labor-intensive, low technology methods of operating businesses.[12] While not particularly a wealthy people, they survive and live well. Among the larger problems facing the Amish today is a shortage of good inexpensive farm land for their children and the high cost of formal medical care.[13]

The Amish do not want compulsory public education for their children and particularly do not want their children to go to school past the eighth grade. They devalue formal education to keep their children from being exposed to worldly influences. They likely could not perpetuate their "old fashioned" culture if their children attended college. The Amish purpose of education is not to get ahead in the material sphere but to get to heaven (Keim 1975). However, Amish children do obtain a very good formal education up to the eighth grade and a good informal vocational education from working with their parents. Their rate of literacy is high. They are also bilingual, speaking a German dialect at home and using English to communicate with non-Amish. Chief Justice Burger recognized the adequacy of Amish education as part of his opinion to permit the Amish to take their children out of school after the eighth grade.[14]

How do the Amish survive so well? Their central "success" principle is strict adherence to the Protestant work ethic. The relationship between the Protestant ethic to material success was prominently developed in 1905 by a German Sociologist, Max Weber (Weber 1920). Weber drew primarily on his understanding of the works of John Calvin to define the Protestant ethic.[15] The core of the Protestant ethic is viewing work as a way to glorify God, not as a means to earn income. One has a calling or special mission of work on earth, and one is supposed to engage in doing that diligently, honestly, and morally in a manner of sobriety and frugality (Tawney 1926).[16] If one becomes wealthy or successful on account of that work, that wealth is a sign of God's favor.[17] However, acquisition of wealth is not supposed to be the reigning motivation. Now, this is the important part: If one did accumulate wealth it was not to be squandered on consumption goods but was to be used for holy purposes as a steward for God.[18] Farming, for the Amish, is considered to be a sacred occupation. To survive in family farming using labor-intensive low technological methods requires a devotion to work, and that devotion is inculcated during childhood. As expressed by an Amish person, "if a boy does little hard work before he is twenty-one, he probably never gets to like it afterwards. In other words, he will not amount to much as a farmer" (in Hostetler 1980).

Self-sufficiency is also an important part of economic life. The Amish believe in private property. Farms are owned by individual families. It is not a communal society, but mutual assistance is stressed, and economic rewards as well as misfortunes are shared within the community. In this sense they are not independent but interdependent. Government aid or subsidy of any kind, including farm price support payments and social security, are refused because they undermine their way of taking care of each other. They are not opposed to paying taxes, just to receiving government aid or welfare. Contact with non-Amish occurs because they interact with non-Amish merchants, buyers, and medical care providers. However, this contact is kept limited for fear of contagion with the outside world. This is a motivation for independent farming or craft self-employment because one does not have to work and socialize with non-Amish.[19] For the Amish, "the highest prestige activity is farming, the second highest is self-employment in a nonfarm business, and the lowest is day labor" (Hostetler 1980, p. 144).

Amish strategies in farming include diversity in crops, crop rotation, use of animals for power and fertilizer. raising animals for dairy and meat products, growing crops in hard to farm places (for example, under fences), maintaining large vegetable gardens for growing one's own food, using old equipment but keeping it in good repair, and general conservation of land and energy. These strategies yield several advantages: low overhead, fewer cash flow problems, avoidance of expensive petroleum-based fertilizers, and the end result that they can label products as organic.[20]

To insure survival, consumption expenditures are kept modest. Most clothes are homemade; most food is either made at home or bought from Amish neighbors; expenditures on secular books and toys are very minimal; purchases of electronic entertainment and gadgets are zero; and distant travel is only occasional. Frugality in consumption is made easier by the lack of exposure to television. When the Amish do shop, they look for secondhand goods and go to farm sales or flea markets. The largest consumption expense is for construction and maintenance of a large home so community religious services can be observed there.

In sum, the Amish succeed well economically though very few are monetarily rich. The Amish may earn an implicitly low hourly wage. However, they are able to generate an adequate family income by laboring long hours and having the entire family work. Work, though, is not alienating toil for them, it is worship and a social activity. They are adept at utilizing "ethnic" resources. Though the Amish lack a high level of formal education and do not use high technology in their economic activities, they compensate through informal vocational education, mutual aid, and adherence to the Protestant work ethic.

A RECENT ASIAN REFUGEE GROUP WITHOUT MIDDLE-CLASS ORIENTATION: THE HMONG

The Hmong are a hill tribe group from Laos that arrived in the United States as a group of 54,000 people in 1979/1980. They assisted the United States in the Vietnam War and had to flee Laos because they backed the wrong side. They are refugees, not just an immigrant group. This distinction is important because they would not have chosen to leave their homeland under other circumstances. The Hmong seem particularly unsuited to American culture. Their occupational background was in small-scale farming and warfare, and many of them were illiterate even in their own language. Their exposure to Western culture was very limited prior to immigrating to the United States. Unlike many Vietnamese refugees preceding them, the Hmong were not middle class and educated, and they rely on public welfare support much more than the Vietnamese did.[21]

Fass (1986) studied how the Hmong and their American advisors developed projects to encourage self-reliance. Under an entrepreneurship and experimentation theme, the following avenues to self-sufficiency were explored: movement from public welfare to wage employment, and movement from public welfare or wage employment to self-employment in either individual or collective enterprises. Approaches included sewing projects for women, farming schemes, establishment of small nonfarm businesses, and help in securing wage employment. Of the small businesses, the most common were grocery stores. They often began as food cooperatives to provide foods that the Hmong liked. The cooperatives also began to sell Hmong farming produce and as a by-product were providing initial business experience.

The for-profit grocery stores had greater monthly sales than the cooperatives, hired more people, and were owned by Hmong who were relatively well educated and had prior business experience. Other small businesses included a supermarket wholesaler, a bakery, a credit union, a security agency, a theater, two restaurants, a home-cleaning service, a jeweler, and two manufacturers (woodcrafts and toy assembly).

Obstacles were formidable, but the prerequisites of successful self-reliance, according to Fass, were there: "willingness to venture into the new, to work hard, and to learn whatever it is that can make the venture a permanent fixture" (Fass 1986, p. 375).

The results of these projects were mixed. The most serious problem was the lack of business knowledge of the American advisors. They came mostly from social service backgrounds and did not know much about operating and managing enterprises. Both the American advisors and the Hmong were experimenting in areas they knew little about. Even though clear successes were few, they provided encouraging examples for others: "This kind of evidence is essential to improved self-reliance because it motivates others to make initial efforts, to work harder if they've already begun, and to learn more quickly" (Fass 1986, p. 374).

Another important outcome was that many of the Hmong realized their knowledge limitations and sought ways to overcome them. Some obtained classroom education related to their businesses. Others searched for persons with requisite skills and experience and built networks so that acquired information from one venture could be shared.

The Hmong should be followed to monitor their progress and uncover the processes they used for economic improvement. Their case is a good test to see if immigrants who are more similarly situated to America's own poor can make it, and if they do make it, how much it was due to their own initiative and how much to government efforts. If successful, perhaps, the techniques used to help the Hmong can be used to help America's own poor.

SUMMARY

Aspects of immigrant participation in self-employment can be used by low-income people to start small businesses. These include promoting strong intact nuclear families, encouraging intra-ethnic networking, developing particular industry niches that entire groups can exploit, having employees who will work cheap and responsibly, rewarding employees with informal managerial and entrepreneurial training, using rotating credit associations and trade associations, encouraging low-income people to buy from each other, and knowing when to compete and when to cooperate.

There are aspects, however, that are not easily copied. These concern initially having a high level of economic and middle-class–oriented resources that the more successful immigrant groups brought with them. Also, many native-born poor people will not have the same willingness to tolerate low rates of return and long hours of work as many immigrant groups because they were not raised in a low wage country, nor feel the same isolation and desperation to survive in a strange place.

Three immigrant/ethnic groups that are actively engaged in self-employment but have low levels of formal education are the Gypsies, the Amish, and the Hmong. Lessons from the Gypsies include the following: A permanent business location impedes one's ability to be responsive to changing demand and fully serve markets; survival is enhanced by being flexible so as to be able to engage in several types of economic activity; and filling needs does not have to involve producing a substantial good or service—it can come out of the air. Lessons from the Amish include the following: Frugality and an austere lifestyle can be a source of capital accumulation; religion can inspire sacrifices that enhance business success; businesses can survive using low technology; a lack of sophisticated education need not be a barrier to operating a business; informal vocational training through the family can be an important source of skill acquisition; commitment to the intrinsic aspects of a business enhances survival; and mutual aid can be a substitute for commercial services. While it is too early to tell how successful the Hmong will be, lessons from their residence in the United States so far point to the importance of experimentation, finding advisors with business experience, and networking. All three groups demonstrate the importance of family as an economic resource.[22]

NOTES

1. Fratoe (1986) calculated self-employment rates by dividing the number of persons in a particular ancestry group who identified themselves as self-employed by the total number of persons in that ancestry group. Everything else the same, groups with high birth rates would have lower self-employment rates because more of that group would be younger and out of the labor force.

2. Jews could not enter this analysis as Jews since Judaism is a religion, not a country of origin.

3. I would expect that also correlated with rates of self-employment are family size (neg.), percent of group with parents who were self-employed (pos.), and education level (pos.).

4. For Eastern European Jews, some of these internal mechanisms were religious schools, religious courts, religion-sponsored welfare systems, net-

working through synagogue contacts, shared language (Yiddish) which could not be understood by non-Jews and could be used to conduct trade with foreigners, *landsmanschaften* (immigrant clubs based on European town origin), immigrant aid societies, and emphasis on a strong family life. At one time, 650 Jewish organizations existed to help fellow Jews (Howe 1976).

An important factor in the success of Eastern European Jews in America was the early existence of reasonably successful German Jews in America who aided their coreligionists when they came in large numbers at the turn of the century. Fear of being embarrassed by "uncouth" less-educated immigrants and of being lumped together with them caused many of these successful German Jews to create immigrant aid societies to Americanize them (Rosentraub and Taebel 1980, p. 196).

5. Rosentraub and Taebel (1980) consider five components of collectivist self-help which Jews, as well as other ethnic groups, have practiced: immigrant-supporting institutions, charities, employment of co-ethnics, selling businesses only to co-ethnics, and purchasing from co-ethnic businesses. From a survey of Jews in Texas in the 1970s, Rosentraub and Taebel found that while there is still high participation in Jewish organizations and charities, very few Jews engage in business hiring-purchasing practices that favor Jews.

6. As a thought experiment, I have constructed a scenario of how low-income groups could copy the success Jews have in America. It is extremely harsh and immoral, and I don't recommend it, but I think it would work. First, restrict the group into only mercantile ways of earning a living or certain professions such as medicine. Second, cut them off from all government assistance so they would develop internal mechanisms of self-help. Third, periodically take their physical possessions, so that the only capital they could keep would be human capital—that is, education. Fourth, restrict entry into most schools. This would necessitate their religious institutions to operate schools to teach literacy and engage students in philosophical debate on arcane religious laws. Fifth—now this is the most important part—keep this up for about 2000 years and then have them immigrate to a country that offers relatively open opportunities.

7. It is unclear what is meant by success. Possible conceptualizations include a high rate of self-employment, high income (e.g., top quartile), at least a middle-class income (e.g., median family income), an income comparable to white male native Americans of similar education and experience, independence and life-style flexibility in one's job, and cultural preservation. Some groups (e.g., Asian Americans) may have a high rate of self-employment and middle-class incomes but may be underemployed compared to whites of similar education and experience (Chung 1979).

8. Portes and Bach (1985, p. 343), commenting on ethnic enclave firms, claim "If employers can profit from the willing self-exploitation of fellow immigrants, they are also obliged to reserve for them those supervisory positions that open in their firms, to train them in trade skills, and to support their eventual move into self-employment."

The situation of the immigrant business owner paying low wages to immigrant workers as a factor for business success is discussed in Bailey (1987), Portes (1987), Bonacich (1987), and Sanders and Nee (1987).

9. In addition, for the Cubans, Portes (1987) cites a fortunate confluence of circumstances which has assisted Cuban businesses in the past but which may not be repeated for Cubans or copied by other groups. These circumstances were class heterogeneity (simultaneous appearance of workers and business owners), institutional diversity, and blockage of returning. However, Portes does suggest that:

> social networks within an ethnic community can play a decisive role in promoting its economic well-being....Their sole differential advantage frequently lies in the informational and economic resources within their group. Thus premature cultural assimilation, with its concomitant weakening of ethnic ties may be inimical to economic progress. The alternative suggested by the Cuban experience and those of other entrepreneurial minorities is instrumental adaption to the realities of the host economy and labor market, a circumspect approach to the new culture and selective adoption of its traits, and preservation of strong bonds of group solidarity. (Portes 1987, p. 368).

10. Kim and Hurh (1985) interviewed a sample of one hundred Korean business owners in Chicago who operate in the predominantly black South Side. It took an average of 2.7 years for them to initiate their businesses in the United States. Over half had completed their college educations in Korea. Korean churches were the only ethnic organizations in which they actively participated. The majority obtained most of their capital in the United States by husband and wife both working in wage jobs and saving and borrowing from family and friends. Three-fourths invested $30,000 or less in their initial business; one-third invested $10,000 or less. The distribution of initial businesses consisted of clothing stores (19%), variety shops (selling jewelry, handbags, etc. [21%]), wig shops (20%), and other types (40%). Owners and their spouses worked on average over 50 hours a week at the business, and the majority were open seven days a week. They used Korean suppliers whenever possible, and a majority hired Korean workers, although half reported also having black employees.

11. Letter to Steven Balkin from Matt Salo, November 23, 1985.

12. Through intermediaries, notably the Mennonites, the Amish are able to have limited access to high technology. For example, the Amish are permitted to use the telephone for important reasons. If they want to use the telephone, they will either go to a nearby pay phone or use the telephone of their Mennonite neighbor. While they can't use an electric freezer in the house to store perishables, they can rent space at a locker. While they can't use a computer at home to do their accounting, they can use the services of an accountant who does use a computer.

13. The Amish are not permitted to buy commercial insurance as this would show lack of faith. Instead they rely on mutual assistance. For health care, the first line of defense is home remedies and Amish healers practicing various types of folk medicine. If the condition still persists, they do use the services of the formal medical care system (Schwieder and Schwieder 1975).

14. In his Supreme Court opinion (1972), Chief Justice Burger stated,

> that since accommodating the religious objections of the Amish by foregoing one, or at most two, additional years of compulsory education would not impair the physical or mental health of the child, nor result in an inability to be self-supporting, or to discharge

the duties and responsibilities of citizenship, or in any way materially detract from the welfare of society, the state's interest in its system of compulsory education was not so compelling that the established religious practices of the Amish had to give way.... (in Keim 1975)

15. Versions of the Protestant ethic were espoused by many theologians during the Reformation. While Calvin is often associated with the Protestant ethic, he and his followers were persecutors of Mennonites.

16. One doesn't have to be a Protestant or even Christian to hold to the Protestant Ethic. In an empirical study of the relationship between religion and economics, Lenski (1963) interviewed four groups in Detroit: white Protestants, white Catholics, black Protestants, and Jews. In a question to approximate the Protestant Ethic on attitudes towards work, Jews were the most likely to express a positive attitude toward work (42%), compared to white Protestants (30%), black Protestants (24%), and white Catholics (23%).

17. Generating wealth by utilizing immoral practices was not a sign of God's favor or grace.

18. Weber observed that this seemed irrational according to the conception of economic man who sought enhanced consumption as the reward for work activity. Yet it propelled industry by accelerating capital accumulation (Viner 1978). At the other extreme are Gypsies. First Gypsies, generally, are not Protestant. Second, a goal of Gypsy life is to spend a lot of money, not necessarily to earn a lot. A Gypsy would rather spend a million dollars during his/her life rather than earn a million dollars.

19. A large proportion of the work of the nonfarming Amish involve trades and businesses that serve the Amish community, such as carpenters, carriage makers, blacksmiths, butchers, tool sharpeners, and bicycle repairers. Amish shops are generally on farms and not advertised. Roadside markets selling produce and baked goods are also common. The granola my family eats is obtained by mail from an Amish woman. If personal contact with the non-Amish in a business transaction is necessary, the Amish would prefer to sell to non-Amish through an intermediary.

20. Because of recent reports of contaminants found in chicken, I know of restaurants that advertise they cook with Amish-raised poultry.

21. The evidence on refugee economic adjustment is impressive. For all refugees in the United States in 1982, those that have been in the United States less than six months faced an unemployment rate of approximately 75 percent, and 82.7 percent received some sort of cash (welfare) assistance. Those refugees who have been in the United States over three years faced an unemployment rate of only 14.8 percent, and 23 percent received cash assistance. The source of this data was the U.S. Department of Health and Human Services found in Fass (1986, p. 357).

22. According to Sowell, stability of family life is not a sufficient condition for economic attainment. However he found no highly successful ethnic group who has unstable families. The effects of a stable family life are in the realms of providing emotional support and transmitting values. This can have impact on economic improvement but it depends on what the values are and to what uses they are put (Sowell 1975, p. 130).

5

Black Business Movements

INTRODUCTION

While the business sector of black ethnics has been underdeveloped in U.S. history, there have been periods where black business formation was promoted. This section briefly describes such times in the nineteenth and twentieth centuries. In the nineteenth century, at least two situations occurred in which blacks attempted to start businesses on a large scale. In pre–Civil War America, a significant black business class emerged among free blacks. This occurred due to indigenous self-help efforts, and its characteristics were similar to those of European immigrant groups. After the Civil War, federal programs were instituted to assist the economic status of freed slaves and promote self-employment via land ownership. These programs were The Freedmen's Bureau and The Freedmen's Bank. In a sense they can be considered to be the first federal welfare programs. Both programs were sensible in their original purpose and design, but shortcomings in implementation and political support doomed them to failure.

From the twentieth century, four black business movements are described: the National Negro Business League (Booker T. Washington), Divine Peace Missions (Father Divine), Black Muslims (Elijah Muhammed), and Black Capitalism (Richard Nixon). Three of the four (perhaps all four) were attached to religious movements. They were all successful to a degree. Further research is required to determine their ultimate effectiveness. Nonetheless, I think there are lessons and formats to be learned from these experiences which may be translatable, with modification, to current policies and programs.

NINETEENTH CENTURY BLACK BUSINESS

Antebellum America

In a study of pre–Civil War free blacks in the 15 largest cities, Curry (1981) found a modest amount of participation in self-employment. The rate of self-employment was greatest in the lower Southern cities, and the city with the highest self-employment rate was New Orleans. This occurred because Southerners were accustomed to using black slaves as artisans, there was an urban labor shortage, and free blacks in the South came from the most able elements of the slave population. The existence of free blacks in the South was mainly the result of manumission, on account of slaves buying their own freedom, receiving a reward for loyalty, or being related to the slave owner (Curry 1981). In the Northern cities, black self-employment was related to residential segregation, creating enclave opportunities.

The institutions that primarily assisted free blacks in their economic endeavors were their churches and associations. However, active churches and associations were primarily Northern phenomena at this time. Black associational activity was outlawed in the South for fear that it could lead to slave revolts. Black churches provided burial sites, Sunday schools which assisted in producing literacy, secular day schools, moral affirmation, and community emotional support (Curry 1981). According to W.E.B. Du Bois, "a study of economic cooperation among Negroes must begin with the Church group" (cited in Frazier 1964, p. 40).

Black associations grew out of the church and were sometimes formally tied to churches. Black associations were of several types: benevolent and beneficial mutual aid societies, fraternal associations, and literary societies. Mutual aid societies were of two types: benevolent and beneficial. Benevolent mutual aid was more like charity; beneficial mutual aid was more like insurance. Benevolent societies redistributed income from better-off blacks to those in dire circumstances (e.g., widows and orphans). Beneficial societies collected money from poor blacks and distributed it among poor blacks on the basis of extraordinary needs such as unemployment, illness, and death. The way the beneficial societies worked was simple: "Once admitted to fellowship, members paid small weekly dues (usually 25 cents). Benefits were dispensed by committees and consisted of payments to members who were ill, the burial of any member whose estate was insufficient to provide for interment, and the support of widows and the training of orphans of members" (Curry 1981, p. 198).

The first of the beneficial societies established in a major city was the Free African Society organized in 1778 in Philadelphia by Richard

Allen and Absalom Jones. Allen later founded the African Methodist Episcopal (AME) Church, the first independent black denomination in the United States. In 1840, there were over 200 various black mutual aid societies in the major U.S. cities. In Philadelphia before the Civil War about half of the adult black population reported that they belonged to one (Curry 1981, p. 202). These mutual aid societies also provided banking and financial services on a limited scale (Walker 1986, p. 370). Out of these mutual aid associations grew the black insurance companies of today.

Free blacks in antebellum America exhibited many of the same characteristics as European immigrants: self-selection, an enterprising orientation, small size, self-help institutions, and occupational niches. According to Frazier, out of the free blacks in antebellum America came a substantial proportion of the black middle class up to the present (Frazier 1957). If slavery had not existed, there would have been no large number of blacks entering the U.S. economy, ignorant and penniless. If that were the case, blacks would have started in America on a firmer economic foundation and racism might be less virulent today. Not only might there be no black underclass today, but blacks might possibly have become one of the more successful groups in America.

Emancipation and Reconstruction

Emancipation of the slaves inflamed anti-black sentiments that exacerbated the problem of discrimination in both the North and the South. This hampered the progress of the then emerging black business class and significantly impeded the economic potential of the freedmen. Slaves had been kept purposely illiterate and dependent. When emancipation occurred, all at one time the slaves found themselves "liberated" but without economic resources. This produced confusion, desperation, and made them vulnerable to various forms of peonage (sharecropping).[1] In addition, many whites conspired to prevent freedmen from owning land. At the end of the Civil War two significant federal interventions were begun the avowed purpose of which was to assist the freed slaves to gain a foothold in the economy—The Freedmen's Bureau and the Freedmen's Saving Bank.

The Freedmen's Bureau

The formal name of the Bureau was the Bureau of Refugees, Freedmen, and Abandoned Lands. Established in 1865 by an act of Congress, its purposes were to provide emergency relief to freed slaves and displaced whites, establish schools and hospitals, and manage confiscated and abandoned lands. Financing of the Bureau was to come from the sale and rental of confiscated and abandoned Southern land. It was proposed originally that the Bureau would distribute land to the freed slaves consisting of 40 acres and a mule.[2] With such capital, freed slaves could become small independent self-employed farmers. However, no such distribution ever became written into law, and very few freed slaves were able to obtain land anywhere. No mules were ever distributed. Essentially, the Bureau and its aims were anathema to landed white Southerners. So, in the interests of reconciliation, the Bureau's powers were continually stripped away until its death in 1872.

As part of the actual law that did initiate the Freedmen's Bureau, the commissioner of the Bureau could set aside abandoned tracts of land of up to 40 acres to lease to freedmen at a low rent. Freedmen would then have the right to buy the land at the end of three years. However, this provision was seldom implemented, and when it was, the land was usually of poor quality and inaccessible (Magdol 1977). In 1865 and 1866, numerous tracts of land were leased by freedmen, but many were soon forced to leave as white Southerners pressed for the return of their land. Returning land back to white Southern landowners was also endorsed by many Northern industrialists who feared that assisting freedmen to own and rent confiscated land would set a precedent and lead to forced distribution of factories to workers.

In 1866, the Southern Homestead Bill was enacted. Freedmen and whites could apply for 80-acre tracts of land to be held for two years, and then the land would be theirs. To make land available, 44 million acres were set aside from public lands in the South. However, freedmen were generally too cash and credit poor to gain much from this.[3] They knew little about financing and had poor access to it. A few years of bad harvests would wipe them out. Some lands were remote and made freedmen inhabitants vulnerable to acts of violence undertaken with the intention to drive them out. Only about 4000 freedmen made claims out of a freedmen population of about 4 million (Cruden 1969).

The Freedmen's Bank

There was no formal connection between the Freedmen's Bank and the Freedmen's Bureau. The former was a quasi-independent bank set up by Congress while the latter was a part of the War Department of the executive branch of the federal government. However, there were many close connections between the two. In the minds of most freedmen (and many others), the Freedmen's Bank seemed to be an institution guaranteed by the United States government. This was a major reason for its tragic failure. First, the mostly sensible programmatic function of the Bank will be discussed and then we will return to why failure occurred.

The Freedmen's Saving and Trust Company was chartered in 1865 by an act of Congress. Its mission was to develop concepts of industry and thrift among freed slaves. The model for it originated from banking institutions set up for Northern black soldiers to help them save money earned as soldiers because they, like white soldiers, might squander it on payday or be swindled. The idea for the Bank emanated from John W. Alvord, a Congregational minister who was attached to Sherman's army (Fleming 1970).[4] The notion of using the bank for investment in the black community was unfortunately absent. A lending bank extending credit to freedmen before they were trained in self-discipline was not considered prudent. The bank was to be a simple savings bank and its ultimate function was to inculcate the Protestant work ethic. The following is a quote of Alvord in 1866: "Pauperism can be brought to a close; the freedmen made self-supporting and prosperous, paying for their educational and Christian institutions, and helping to bear the burdens of government.... That which savings banks have done for the working men of the north it is presumed they are capable of doing for these laborers" (Osthaus 1976, p. 9).

The Bank was called upon to preach the virtues of thrift, sobriety, and industry. To do this, public meetings were held, advertisements were taken out in newspapers, and miniature savings programs were instituted in schools. Freedmen's Bureau agents regularly exhorted their clients to use the Freedmen's Bank. Cashiers of the bank urged their depositors to use their savings to become independent farmers and not to "use tobacco, frequent lottery dens or candy shops, wear cheap jewelry and flashy clothes, or drink liquor" (Osthaus 1976, p. 52).

In helping dirt-poor freedmen save in order to accumulate capital, the Freedmen's Bank was a success. Over its history, it is estimated that there were well over 100,000 depositors among its 37 branches (Osthaus 1976, p. 96). Even those with no account at the Bank could be influenced by it. The Bank was a source of pride and hope.

The basic reasons for failure were trustee mismanagement and lack of depositor insurance. The first set of trustees included important business and philanthropic people. None of the original trustees were black. Most of the cashiers were drawn from missionaries, the Freedmen's Bureau, and the black community. None had prior banking experience.

The Bank was to invest all its nonreserve assets in U.S. government securities. Because of expansion and rising costs, the bank sought to earn a greater return on its assets. In 1870, the Bank was allowed to invest in notes secured by real estate. This led to more speculative loans of which some big ones went sour. The Bank was forced to close in 1874. The real tragedy of the Bank was that the U.S. government refused to reimburse depositors fully. Depositors received 61 cents on the dollar, and that took some years. On the closing of the Freedmen's Bank, Du Bois commented, "Not even ten additional years of slavery could have done so much to throttle the thrift of the freedmen" (Du Bois 1903, p. 36).

TWENTIETH CENTURY BLACK BUSINESS

National Negro Business League

Booker T. Washington, former slave, was a pragmatist, educator, and the leading black spokesman at the turn of the century. He founded the Tuskegee Institute and stressed the vocational aspect of higher education, self-improvement, accommodation with whites, and patronage of black businesses.[5] He was supported by some of the leading white Northern businessmen of the time (Andrew Carnegie, George Eastman, and Julius Rosenwald).

In 1900, Booker T. Washington organized the National Negro Business League and was elected as its president by delegates from 20 states.[6] Its purpose was to encourage the formation and expansion of black businesses. Its aims were to promote black economic development and to gain the respect of the white community as a means of combating prejudice.

After calling this first meeting, Washington noted:

As I have travelled through the country from time to time I have been constantly surprised to note the number of colored men and women, often in small towns and remote districts, who are engaged in various lines of business. In many cases the business was very humble, but nevertheless it was sufficient to indicate the opportunities of the race in this direction. . . . The meeting was called with two objects in view: first to bring the men and women engaged in business together, in order that they might get acquainted with each other and get information and inspiration from each other; secondly, to form plans for an annual meeting and the organization of local business leagues that should extend throughout the country. (Scott and Stowe 1918, pp. 186–187)

At the eleventh annual meeting, Washington exhorted the members to go out from the meeting:

determined that each individual shall be a missionary in his community—a missionary in teaching the masses to get property, to be more thrifty, more economical, and resolve to establish an industrial enterprise wherever a possibility presents itself. (cited in Frazier 1957, p. 134)

The National (Negro) Business League still exists today. Out of it have come various other black business and professional associations. As of 1918, they included, "The National Funeral Directors Association, The National Negro Press Association, The National Negro Bar Association, The National Negro Retail Merchants Association, and The National Association of Negro Insurance Men" (Scott and Stowe 1918, p. 221).

The National Negro Business League encouraged the local leagues to consider various issues and strategies for encouraging black enterprises such as developing an employment service, protecting the community against fraudulent schemes, determining what business and professional men can do for each other, encouraging patronage of black businesses, and determining what new businesses could be established. The League declared that black health insurance agents should constitute themselves unofficial health inspectors. Black newspapers should set up bureaus of information; buyers co-ops should be established; several small shopkeepers should group together and employ one expert bookkeeper; a social survey of the black population should be conducted each year and the results should be reported in a directory of black establishments (Scott and Stowe 1918, pp. 196-197).

The League was a forum for confidence building. Members of the black community were told, "If these men succeeded, so can you." Meetings were filled with testimonials of business success, how an individual started out from humble origins and overcame adversity. To be sure, this resulted in exaggerated claims. Frazier (1957) argues that the National Negro Business League institutionalized the myth that black business can provide a significant black economic base.[7] While this claim has some validity, the National Negro Business League did succeed in establishing black ethnic business networks and was associated with a rise in business formation from 20,000 black businesses in 1900 to 45,000 in 1915. These newly formed enterprises were mostly very small, specialized in local services, and took the forms of small grocery stores, general merchandise dealers, barbers, undertakers, saloons, drugstores, and restaurants (Scott and Stowe 1918, p. 194). After Washington's death there appeared to be continued growth in black business formation, which was halted at the onset of the Great Depression. The smaller black businesses did not have the capital to sustain themselves as many white businesses could.

Light (1972) claims, similarly to Frazier, that the League overall did not significantly increase the proportion of blacks in business. He lays the blame on his perception that the League was not an "organization of community participation." Only businessmen were allowed in the League—thus its ranks included only elite blacks. The orientation of the organization was middle class, and the profit motive was the League's primary social value. According to Light, the League stressed individualism rather than mutual aid which was the hallmark of Oriental business network organizations. To grow, the League would have had to actively recruit among lower-class black youths who had interests in business because this is the group most likely to view small business as a route to upward mobility. When a young immigrant was provided a job through an Oriental business network organization, often employers felt a moral obligation to sponsor him later in a business or grant him some sort of partnership. In contrast, "The League's bourgeois ethos provided no reason for profit-maximizing businessmen to take an economically irrational interest in the welfare of some poor Black youth" (Light 1972, p. 117).

Unofficially, the League sought to expand business through promulgation of the "double-duty dollar."[8] This was an exhortation to blacks to buy from black-owned enterprises as a matter of racial pride. A dollar spent at a black merchant would purvey goods and services plus provide jobs and capital to the black community. But whites still control the majority of ghetto revenues. One reason is that white merchants were able to extend credit. Light (1972) claims that had the promotion of the "double duty dollar" been accompanied by moral solidarity generating mutual trust between black merchants and black customers, credit could have been safely extended to poor black customers by black merchants at interest rates below what white merchants charged. That this black community mutual trust did not occur explains why white merchants in the ghetto gained a competitive advantage on credit availability.[9]

Light describes what he considers to be the differences between black and Oriental trade associations. The black trade associations were voluntary and able to recruit only a fraction of the relevant businessmen pool. "Because these associations were not immigrant brotherhoods, they lacked informal social sanctions so extensive as those of the Oriental trade guilds. This lack deleteriously affected their ability to recruit membership, to conduct mutual aid, and to organize guild-style cooperation concerning wages, price and so forth" (Light 1972, p. 125). Black trade associations lacked internal discipline to force cooperation among their members. This impeded their ability to reach economic objectives.

Divine Peace Mission

Divine Peace Missions were established by a clergyman, Father Divine, who claimed to be God.[10] During the Depression, he was able to organize widespread black-owned businesses and was considered to be the most powerful man in black America. The Divine Peace Mission was the name of the movement and the name given to its religious centers scattered about the country but centered in the East, particularly in Harlem.

Members of the movement had to ascribe to various prohibitions: no alcohol, no drugs, no smoking, no sex, no insurance, no welfare, no thievery, no racial discrimination, no gambling, no credit purchases, and no chain letters.

Members were exhorted to get jobs, and if a job didn't exist, they were encouraged to start a business with fellow members along the lines of a cooperative.[11] All income, after bare necessities were taken care of, was supposed to be given to the Divine Peace Mission. The focus of the businesses was not on profit but on creating jobs, service to God, and spreading the teachings of Father Divine. Members could live in Divine Peace Mission dormitory-type residential buildings for free and share among themselves the expenses for providing meals. The low cost of living for members allowed Divine Peace entrepreneurs to charge prices below existing market prices: Thus they significantly expanded and thrived.

Weisbrot (1983) reports that most businesses required small initial capital investment and were mostly involved with retailing. According to Light (1972), the followers of the Divine Peace Mission during the Depression became the leading landlords of Harlem. The most numerous businesses were laundries and restaurants, but they also operated grocery stores; barber shops; dry-cleaning establishments; huckster wagons of vegetables, fruit, and fish; and a coal business (Light 1972, p. 144). After the Depression, membership decreased but business expansion continued. With Divine advancing in age, the organization dwindled. Many poor consumers were grateful to Father Divine for providing businesses that charged low prices because this assisted their survival, especially during the Depression. Father Divine was also known for providing huge free banquets for those members and nonmembers who needed food.[12]

Divine, an ardent integrationist, discouraged his flock from relying on racial solidarity for customers. His strategy was for member businesses to gain economic advantage through low prices. In a sermon, Father Divine declared:

"When you can get a soda-pop for three cents, you come in at times and buy from four to five because they are only three cents. If you were obliged to pay 10 cents for them, maybe you would not buy any.... Take Mr. Ford as a sample and as an example, building the cheapest car that could be built at one time. He did not build a car costing fifteen, twenty or thirty-five thousand dollars, yet he came to be the richest man in the world." (cited in Weisbrot 1983, p. 124)

Divine had a personal hand in directing many of these businesses and provided frequent advice. Divine often exhorted, "If you love me so much as you say you do, let your love and devotion become to be practical, profitable, and good-for-something" (in Weisbrot 1983, p. 127). He helped pick managers and close deals. Because purchases, even large purchases, were made in cash, Divine was in a strong bargaining position with outsiders. A prominent black educator observed, "I am waiving Father Divine's divinity, but as a business genius, we must lift our hats to him."[13]

Divine's endorsement was sought by numerous politicians. While never running for office, he issued a political agenda at a 1936 Divine Peace Mission convention. The Righteous Government Platform was a document aimed chiefly at civil rights, but it also contained an economic program. In addition to proposing the establishment of a minimum wage, it called for: "government control of all idle plants and machinery, tools and equipment, where owners are unwilling to operate them at full capacity; such facilities to be made available to workers on a cooperative, non-profit basis under supervision of government experts, with temporary provision for materials" (Weisbrot 1983, p. 153). In this, one can see Divine's belief in free enterprise insofar as it generates jobs and decent wages, but sometimes government or centralized intervention was necessary to accomplish this.

Light finds in the Divine Peace Mission movement similarities to Oriental regional and kin groupings. They "institutionalized a mutually supportive moral community which was based on active participation and a public way of life. . . . The Peace Mission Movement's internal solidarity facilitated small-business operations and mutual aid. . . . The secret of Father Divine's miracles was his special ability to induce sect members to cooperate" (Light 1972, p. 148).

When working for God, this seems more easy to facilitate. Howard Brotz, a researcher on black religious movements, observed that "an ideology together with an organization can do things which individual entrepreneurship among Negroes cannot achieve" (Brotz 1964, p. 104).

Robert Weisbrot responded to my question concerning the applicability of Father Divine's economic development plans to the black underclass of today:

Tentatively, I'd say aspects of his program are still valuable today: emphasis on education, discipline, avoidance of luxury spending and efforts to develop institutions for pooling funds for business investment, reliance on low prices and volume trade rather than racial solidarity to insure patronage, provision of goods and services sought by a wider community rather than simply those limited to a narrow clientele. . . . Still one must keep certain limiting factors in mind. . . . Father Divine's charisma was at the center of his successful cooperative movement. In the absence of such a charismatic basis for communal living, one would have to develop quite different, very tangible economic incentives for attracting funds to a common pool, or even for insuring the strict economy that could keep profit margins adequate, especially in the early stages of a business. Also, if one is seeking to transform the lives of the black underclasses as a whole, as opposed to a few fortunate upwardly mobile people, one has to ask broader questions like: would Divine's system have worked for all of Harlem? Well, it might have helped, but then as now there were obstacles. Chief among them was that the great bulk of national wealth lay outside the ghettos. Even with pooled funds, ghetto resources were, and are, limited. Divine solved this problem in part by attracting funds from wealthy white (and some black) disciples. One would need to attract much more of that wealth in order to help entire black districts. Also, businesses as a whole are becoming far more dependent on skilled labor than ever before; that requires either upgrading the levels of training among poor urban blacks, creating jobs for less skilled workers, or some combination of the two. For long-run success, in other words, at least one eye should be kept on broader economic currents in the nation—don't let the computer age wholly pass the ghetto by.[14]

The Nation of Islam

The Nation of Islam has its roots in the Moorish-American Science Temple founded by Noble Drew Ali, née Timothy Drew, in 1913. This movement experienced a factional split, and the Nation of Islam emerged under the brief leadership of W. D. Fard. The leadership then passed on to Elijah Muhammad, née Robert Poole (Essien-Udom 1962, pp. 33-45).

The Nation of Islam is a black nationalistic movement and advocates separatism. It emphasizes self-help and business development which is a natural response to the need to build infrastructure for an expected separatist state.

In the 1950s, Elijah Muhammad revealed his five-point economic development plan, "Economic Blue Print for the Black Man." The first four points emphasize the need for unity. The fifth point concerns emulating Muhammad's perception of white men in their approach to business: "Observe the operations of the White Man. He is successful. He makes no excuses for his failure. He works hard—in a collective manner. You do the same. . . . (quoted in Ofari 1970, p. 54).

Muhammad's view of the business world is that white businessmen operate in a collective and cooperative manner and that whites deliberately patronize and favor white businesses. This forms the basis for his economic development plan: Black people should favor black businesses (double-duty dollar); black people should try to start their own businesses and employ black people (Muslims should not look to the white race for jobs); members are required to tithe to the Nation (one-tenth of income); the Nation should be actively involved in setting up communal businesses; members should live frugally (one meal a day), eschew vices (no gambling, smoking, liquor, tobacco, fornicating, or popular entertainments), and save and pay for things in cash—no borrowing from banks.

I could find no information on the rate that Muslims started their own independent businesses. However, information exists about the "communal" businesses initiated and managed by the Nation itself. Essien-Udom (1962) reported that the enterprises owned by the Nation were small businesses traditionally operated by blacks: barbershops, restaurants, grocery stores, clothing stores, bakeries, and a dry cleaning plant. They also owned some large farms. Most of these businesses provided goods and services particularly required by Muslims (e.g., porkless meals). These businesses hired Muslims as managers and employees. It is Essien-Udom's view that Muslim employees were paid lower wages than they could receive elsewhere. However, these positions were very useful as providing jobs particularly for Muslims converted in prison and needing a job upon release.

The most successful of the Nation's businesses was its newspaper, *Muhammad Speaks*. This newspaper was the result of a consolidation of other Muslim publications and was organized by Malcolm X. Members were required to sell a quota of newspapers or else pay for the copies themselves. The Nation had considered entering large-scale manufacturing, but they were limited by capital and lack of skilled and experienced personnel.[15] Most members were recruited, purposely, from the lower status segment of the black community. Internal turmoil following the death of Elijah Muhammad in 1973 led to a dissolution of these businesses. The Muslims are now split into two factions: one headed by Wallace D. Muhammad (Elijah's son) called the American Muslim Mission; the other headed by Louis Farrakan, still called Nation of Islam. Mr. Farrakan has continued many of the business ideas of Elijah Muhammad under the name of "POWER plan" (People Organized and Working for Economic Rebirth).[16]

Black Capitalism

Black Capitalism refers to the economic development strategy of encouraging black business formation and expansion in black communities. As a political movement, it reached its greatest influence during the 1968 presidential campaign. The term was used to describe Richard Nixon's private sector approach for black economic development in opposition to Hubert Humphrey's public sector approaches via Great Society programs.

Nixon's "Bridges to Human Dignity" speech, delivered on April 25, 1968, outlined his platform on this issue:

To have human rights, people need property rights—and never has this been more true than in the case of the Negro today. He must have the economic power that comes from ownership and the security and independence that come from economic power.... Private enterprise, far more effectively than government, can provide the jobs, train the unemployed, build the homes, offer the new opportunities which will produce progress—not promises—in solving the problems of America.... Much of the Black militant talk these days is actually in terms far closer to the doctrine of free enterprise than to those of the welfarist 30's—terms such as 'self-determination,' 'ownership' and 'self-help.' What most of the militants are asking is to be included as owners, as entrepreneurs, to have a share of the wealth and a piece of the action. (Quoted in Blaustein and Faux 1972, p. 18).

In a TV commercial following the Bridges speech, Nixon is shown exclaiming, "With your help, I will begin a new program to get private enterprise into the ghetto and the ghetto into private enterprise. I call it, 'Black Capitalism' " (quoted in Blaustein and Faux 1972, p. 16).

Roy Innis, of the Congress of Racial Equality, was very favorable to this approach. He observed that Nixon made more sense on racial matters than any other aspirant to the presidency, including Robert Kennedy (Blaustein and Faux 1972, p. 21).

The reaction in the white community was generally favorable, but the reaction in the black community was mixed. In a letter to Stokely Carmichael, of the Student Non-Violent Coordinating Committee, Eldridge Cleaver, of the Black Panther party wrote: "The Black Panther Party tried to give you a chance to rescue Black Power from the pigs who had seized upon it and turned it into the rationale for Black Capitalism.... In effect your cry for Black Power has become the grease to ease the Black bourgeoisie into the power structure" (Blaustein and Faux 1972, pp. 22-23).

Black Capitalism as a government policy turned out to be a continuation of policies started under the Johnson administration which involved government underwritten loans from the Small Business Administration (SBA) and minority set-asides for government contracts. There was little support to encourage the small entrepreneurial efforts of uneducated, unskilled persons at the bottom of the income distribution. Instead, efforts went to assist largely middle-class blacks to start businesses and expand one's businesses. In a book review, Robert S. Browne exclaims: "The support to black businesses during the Nixon years, although grossly inadequate, far surpassed what most blacks would have predicted and probably inspired the most rapid period of growth black businesses has ever experienced" (Browne 1985, p. 102).

The idea for the Small Business Administration did not grow out of any notion to assist black economic development, though it did have some impact in this realm. The SBA was established in 1953. This independent federal agency was authorized to provide financial and advisory aid to small businesses who could not obtain reasonably priced financing elsewhere. The precursors of the SBA were the Reconstruction Finance Corporation (initiated during the Depression), the Smaller War Plants Corporation (initiated during World War II) and the Smaller Defense Plants Administration (initiated during the Korean War) (Wollard 1973). These agencies focused on insuring the viability of the small firm in the defense sector.

As part of the War on Poverty, the 1964 Economic Opportunity Act, sometimes referred to as the Equal Opportunity Act was passed, authorizing the Equal Opportunity Loan Program (EOL). The SBA was permitted to make loans of up to $25,000 for 15 years with low interest rates, and collateral was not required. It was initially geared to help disadvantaged low-income micro-entrepreneurs.[17] However, this program's target clientele was quickly abandoned in favor of those who would operate larger, more sophisticated businesses.[18]

During the Nixon administration a whole set of initialed programs sprang up to assist the minority business sector. There were the Local Business Development Organizations (BDO), Minority Enterprise Small Business Investment Companies (MESBIC), Business Resource Centers (BRC), and Office of Minority Business Enterprise (OMBE). The last body, created in 1969, as an agency of the Commerce Department under Secretary Maurice Stans, served mainly as an advisory and organizing agency. Actual federal loans to small businesses were still in the jurisdiction of the independent SBA. Today the OMBE is referred to as the Minority Business Development Agency (MBDA).

An objection could be raised that almost all the effort of these programs has been directed to the higher-income, more sophisticated, better-educated minority entrepreneurs, rather than the lower socioeconomic status minority potential business person. Timothy Bates (1981), in his studies of minority business programs, concludes that all minority assistance programs focusing on helping the truly deprived minority enterprise have been unsuccessful. He assumed economic development and parity as the goal of the SBA programs rather than poverty alleviation. Bates (1981, p. 69) concluded that the SBA loan and procurement programs that assist economically and socially disadvantaged individuals should be abandoned because promising minority firms were ineligible while eligible recipients had high loan default rates. It would be useful to conduct further research on the history of SBA's provision of small loans to economically disadvantaged individuals to evaluate its using measures of success other than loan default rates (e.g., shifts in lifetime earning streams). The experience of early SBA efforts, while informative, should *not* be taken as precedent that a new type of assistance to low-income persons to start small businesses will fail.

Besides being easier to conduct, arguments in favor of assisting the higher income entrepreneur often go like this:

These rapidly growing, economically viable firms promote economic development by creating jobs in minority communities. Their profits support investments that, in turn, permit further business expansion and job creation. The presence of business success stories lures younger, better educated minorities into self-employment, thus further promoting the economic development thrust of minority entrepreneurship. Similarly, existing minority-owned firms in less profitable lines of business are induced—by the success story phenomenon—to reorient their operations to areas that offer greater profit potential; once again economic development is promoted. All of the above describe the process whereby the vestiges of discrimination are gradually overcome, allowing minority enterprise to approach parity with the non-minority enterprise universe. (Bates 1985, p. 52).[19]

As a poverty alleviation strategy, objections can be raised to this rationale on several grounds. First, government efforts ought to be directly targeted toward the truly needy as an equity issue. If jobs trickle down, they may well be low mobility secondary labor market positions. Small business ownership may be a potentially good route for economic advancement for low socio-economic status individuals, but this route is hampered if larger businesses exclusively get the government funds. Second, to the extent they do provide role models for youth, these larger businesses are difficult to emulate. Low-income minority youth may find it difficult to identify with the efforts of middle-income minorities to become even richer. It is likely to be more inspiring to identify with an underclass person making it to the middle class. Third, information about economic mobility through particular small business routes should be based upon sound observation, case studies, and statistical analyses, not on "stories of success." It is a principle of probability that rare events do occur occasionally. Fourth, while it may make sense to encourage low-income people to engage in business ownership, it seems preferable to encourage well-educated minority youth to obtain higher levels of formal education and then enter the professions or a good corporate job. To the extent that they do engage in business ownership, this should occur after they have gained significant on-the-job experience as an employee. Finally, the goal of government intervention is to effect a change that would not occur without the stimulus. It seems imaginable that many higher income, more highly educated entrepreneurs would have succeeded without government assistance. It is more difficult to imply that a low income, minority nascent entrepreneur would succeed without intervention.

To the extent that Black Capitalism calls for developing the ghetto and for separatist economics, further objections can be raised. Exhorting ghetto residents to buy from black businesses only, the double-duty dollar acts as a tariff imposed by the ghetto economy. White businesses are placed at a competitive disadvantage. If effective, black customers buy from black businesses even if prices are higher or products are of lower quality. This raises the cost of living for an already impoverished group. In addition, it artificially shields ghetto businesses from market discipline. Black businesses may not develop efficient enterprises if they do not have to compete with white businesses. Of course as a temporary measure, it can serve the same useful function in black communities as it does in international trade. This is the infant industry argument. It can provide an environment where businesses can develop, and once on a sure footing, the tariffs can be removed. A problem is that temporary tariff policies may become permanent.

The "double duty dollar" policy presents a dilemma to black business persons. Segregation is complementary to the "Buy Black" campaigns. A separate black community is conducive to discourage white businesses from selling to blacks. Policies that open up housing to blacks in white neighborhoods allow blacks access to white-produced goods and services previously unobtainable in the ghetto. Policies geared to the development of black ghetto businesses have a vested interest in maintaining segregation (Myrdal 1944, p. 305).

Related to this are the views of Kain and Persky (1969). They argue that economic opportunity is dispersed throughout the metropolitan area. Policies that strengthen the ghetto impede efforts to leave it. Emphasis on improved access to jobs in the suburbs will lead to higher income and eventual housing desegregation.

From Brimmer's (1969) analysis of Washington, D.C., businesses, he concludes that a ghetto community provides an inadequate market for black businesses to develop: "the Negro market is by no means a strong one. Consequently, entrepreneurs who limit themselves to these markets will be denied the economies of scale which are a precondition for long-run development.... I am personally convinced that the most promising path of economic opportunity for Negroes lies in full participation in an integrated national economy" (Brimmer 1969, p. 172).

I am suggesting the goals of Black Capitalism be modified. In sum, I think that low skilled blacks should be targeted for assistance to business ownership rather than just middle income blacks, and that both groups be encouraged to sell in non-minority markets, wherever the markets are located.

Black Business Movements of Today

I perceive a new black business movement is emerging. It, of course, has its roots in the movements mentioned in this chapter.[20] This new movement is evident mostly among the poor.[21] It can be found: (1) in the public housing projects where tenants are pressing for the management of their housing and creating new businesses on the premises, (2) in churches where people are striving to provide a better life for their children and making use of group economic action, and (3) in community organizations trying to help neighborhoods cope with the loss of good paying manufacturing jobs by developing new enterprises. It is also found among the self-employment programs mentioned in this book. The focus of this new black business movement is to translate the work ethic into the ownership ethic.[22]

SUMMARY

There does seem to be significant potential for black business, and it has surfaced at various times during American history. A substantial black middle class has arisen partly on account of business ownership efforts. The challenge will be using business ownership as a tool to assist the economic development of underclass blacks of today. From the aftermath of the Civil War, the notion of assisting poor blacks to obtain land to form independent self-employment can be translated today into helping poor blacks (and whites) to obtain capital to start small businesses. The notion of promoting thrift and industry through a banking institution with missionary zeal and purpose is also an idea applicable today. The Freedmen's Bureau and the Freedmen's Bank were developed on sound principles. What they lacked was expertise in implementation and political support. Political support for economic development efforts directed at the underclass is certainly valuable but even more important is obtaining expertise in implementation of programs.

From Booker T. Washington, Father Divine, and Elijah Muhammad, we can learn about organizing efforts to promote business development. It seems to require religious zeal. From the shortcomings of the National Negro Business League, we learn that a successful business involves cooperation with other business persons as well as competition, and that successful business cooperation involves sanctions for not following rules. Further, the pool of poor blacks should be viewed as a source of business apprentices.

From Father Divine, we learn of the economies of communal living and strategies for developing businesses even in times of high unemployment. The Nation of Islam demonstrates that even the poorest blacks can be reached to engage them in business activities. The era of Black Capitalism points to the potential for substantial growth in black business even when government is involved. But the problem is, again, how can business ownership reach the lower income masses. Some principles for developing black businesses are the following: An ethnic enclave produces a sheltered market; reliance on ethnic solidarity for a market should only be a temporary strategy; and urban economic opportunities are dispersed throughout metropolitan areas—hence, ghetto markets are limiting.

NOTES

1. Sharecropping is a form of self-employment, but it entails dependent enterprise in a way that permits exploitation and inhibits capital accumulation and economic mobility. An example of the white Southern argument for fraud in the treatment of sharecroppers was mentioned in a report "The Negro American Artisan" by W.E.B. Du Bois in one of the Atlanta University Conferences. A nineteenth century white Southerner would exclaim,

These Negroes do not need this money—if I give it to them they'll squander it or leave the plantation; therefore give them just enough to be happy and keep them with me. In any case their labor rightfully belongs to me and my fathers and was illegally taken from us. (Quoted in Katz 1968, p. 135).

Sharecropping as an interim system would not have been an evil if sharecroppers had job alternatives, contracts were fair, and credit were available for progression to share tenancy (the tenant provides the tools) and eventually to land ownership.

2. The practice of distributing land to freedmen originated with General Sherman's Field Order No. 15 on his march to Savannah in 1864 (Magdol 1977, p. 139).

3. One approach to counter this was evidenced by some groups that combined resources and formed cooperative associations to buy land. This occurred particularly in the South Carolina Sea Islands (Cruden 1969, p. 45).

4. The Congregational (Puritan) Church was very active in Reconstruction efforts to help freed slaves. General Oliver Otis Howard, who headed the Freedmen's Bureau, was a member of the Congregrational Church. Many people working for the Freedmen's Bank were from Oberlin College and the American Missionary Association (AMA). Both were associated with the Congregational Church. The AMA was the foremost religious group involved in education efforts in the postwar South (Osthaus 1976, p. 60).

5. An intense split occurred among blacks between the teachings of Booker T. Washington and those of W.E.B. Du Bois. However, both agreed on the importance of promoting black businesses and this is the topic of this chapter. "So far as Mr. Washington preaches Thrift, Patience, and Industrial Training for the masses, we must hold up his hands and strive with him, rejoicing in his honors. . . . " (Du Bois 1903, p. 59).

The disagreements centered on the priority given to political and civil rights and to the importance of liberal arts higher education training for blacks. Today, in terms of the economic development for blacks as a group, I think Du Bois is more relevant. In terms of the underclass of today, I think Washington is the more relevant.

6. In 1899, in an Atlanta University conference titled "The Negro in Business," W.E.B. Du Bois and others passed a resolution that a Negro Businessmen's League be formed. Other parts of this resolution included: (1) that blacks ought to enter into business life in increasing numbers and that they should be in a wider set of industries so that development won't be one-sided and lead to overcompetition; (2) college education is a good preparation for business and English and high school training are a necessity; (3) businessmen should be courteous, honest, and careful; (4) blacks should patronize black businesses; (5) churches, schools, and newspapers should encourage blacks to engage in business careers; and (6) saving and habits of thrift should be encouraged among the young (Du Bois et al. 1899 in Katz 1968, p. 50).

7. Even if true, there is still a role for black businesses as a way to create jobs for the low-income blacks.

8. The current practice of the double duty dollar is the Buy Freedom program where blacks are asked to spend half their purchases with black companies.

9. At a conference on black economic development, I heard it expressed that the largest group of boycotters against black businesses were whites and the second largest group were blacks. Brimmer reports that the share of black income going to black companies has declined from 13 cents per dollar in 1969 to 7 cents per dollar in 1985 (Davidson 1987).

10. Biographers claim his name at birth was George Baker and provide some early history of his life. At a visit to one of their hotels in Philadelphia, where the movement is now headquartered, I was told by followers that his only name is Father Divine and he could not have had a name at birth because he was God and not a born man. He just appeared one day.

11. Divine also assisted members seeking wage jobs. He encouraged people to seek out work no matter how humble, yet he sought to promote dignity and decent wages. Members, by living at low or no cost at the mission shelters, could better hold out for jobs paying decent wages. Divine encouraged this. He instructed domestic workers not to accept employment for less than $10 a week, which was far above the prevailing wage. See Weisbrot (1983), pp. 136-141.

12. Some hold the view that Father Divine was sincerely interested in the well-being of his flock and not concerned with amassing personal wealth. Contributions were dispensed to the missions, not to Father Divine himself. Titles to business properties were in the names of members, not Divine. Others have viewed Divine merely as an opportunist creating personal wealth and power for himself.

13. This was in a letter by George Hancock dated 1939, quoted in (Weisbrot 1983, p. 121).

14. This was excerpted from a letter to me dated January 3, 1985.

15. In 1970, it was reported that Black Muslim enterprises included a large

printing plant, producing 500,000 copies of *Muhammad Speaks,* a $125,000 meat processing plant, and a 600-seat restaurant-supermarket complex. (Fortune 1970, January). Lincoln (1973, p. 96) reported that the Nation owned and operated an ultramodern, multi-purpose building in Chicago, housing a department store, doctor's offices, and a showplace dental suite.

16. In a copy of Farrakhan's newspaper, *The Final Call* (March 19, 1988) the headline on the front page was, "Cast down your buckets where you are!—Booker T. Washington, 1885—Minister Louis Farrakhan, 1988." Wilson (1987, p. 125) noted similarities between the teachings of Booker T. Washington and the black nationalistic movement of the 1960s. Both stressed self-sufficiency as a way to develop inwardly in response to the practices of segregation.

17. The predecessor to the EOL program was the "6 by 6" program which offered loans of up to $6,000 for terms up to six months. At this same time, SBA Opportunity Centers were initiated to develop and finance businesses in target poor minority communities. These would later be renamed Small Business Development Centers (SBDCs). Initially, the Office of Economic Opportunity controlled policy for these programs and its focus was to address the needs of persons in poverty. Later the focus would switch to addressing the needs of nonpoor minorities because they were considered disadvantaged by virtue of their membership in a disadvantaged racial group (Garvin 1973).

18. The definition of an eligible small business includes some rather large enterprises. In 1968, small businesses meant wholesale firms with annual revenues under $5 million dollars, retail firms with annual revenues under $1 million, and manufacturing firms with fewer than 250 employees (Blaustein & Faux 1972, p. 118). This definition has since expanded to firms with fewer than 500 employees.

19. This is similar to the view taken by Theodore Cross in his pioneering book on black capitalism. He is concerned with the reverse face of poverty:

that almost nobody in the ghettoes of America is rich or even affluent. . . . that the skills and benefits of entrepreneurship must be transferred to the residents of black slums. . . . Therefore, I offer programs for whites to assist black entrepreneurs in production and marketing. Black capitalism grounded on credit and skills borrowed from the white economy is a temporary but necessary foundation for creating viable and enduring businesses in the black slums. (Cross 1970, pp. viii–x).

20. There is a continuation today of many of the black capitalism programs. The Buy Freedom campaign is a version of the double duty dollar. NAACP's Fair Share program attempts to promote blacks in jobs and businesses in sectors where they are underrepresented. Operation Push operates similar programs. There are set-aside programs in most government jurisdictions.

21. See Woodson (1987) for a description of recent black self-help projects. Robert Woodson was founder of the Council for a Black Economic Agenda and operates the National Center for Neighborhood Enterprise in Washington, D.C., which provides technical assistance for self-help projects targeted to the poor.

22. One could raise the following objection: "Why should blacks be encouraged to start micro-enterprises when their self-employment participation is mainly in these types of businesses already?" Blacks shouldn't be encouraged

to be small-scale business people, but a micro-enterprise ownership strategy does make some sense for the goal of poverty reduction for low-income people, black or white. Further, suggesting that self-help strategies are useful to promote the economic mobility of low-income blacks is not the same as suggesting that it is the only approach to use. A mix of approaches are required using macro and micro, public and private sector orientations.

II.

Program Descriptions

6

Self-Employment Programs in the Third World and Europe

INTRODUCTION

Four major efforts at encouraging self-employment in foreign countries will be examined.[1] From the Third World, the PISCES Project and the Grameen Bank are presented.[2] From Europe, the British Enterprise Allowance Scheme and the French Chomeur Createurs are presented.[3] The PISCES Project involved several demonstration programs in Third World countries to help existing micro-enterprises become more profitable and expand. The PISCES Project combined some technical assistance with financial assistance. The Grameen Bank is a bank for the poorest of the poor in Bangladesh. It combines elements of social support and financial assistance to create micro-enterprises. In contrast the two European efforts are basically just financing mechanisms. They are government systems providing unemployed people with funding to start small businesses. Technical assistance is available through existing small business assistance organizations in each country but using them is not mandatory. All four efforts seem reasonable models to consider for replication in the United States.

PISCES PROJECT

In 1978, the United States Agency for International Development (AID) funded the *Program for Investment in the Small Capital Enterprise Sector* (PISCES Project).[4] Demonstration projects were designed in four countries: Dominican Republic, Costa Rica, Kenya, and

Egypt. The target groups were owners of micro-enterprises in the informal sectors of large urban areas.[5]

Informal Sector

This sector has been considered a nuisance due to its unregulated ways of operation. However, it is now recognized that this sector contains among the most dynamic, entrepreneurial, and economically efficient firms in the Third World. Firms are small, adjustments are quick, and market prices are not too distorted by the forces of government intervention. In keeping with the mission of AID in promoting economic development through the medium of the private sector, the PISCES Project seemed like a compelling approach.

Businesses in the informal sector are generally small-scale, labor-intensive, and serve mainly local markets. They consist of individuals commonly working alone or with unpaid family members. There is little division of labor, equipment is simple, and start-up capital is minimal.

The informal sector in less developed countries is often the largest and fastest-growing sector. Ashe (1985a, pp. 4-8) provides numerous reasons why assisting this sector is so important: This will be the sector that provides the majority of new jobs in less-developed countries; there is ease of entry because of low capital requirements; there is flexibility in that product lines can be shifted rapidly; there is avoidance of regulations that mire larger businesses in red tape; and there is often tradition and knowledge for starting and managing a tiny business. This sector is a major source of affordable goods and services to the poor, vocational and entrepreneurial training, and employment for women. Work hours can be built around child care, and self-initiated enterprises are an alternative to discriminatory hiring practices. Production tends to be efficient. This sector is a source of linkage between modern manufacturers and rural areas. These types of businesses are more likely to survive during economic contractions. They also mobilize cash flow through facilitating informal credit.

A rich variety of programs were funded during the PISCES Project. See Ashe (1985b) for a description and evaluation of these programs. Just to provide some of the flavor of these programs, the Dominican Republic program will be described here.

PISCES: Santo Domingo, Dominican Republic.
Program for Development of Micro-Enterprises
(PRODEME)

PRODEME was operated by the Dominican Development Foundation, a private and voluntary organization (PVO), with assistance from

ACCION, a nonprofit organization which creates and manages business development programs in the Americas.[6] PRODEME became operational in May 1981. It had two components: (1) solidarity groups and (2) individual micro-enterprise assistance. The goals of both these programs were to increase income and employment. The solidarity component had an additional goal of enhancing mutual support and leadership through group processes.

Solidarity Groups

The unit of operation is a five-person cluster called a solidarity group. A newly formed group attends a four-hour course. This course emphasizes the notion that all members are mutually responsible for paying back each other's loans. Each group member is a cosigner for the debt of the others. This is a substitute for collateral. Members then select a group president. The group attends barrio level meetings for one to two months before a credit request is submitted.

Eighty-three percent of businesses in the solidarity group program are tricycle cart vendors. They receive $249 toward the purchase of their vehicle plus $21 for working capital, for example, to finance current assets like inventory. This amount of $270 is to be repaid in 52 weekly payments at a flat interest rate of 24 percent per annum.

The remaining 17 percent of clients are known as the working capital group. These are seamstresses, food vendors, or market stall holders. They receive $249 to be used for working capital only. This is also to be paid back in one year at the 24 percent per annum interest rate. Access to credit at the rate of only 24 percent per annum is thought to be a great help to the Dominican poor. This is an alternative to taking loans from street money lenders at rates up to 20 percent a day. In addition, the project provides a mechanism for generating mutual support.

All the tricycle cart vendors are male and are, on average, 30 years old. Seventy-five percent of the working capital group are female and are, on average, 40 years old. Almost all clients of both groups are immigrants to Santo Domingo from rural areas.

Micro-Enterprise Component

The businesses of the micro-enterprise component are larger than those of the solidarity group businesses, involve greater investment, and the owners are more educated. The clients of the micro-enterprise component tend to be among the upper strata of the poor. Intensive assistance is provided to these individual enterprises. In addition to loans effort goes into setting up a bookkeeping system and improving management.[7]

Evaluation: Solidarity Group

In 30 months, 343 solidarity groups with nearly 2000 members have been financed. A 1982 evaluation identified two major problems: a growing problem of low payback and slowness in the institutions disbursing loans. This latter problem resulted in increased administrative costs and delays for clients. Before April 1982, the payback rate was 100 percent. It then decreased to 80 percent, and by September 1982, it was 67 percent. When enthusiasm of new clients fades, other needs arise, and payback often becomes a second priority. Solidarity group coordinators estimated that they spent half their time with repayment problems. Measures were suggested to provide incentives to repay loans— make a clearer policy on late payments and enable easier repossession of the tricycles by coordinators. Second loans should be granted as quickly as possible after the first loans are paid. If second loans are not considered, there is less incentive to pay the first loan back.

Another recommended change was to arrange for providing working capital loans having shorter terms. Before this program, almost none of these clients had experience with business loans that lasted more than one week.

When asked to rank possibilities for new types of services, 56 percent responded they would like a savings and loan cooperative; 28 percent would like a place to buy cheap merchandise; 14 percent wanted a business course; 2 percent said trips or parties.

It was calculated that at least a 16 percent increase in yearly business income occurred due to avoiding the rental fees for the tricycle. An additional $50 was saved if they kept the tricycle at home rather than at the central marketplace. The new tricycles also allowed the sellers to expand their market, as these vehicles allowed them to travel farther and faster.

Evaluation: Micro-Enterprise Component

The evaluation of this component utilized a control group consisting of those who made contact with the project but dropped out early.[8] The project group outperformed the businesses of the control group on every measure of business success.

The project group showed an increase in investment of 31 percent, monthly sales of 25 percent, and (in value added) of 20 percent, all above that of the control group. Of the 101 project businesses in the evaluation, 141 full-time equivalent jobs were created, a 65 percent increase in employment above the control group. The $115 average monthly salary paid to the project's new employees was above the $104 minimum wage in the Dominican Republic. In a year, the total amount of new salaries was slightly greater than the total value of the loans ($194,033). The project also increased incomes of owners by 27 percent. The payback rate started at only 56 percent but has increased to 71 percent.

The main complaints of the clients concerned bureaucratic arrangements of the projects. It was suggested that the granting of a purchase order redeemable only at certain merchants restricted their ability to purchase efficiently. It was also felt that there was too much delay in delivering loans and too many pre- and post-loan monitoring visits.

A cost/benefit analysis of PRODEME was performed using data for 1981 and 1982. Both the micro-enterprise and solidarity components showed substantial net benefits, approximately a half milion dollars each in 1982 U.S. dollars. See Kilby and D'Zmura (1985).

Characteristics of Successful Projects

According to Ashe (1985a, pp. 13–17), the characteristics of effective projects studied and implemented by the PISCES Project include having good leadership (imbuing the organization with vision, making hard decisions, and keeping the project on track), having a concerned staff, respecting clients' ideas and needs, selecting responsible clients based on community information, reaching clients efficiently without exhaustive analysis and undue delay, creating a program structure clients can easily understand and participate in, being flexible to meet clients' changing needs, being concerned with efficient administration (average costs should decrease as number of clients increase), avoiding paternalism, and avoiding excessive formality.

In addition, the characteristics of the locality which are conducive to project success are a growing local economy, stable political conditions, a government which approves its informal sector, adequate infrastructure (e.g. roads, banks, schools), an entrepreneurial tradition, and proximity to major markets.[9]

GRAMEEN BANK

The Grameen Bank was initiated by an economics professor at Chittagong University, Muhammad Yunus, who obtained his Ph.D. in the United States at Vanderbilt University. Grameen is a Bangla word for "rural," so a translation of the name of the bank is "Village Bank." The Bank began as a pilot project in 1976 to serve an impoverished village near the campus of Chittagong University. At first, Yunus tried to get local banks to lend money to landless poor people so they could begin small businesses. He found this task so difficult that he created a bank to serve the landless poor and those owning a half acre or less exclusively. Yunus's work expanded to other villages and, in 1979, it became a formal project. In 1982, it was recognized by the government of Bangladesh as a specialized bank. As of 1986, 60 percent of the capitalization of the bank came from the government and outside agencies and the remainder from Grameen clients (Hossain 1986).

A key aspect of Yunus' approach is his respect for the survival skills of illiterate landless poor people. He observed what poor people do to survive and determined the things that restrict their upward mobility. His view is that the "planner's job is to design a programme which will make constraints crumble away, help the poor use their full potential, and then gradually let them go beyond their initial capacity" (Yunus 1982, p. 5). An important impediment to their upward mobility was access to credit, without the requirement of collateral, at reasonable rates of interest. Loan money was available from village loan sharks, but exorbitant rates were charged—often 10 percent per month and sometimes even 10 percent per day. The central goal of the Grameen Bank was to provide small loans at "national" market rates of interest (approximately 16%) and to substitute the good character of the borrower, reinforced by peer pressure, in lieu of collateral.

Here is how the Bank is organized. A Bank unit covers an area of 15 to 20 villages and is headed by a field manager, who has Bank workers under him. Any person who owns a half acre of cultivable land or less is eligible for a loan but must be in a self-formed group of five similar people, all of the same sex. The same sex rule is in keeping with local Islamic traditions. These self-formed groups of five are very similar to the "solidarity groups" used by the PISCES Project. When a group is formed, it enters into a probationary period of a month to determine if it is conforming to the rules of the bank and to make sure every member of the group can write his or her own signature. Each "group" elects a chairperson and secretary and must hold weekly meetings. A number of groups are formed into a "centre," where an elected leader holds weekly meetings. At the weekly meetings, loan proposals are discussed, disbursements are made, and payments are collected. Thus, the bank comes to the village to reach out to its potential clients rather than waiting for clients to initiate a visit to a branch bank.

After the probationary period is completed, two members of a group are permitted to take out individual small loans for any productive activity of their choice. When the first loans are repaid, they are eligible to take out larger loans. The maximum loan is 5000 taka, which is equivalent to $150, using an exchange rate of 1 taka = 3 cents. The loan is repaid in weekly installments of 2 percent of the principal plus interest. Most loans are repaid in about a year, that is, 50 weeks × 2 percent = 100 percent. The behavior of the first borrowers are observed for one or two months, and if they comply with the rules, the other members of the group become eligible for loans. If anyone of the group defaults, the whole group becomes ineligible to obtain loans and is responsible for repaying the default amount.

Besides loans for productive activity, loans for personal and emergency purposes are available through the Group Fund and the Emergency Fund. The Group Fund is established from forced saving to enable bank members to borrow interest free for personal purposes. This fund enables members to meet personal needs so that funds from the productive loans don't have to be diverted for consumption purposes. The problem of diversion of loan money was also a problem in the PISCES Project. The Group Fund concept seems a good solution to this problem. The forced savings is obtained from two sources. The first is requiring each bank member to save one taka (3 cents) every week. The second source is a withholding of 5 percent of the main loans. While members have easy access to loan money from the Group Fund, a member does not have any individual claim on his/her group fund account and cannot take it upon leaving. This would seem to create a strong incentive to stay in the bank program.

The Emergency Fund is really an insurance pool. It can be used to repay loans when there is a volitional default, death, or an accident. It is funded from forced payments of a surcharge of 25 percent of the interest paid on a loan after the loan is fully repaid. It is used by groups when a member of a group can not repay their loan. This is a back-up mechanism to preserve the eligibility of members to obtain future loans.

Great thought has been put into developing this process. An important rationale in the process is to discourage participation by well-off people who are very skilled at diverting scarce resources to themselves. The commercial rate of interest charged to borrowers is much lower than the interest rates charged by loan sharks. The bank rate could be reduced further, but then higher income people would want to participate. Further, well-off people do not want to borrow small amounts, nor attend meetings with people at the bottom rungs of society. Another important rationale is to integrate the process of the bank with the natural cycles of local economic life. Small weekly payments, made in the process of a social gathering, enable relatively large amounts of money to be paid back in a way manageable to poor landless struggling people. The networking and mutual assistance that occurs in the process of group and center meetings is an important element for providing informal technical assistance.

According to Tendler (1987), there are five characteristics to describe the Grameen Bank that were also shared by three somewhat similar organizations in India:[10] The Bank started out as a credit brokering organization linking clients to existing financial institutions;[11] clients were required to save in an account as a prerequisite to borrowing; businesses that were financed were mainly in the trade and commerce sector; "minimalist" credit was provided which meant no formal evaluation of the merits of client investments, no technical extension, and selection was shifted to peer groups of borrowers; and social and other services were provided, after the Bank started with providing just plain credit (Tendler 1987, p. 15).

Another key element in the Grameen Bank process is the promulgation of a set of slogans which forms a practical code of life called the 16 Decisions. Their acceptance is voluntary, but they are heavily promoted by bank workers, and members are expected to have them memorized. They seem to be a secular creed sharing common characteristics with the Protestant work ethic, and read as follows:

1. We shall maintain unity, discipline and hard work in daily life.
2. We shall bring prosperity to our family.
3. We shall not live in dilapidated homes. We shall construct tin-shed houses.
4. We shall grow vegetables year round.
5. We shall plant seedlings of trees during planting season.
6. We shall keep families small and look after our health.
7. We shall send children to school.
8. We shall keep our homes and environment clean.
9. We shall have latrines in every home.
10. We shall drink water from tubewells. Otherwise we shall boil drinking water.
11. We shall arrange for dowry free marriages for sons and daughters.
12. We shall not inflict any injustice to anyone, nor shall we allow anyone to do so.
13. We shall undertake collective enterprises for raising incomes.[12]
14. We shall cooperate with fellow members and help each other in difficult times.
15. We shall not allow breach of discipline in any center. We shall offer help in restoring discipline in other centers.
16. We shall do physical exercises and take part in collective social activities.

Besides being just good commonsense advice, they represent an attempt to transform local culture in a way that is conducive to capital accumulation. Most program attempts at promoting individual economic improvement stay clear of trying to change personal behavior. It is refreshing to see an economic organization actively become involved in explicitly changing culture in ways conducive to economic improvement.

Evaluation

An assessment of income generation programs in the Third World, funded by the Ford Foundation, states, "the Foundation's most successful grantee organization was not in India but in Bangladesh—the Grameen Bank, whose 160,000 borrowers place it head and shoulders above any other Foundation project in terms of the number of persons reached" (Tendler 1987, p. 3).[13]

Coverage and Cost

As of 1986, the Grameen bank had 232 branches, covering 4192 villages, and served 191,000 persons.[14] Overall this is considered to be 3.1 percent of the target population (agricultural households operating with less than one-half acre of land) of Bangladesh. In one district almost 25 percent of the target households were members of the Grameen Bank. The amount of credit disbursed per year was only 17 million taka in 1980, but this steadily increased each year to 425 million taka in 1985. The Bank approves about 80 percent of loan applications. Average savings per member as of 1986 was 524 taka, which is 12 percent of the per capita income of Bangladesh. Cumulative savings were equal to 40 percent of outstanding loans.

In 1986, women accounted for almost 70 percent of the total members and received 55 percent of loan disbursements. Women borrow smaller amounts than men. Average loan size in 1985 was 2505 taka ($75) or about 60 percent of per capita income for Bangladesh. The Grameen Bank mainly finances activities in noncrop agriculture and nonfarm activities.[15] In 1985, of six industries, the largest share of loans (37%) went into the livestock/fishery sector, followed by trading and shopkeeping (28%).[16]

The Group Fund, comprised of forced savings, disbursed 11 million taka in loans in 1985. This was only 15 percent of the Fund. Fifty-one percent of the loan disbursements were for personal reasons (social/household needs; health; repayment of old loans), and 49 percent were for purposes for which members could obtain regular loans. An advantage of Group Fund loans is that loans are interest free, and repayment is more flexible.

In 1985, the cost of its credit operation, overall, was about 20 percent of loan disbursements.[17] The bank charged an interest rate of 16 percent. Therefore, a shortfall existed of 4 percent. This shortfall was paid from the Bank's earnings from investing in short-term deposits with other banks.

As of 1986, 97 percent of loans were repaid within one year. The reasons for the high recovery rate are attributed to the following four factors: close supervision by the managing director; the motivation of bank workers to help the poor; providing loans that generate regular incomes; and collecting payments in small weekly installments.

Impact

One should expect income to be higher for Grameen Bank members compared to a similarly situated control group for the following four reasons: improved access to capital; participation in self-employment, an alternative to low-wage employment; lower capital input costs through avoidance of the village loan shark; and lower information costs from networking through peer support groups.[18]

A survey of borrowers of the Grameen Bank was conducted in 1985. The results were compared to data taken from applications to join (approximately 2.25 years earlier) to obtain before-after measures of outcome.[19] The Bank "caused" members to utilize capital more in economic activities, a before-after 74 percent increase in utilization of working capital. Average amounts of working capital loans increased from 743 taka before membership to 2811 taka at the time of the survey for a 278 percent increase. Even after taking account of inflation (at approximately 10% per year), there was a substantial increase of at least 200 percent.

There was an overall improvement in the occupations that people held. Before joining the Bank, 10 percent of members were employed as agricultural wage laborers, and 31 percent were unemployed or out of the labor force. At the time of the survey, only 1 percent were working as agricultural wage laborers, and 11 percent were unemployed or out of the labor force. Most of the increase in employment was the result of female members changing from working at home to income earners.

Data on control groups were obtained to determine what would have happened to members in the absence of the Bank. The control group consisted of a stratified random sample of people in two villages where the Grameen Bank was not present but met the target group criteria of being landless or near landless. The demographic characteristics of the control villages (e.g., household size, age distribution) were similar to the five Grameen Bank villages used for the survey.[20]

If the Grameen Bank is stimulating economic activity, members of the Grameen Bank should have higher labor force participation. For Grameen Bank members (in the village sample), a measure of labor force participation was 25 percent greater compared to the target group sample in the control villages.[21]

Estimating household incomes is difficult because the borrowers do not keep business records. Nonetheless, an attempt was made to do this from survey information for both Grameen Bank and control villages. Average household income was estimated to be 50 percent higher for members of the Grameen Bank compared to the target group in the control villages (18,133 taka vs. 12,106). Per capita income was estimated to be 40 percent higher for Grameen Bank members compared to the target group in the control villages (3524 taka vs. 2523).

Further comparisons of income were made using the variables degree of poverty and household income levels by level of landholding. These comparisons were made between Grameen Bank villages and control villages, but here the data represents whole villages to capture entire village impacts. A greater proportion of the population live in poverty in the control villages. The percent of the population in Grameen Bank villages that have an income below the Bangladesh poverty income level (approximately 2700 taka per person) was estimated to be 50 percent as opposed to 71 percent for the population of control villages.

For the lowest landholding group (no land ownership), average household income was estimated to be 27 percent higher in the Grameen Bank villages compared to the control villages (10,256 taka vs. 8090). The same type of comparisons for four other landowning-size groups shows some redistribution of income from rich to poor because the relative differences become smaller the larger the land holdings. For the largest two landowning groups (nontarget populations), incomes are larger in the control villages. This implies that the rich were worse off in the Grameen Bank villages. This would be the case if real wage rates rose, redistributing income from landowners to labor.

Still another measure of outcome considered is the impact of the Grameen Bank on population growth. Because of the increased participation of women in market economic activities, it was expected that members of the Bank would participate more in family planning. From a survey, it was estimated that 24 percent of Grameen Bank women used family-planning methods. This compares to a national estimate that 19 percent of married women under 50 in Bangladesh used contraception.

Related to the 16 decisions are a whole list of specific behaviors that were expected to change. Data indicate that favorable behavioral changes occurred with building latrines, using tubewells or boiling water to drink, improving housing, growing vegetables, and exercising.

Applications to the United States

Although the Grameen Bank is mainly a rural bank in the Third World, elements of the Grameen Bank seem applicable to programs assisting low-income people to start small businesses in developed countries, even in the United States.[22] Bangladesh has a very high population density of 1763 persons per square mile. This makes it more applicable to urban programs than would occur from rural programs in other countries.[23]

The following four concepts of the Grameen Bank, translated into Western principles, seem paramount. First, collateral, if unavailable, should not be required to acquire a loan. Instead, requiring borrowers to form themselves into small peer groups where each cosigns each other's loan seems a good alternative way to ensure repayment. Substitute peer group pressure, and access to further credit, as motivators to repay loans. Second, provide a credo of Protestant ethic–like principles that borrowers become infused with. Third, initially provide only small loans to clients. After they establish reliability (i.e., a credit history), larger loans can be provided. Fourth, loans should be scaled to the U.S. economy, taking into account American incomes per capita and minimum start-up capital requirements to start low-level micro-enterprises in the United States. For example, as a first approximation, if the average Grameen Bank loan is $75, which is 60 percent of the per capita income in Bangladesh, American loans should, on average, also be 60 percent of per capita income.

The first two principles seem so important I can even envision a Grameen Bank–type program that does not distribute any credit but only organizes people. That is, once people are formed into peer groups and are forced to save, they can merely lend money to each other, much like an ethnic rotating credit association.

However, there are difficulties in adapting the Grameen Bank model to the United States. These concern issues of welfare, alternative economic opportunities, and the underground economy. The big constraint for engagement in self-employment for the landless poor in Bangladesh is credit. They appear to have many self-employment opportunities that pay better than alternative wage labor. Agricultural wage labor pays very little and there are few large-scale retail and service businesses that compete directly with micro-enterprises. Their primary problem is obtaining access to affordable credit. In the United States, because of welfare, minimum wage jobs, and the existence of large chains, self-employment opportunities that pay better than the aforementioned are relatively scarce. In Bangladesh there is no competing welfare nor are there minimum wage jobs. It is good that people in the United States have a safety net so they are not forced into demeaning and unhealthy activities just to eke out a subsistence income, but it does make the circumstances different between the two countries. Abundant self-employment opportunities are a constraint in the United States. To parallel the simple types of unregulated self-employment activities in which people participate in Bangladesh, one needs to look at the informal sector of the U.S. economy. If we want to encourage people to engage in small-scale unregulated self-employment activities in the United States, it may be necessary to provide mechanisms so that they can operate in the moral but marginally illegal part of the underground economy and have access to information on how to do that.

EUROPEAN PROGRAMS

Britain—Enterprise Allowance Scheme (EAS)

This scheme was introduced on a pilot basis in February 1982 and started on a national basis in August 1983.[24] Unemployed people who want to set up a business were paid a flat-rate taxable allowance of 40 pounds a week for up to 52 weeks. They were also eligible for three free counseling sessions with the Small Firms Service. To be eligible, a would-be entrepreneur had to be over 18 years old, have been unemployed for at least 13 weeks, be able to raise 1000 pounds start-up capital of his or her own to invest during the first year, and work full-time at the business. Interested individuals must first attend a workshop where they meet with business service professionals who try to be discouraging, telling of the hurdles they have to overcome. If still interested, persons self-select to become formal applicants.

Evaluation

As of June 1985, 88,000 people had participated in EAS. At that time 47,000 were receiving the allowance; 60,000 slots were available each year. A 15 month–mail survey was conducted in November 1984 for a sample of 1300 randomly selected participants who joined in early Fall 1983 and who completed one full year. The response rate was 65 percent. The three largest categories of businesses were construction, retail distribution, and repair of consumer goods and vehicles. Sixty-five percent had established businesses within the service sector. Fifteen months after entering the program, the median weekly net (pre-tax) income of participants was 80 pounds. On average, for every hundred businesses created, an additional 68 new jobs were created: 24 full-time and 44 part-time positions.

Eighty-six percent of the respondents were still operating their businesses (the survival rate). Two-thirds of the 14 percent of businesses that did not survive closed as they reached the 12-month allowance cut-off period. This indicates that some of the businesses operated just to obtain the allowance. Participants most likely to survive were older, male, and those who experienced shorter periods of unemployment. The four top reasons for business closings were lack of demand, too much competition, lack of capital, and very high costs.

No control groups were used in the evaluations, but some attempt was made at estimating how many participant businesses would have started without the help of the EAS. This is called "deadweight." From survey questions to entrants, it was estimated that deadweight was approximately 50 percent.

From a pilot study, an economic impact evaluation was conducted.[25] For every 100 entrants to EAS, unemployment fell by 32.5. The net cost per person off unemployment in the first year was 2690 pounds. A longer-term two-year net cost estimate was also made, taking into account future lower unemployment benefits and higher tax receipts. Its cost amounted to only 650 pounds.

France—Chomeur Createurs (Unemployed Entrepreneurs)

This program was introduced on an experimental basis in 1979.[26] It became a national policy one year later. Any French citizen entitled to unemployment compensation or welfare could choose to collect his or her cash benefit in a lump sum to help start a business. In addition to individual efforts, when a plant closed, workers were encouraged to pool their benefits to start a new business. This lump sum varied from 8000 francs ($1140) for someone with no eligibility for unemployment benefits to 30,000 francs ($4285) for a regular unemployed worker or 50,000 francs ($7140) if an additional person is hired in the first six months of operation. The amount increases by 20,000 francs ($2860) for every job directly created. The recipient was also freed from social security and unemployment compensation fund payments for the first six months of operation. No consulting or technical assistance was provided, but many entrepreneurial outreach support programs were available. The business proposals, though, were carefully scrutinized, mainly to avoid fraudulent claims. Funding came from general revenue rather than out of the unemployment compensation fund which was used initially.

Evaluation

Since its inception until March 1984, 135,000 people have started businesses under this program. One-third of new businesses in France during 1984 were considered the result of Chomeur Createurs. The failure rate after one year of operation was claimed to be 16 percent.

Recipients in 1983 started new firms (74.2%), bought out existing firms (13.2%), obtained firms from bankruptcy (6%), and started professional practices (6.1%). The industrial distribution of client businesses in 1983 consisted of agriculture and manufacturing (13.0%), construction (19.8%), wholesale and retail trade (25.4%), services

(27.5%), and others (14.3%). Fifteen percent of clients were younger than 25; 79 percent were between 25 and 49, and 6 percent were over 50; 81 percent of recipients were male. In terms of the occupational distribution, 37 percent were skilled workers, 25 percent were unskilled workers, 18 percent were executives, 14 percent were lower managers, and 7 percent were high technology specialists. No economic impact evaluation was available.

Evaluation of the European Programs

Bendick and Egan (1987b) compared participants in the Enterprise Allowance Scheme (EAS) and the Chomeur Createurs (CC) program to the unemployed in their respective countries.[27] They did find evidence that participants in the programs were less severely disadvantaged compared to the general unemployed population. The most typical participant was a male in his mid-thirties, and unemployed less than six months. However, the program did serve severely disadvantaged people. Twenty-seven percent of participants in Great Britain and 17 percent in France were unemployed a year or longer.

Another observation was that approximately 75 percent of the businesses started in Great Britain served local markets. Bendick and Egan argued that to the extent that unemployed participants come from depressed areas, this would reduce the chance to succeed because spending would be weak.

In both programs, Bendick and Egan found that earnings were modest. However, they did approximately match what participants earned in the jobs they held before. Failure rates for participants were similar to failure rates of other small enterprises, in general. Of the participants in the EAS who discontinued their business after operating it for at least a year, 44 percent became reemployed within a year of ending their business, and 67 percent of those reported higher earnings in their new job compared to their previous EAS business earnings.

Job creation for businesses in the two programs conforms to the same patterns of small business job creation in their respective countries. For the CC program, of businesses that survived three years, 25 percent created jobs in addition to the proprietor's. For the EAS program, that number was 38 percent.

For the EAS, participants who were still in business three years after the program were compared to participants who discontinued.[28] The purpose of this was to derive factors associated with success. Participants who discontinued were more likely to be under 30 years old, not be a professional or manager, be unemployed for more than a year before entering the program, have had a relatively low wage before unemployment, have started with an initial investment of less than

$1500, and be in the service sector. From this, Bendick and Egan conclude, "Persons with weaker prerequisites are precisely those who are having the most difficulty finding employment. Thus, programs face a tradeoff between economic objectives and social ones. They can maximize the extent to which they serve the hardest to employ, or they can maximize business survival, profitability, and employment generation" (Bendick and Egan 1987b, p. 538).

I disagree with the above notion of a tradeoff between social and economic objectives. If we consider the objective as programs making the greatest difference in generating new business start-ups, picking participants with weak prerequisites may be the best way to accomplish that objective. They are the least likely to start a business without the program. In terms of a cost-benefit analysis, investing in those weak participants may yield a higher rate of return compared to investing in professionals with good educations, who would more likely start a business or obtain a good wage job on their own. Bendick and Egan's suggestion to improve efficiency, is to screen to pick better participants. My solution is to pick better programs—programs with a track record at helping the most disadvantaged participants.[29]

SUMMARY

The PISCES Project has demonstrated that feasible ways exist for enhancing the micro-businesses of the poor in Third World countries. The PRODEME program did pass a cost/benefit test. However, a greater program emphasis should be placed on achieving enhanced earning streams rather than on high loan payback rates.

The Grameen Bank demonstrated that credit for micro-enterprise development can be efficiently provided to the poorest of the poor on a large scale and at reasonable cost. The Bank increased the acquisition of capital, improved earnings, and effectuated positive lifestyle changes. The process of the Bank, with some modification, does seem capable of assisting the U.S. poor.

The European programs also mainly provide capital rather than training. For unemployed people with skills, close ties to the labor market, and moderate amounts of formal education, these programs seem promising. Further evidence is required to determine applicability to the long-term unemployed.

NOTES

1. The word *evaluate* is used very loosely in this chapter. I use the term to mean a presentation of quantitative data related to program process and

outcomes. Occasionally, control group impact evaluations were performed but none were true classical experiments using random selection.

2. For information on other self-employment programs in the Third World, see Nelson (1986), Hunt (1985), Kilby and D'Zmura (1985), Stearns (1985), Harper (1984), and Fonstad et al. (1982).

3. Systems, similar to Chomeur Createur and the Enterprise Allowance Scheme, have been instituted in Australia, Belgium, Finland, Ireland, Netherlands, Norway, Spain, and Sweden. The Co-operative Action Program on Local Initiatives for Employment Creation (ILE) of the Organization for Economic Co-operation and Development (OECD) is engaged in a study of these. For descriptions of yet other European entrepreneurial assistance programs see Steinbach (1985a and 1985b); Johnson and Rodger (1983); the OECD publication, *Feedback ILE:* and the British publication *Employment Gazette.*

4. Information for this section on the PISCES Project was taken from (Ashe 1985a; Ashe, ed. 1985b).

5. For discussion on the concept of the informal sector as applied to the Third World, see Hart (1973), Sethuraman (1976), Moser (1978), Uzzell (1980), and Todaro (1985).

6. ACCION's goals are to create "effective, innovative, and self-financing programs" to help the poorer communities of the Americas. They are based in Cambridge, MA and publish reports and manuals related to their projects.

7. Micro-enterprise development should be concerned with helping people exit this sector as well as enter it. Projects assisting the more capable poor, should consider the strategy of helping people leave the micro-enterprise sector, with additional education, to enter a higher-pay occupation.

8. Caution should be attached to findings that use dropouts as a control group. It is very possible that such a control group is not equivalent to the project group. Individuals in the project (experimental) group may be more motivated or better managers to begin with.

9. The newest AID project in the field is the ARIES Project, Assistance to Resource Institutions in Enterprise Support. Its focus is on the capacity of intermediary agencies. Issues to be examined include factors affecting sustainability, constraints to extending outreach, the balance of credit and technical assistance, and training needs assessment. In addition, the project will develop training packages and provide technical assistance to local institutions supporting micro-enterprise development.

For a list of 25 nongovernmental organizations active in micro-enterprise development in the Third World see Buzzard and Edgcomb (1987).

10. Tendler (1987) also found these characteristics in three Ford Foundation programs in India which also functioned as trade unions: Self-Employed Women's Association of Amedabad, Working Women's Forum of Madras, and Annapurna Caterers of Bombay.

11. The importance of starting as a credit-brokering institution, rather than obtaining loan funds of the program's own, is that it gives the organization time to learn the loan business from working with established banks (Tendler 1987, p. 16).

12. The vast majority of loans are for individualistic self-employment activities. However, if someone is considering buying an expensive piece of equip-

ment (e.g., a tractor for farming), he or she is encouraged to do this with a larger-scale enterprise organized on a cooperative basis. This is done so expensive equipment can be shared and its costs spread among a large number of owners.

13. Another very similar bank was initiated at the same time as the Grameen Bank but in Indonesia and named the Badan Kredit Kecamatan. See Goldmark and Rosengard (1983) for a description and evaluation of that project.

14. The evaluation section draws mostly from Hossain (1986). For other evaluation literature on the Grameen Bank, see Tendler (1987), Ghai (1984), and Fuglesang and Chandler (1986).

15. According to Fuglesang and Chandler (1986), an insidious leasing of land system operates in rural Bangladesh where large landowners obtain control of peasant lands by lending money which the poor can't pay back. One important purpose of borrowing money from the Grameen Bank is to get these small plots of land back.

16. The six industry sectors that members participated in were agriculture/forestry, livestock/fishery, processing/manufacturing, trading/shopkeeping, transport and other services, and collective enterprises. The major activities in these sectors were cattle fattening, seasonal crop trading, milch cow raising, paddy and rice trading, grocery and stationery shop, rickshaw transport, cattle and goat trading, paddy and pulse husking, crop cultivation, handloom weaving, handloom products trading, cloth trading, fish trading, wood and timber trading, peddling, vegetable trading, betel leaf and nut trading, flour trading, mustard seed trading, gur trading, cane and bamboo works, goat and poultry raising, mat making, rice products making, tailoring, and fishnet making (Hossain 1986, pp. 21-22).

17. Salaries represent 10.4 percent of loan disbursements. Cost of money represents 5.8 percent, and other expenses represent 4 percent for a total of 20.2 percent.

18. One could also expect income of nonmembers in a village to have increased due to the presence of the Bank in their village. Two mechanisms which could cause this are workers leaving wage employment for self-employment, effecting a reduction in labor supply (which increases wage rates and work hours), and the increased presence of peddling activity expanding the market for locally produced goods.

19. A major weakness for before-after comparisons is that many things change together over time. There might have been similar changes over time to those who were not members of the Bank. Fortunately, this evaluation does utilize control groups to measure other outcomes.

20. A second control group sample was constructed from the random sample of those who lived in the Bank-served villages and who met the target group criteria but were not members of the Bank. I reported the results using only the first control group because selection bias would not be as strong.

21. Seventy-one percent of adult bank members are workers (including self-employed workers) as opposed to 57 percent of the adult target group who are workers in the control villages.

22. Dr. Yunus has had close association with the South Shore Bank in Chicago. This bank has used principles of the Grameen Bank to develop the

Women's Self-Employment Project in Chicago and the Good Faith Micro-Loan Fund in Arkansas.

23. In 1980, the population density of Los Angeles County was 1837 persons per square mile. This is only slightly greater than the population density for the mostly rural Bangladesh.

24. Information about the Enterprise Allowance Scheme was obtained from Allen and Hunn (1985), and Informisep (1984).

25. The following key parameters were used in the calculations: a dead-weight percent of 50 percent (adjusted), a displacement rate of 50 percent (estimated from other studies), and a growth rate of 50 to 65 percent (50 to 65 additional jobs were created for every 100 new businesses).

26. Information about the Chomeur Createur program was obtained from Steinbach (1985), *Transatlantic Perspectives* (1985), *Feedback ILE* (1985), and Folques (1984).

27. This section is based on information from Bendick and Egan (1987b).

28. It should be remembered that discontinuances are not the same as failure. People may leave their businesses for better opportunities even when businesses are not doing badly.

29. Experimental programs to test the applicability and viability of the European approach to the U.S. unemployed are underway in four states. See Chapter 7.

7

Self-Employment Training Programs in the United States Targeted to Low-Income People

INTRODUCTION

The concern here is with programs the purpose of which is to assist low-income people in starting a business after the initial training part of the program is completed.[1] There is presently high growth in the number of these programs. The growth in these entrepreneurial training programs is a response to the increase in demand for them by individuals, and an attempt by organizations to provide alternative private sector–oriented training options. The increased demand for self-employment training programs is due mainly to reasons cited in Chapter 3 for the increase in rates of self-employment since 1970. The increase in the supply of self-employment training programs is a creative response to attempt to provide new training programs that will lead to additional jobs. Momentum for this has come from the recognition that America has serious structural unemployment. That is the problem. There is wide acceptance of the idea promulgated by David Birch (1987, 1981) that small businesses create the majority of jobs. That is thought to be the solution. Therefore, you put the problem with the solution, and you get a policy.[2]

There is a debate on whether Birch's analysis substantiates his conclusion (Armington & Odle 1982; Maier 1985; and Kaladonis 1988). However, Birch's conclusions do not have to be correct to rationalize helping low-income people start businesses. Good reasons for doing it include reducing poverty, providing training options, assisting entry into the job market, and assisting the quest for self-sufficiency.

The immediate precursor to today's self-employment programs occurred during the late 1970s and early 1980s under the Comprehensive

Employment and Training Act (CETA). A brief summary of this is followed by the results of an enumeration of contemporary programs operating through a variety of sponsorships and arrangements.

CETA ENTREPRENEURIAL PROGRAMS

Only a very small portion of progams that operated under the Comprehensive Employment and Training Act (CETA) involved entrepreneurial training and their existence largely went unnoticed. These programs were established under Title VII of CETA, the Private Sector Initiatives Programs. Some of those programs continue today under the reincarnated CETA, the Job Training Partnership Act (JTPA). June Sekera and I conducted a national mail survey in 1982 requesting that all CETA prime sponsors enumerate and describe these programs. The results of that survey, including case descriptions and addresses, are in Balkin and Czechowski (1986) and Balkin (1988e).

From a mail survey to 542 CETA prime sponsors, 49 entrepreneurial training programs were discovered. Of those 49, detailed information was provided on 38 of them. Eighteen of the 38 programs were ownership oriented and the remaining 20 just taught business skills in one form or another. The average cost per enrollee for the 35 programs which provided cost information was $5600 with a range from $300 to $19,000. This was high compared to other CETA programs.

On average, 77 percent of clients enrolling in these programs completed them. For clients completing the ownership-oriented programs, 34 percent started businesses. Only seven out of the 18 ownership programs provided follow-up information. These programs conducted follow-up on their clients ranging from six to 20 months after progam completion. For those seven ownership programs, the client success rates (still in business) was high: Six out of the seven programs had follow-up success rates of 85 percent or higher. It seems once CETA ownership programs helped clients start businesses, they were able to keep them in business.

PROGRAM TYPOLOGY: CONTEMPORARY
PROGRAMS

Self-employment training programs for low-income people can be classified according to the following three dimensions, measured dichotomously: Target population—group specific (e.g., women, youth, dislocated workers, ex-offenders) versus low-income in general; type of training—industry-linked training for specific types of businesses (e.g., child care, street vending, home sewing) versus training for self-employment in general; and program focus—a business plan is an

Table 7.1
Relative Frequencies for Eight Types of Self-Employment Training
Programs for Low-Income/Disadvantaged People (N=50)

	Specific Target Pop.		General Target Pop.	
	Business Plan Important	Business Plan Unimportant	Business Plan Important	Business Plan Unimportant
Industry Linked Training	(1) 2%	(2) 12%	(3) 2%	(4) 2%
General Self-employ Training	(5) 42%	(6) 4%	(7) 32%	(8) 4%

important program outcome (e.g., two-year cash flow projections, projected income and balance sheet statements, formal marketing strategy) versus business plan preparation is not emphasized. By considering all combinations of these three program attributes, eight mutually exclusive program types emerged. Other attributes that could be used to categorize programs are presence or absence of a screening process, extensive academic classroom work, extensive self-confidence improvement work, client access to a loan fund tied to the program, extensive post-training follow-up assistance, use of formal mentors or internships, and reliance on government funding. The three dimensions chosen seem among the most important and easiest to discern.

ENUMERATION OF PROGRAMS

The eight possible program types are the cells in Table 7.1. The percent inside each cell is the relative frequency from an enumeration of 50 programs that I found across the country that currently operate or recently operated.[3] The list of programs is in Table 7.2.

Programs that provide general self-employment training are much more common than industry-linked programs (82% vs. 18%). Programs that target a specific group are slightly more numerous than ones that do not (60% vs. 40%). Programs that focus on a business plan are much more common than ones that do not (78% vs. 22%). The most common program is Type 5: general self-employment training, focusing on a business plan, and serving a specific target group. Programs of Type

5 and Type 7 (serving general low-income clients) together comprise 74 percent of the programs.

I think the reason for the predominance of the business plan focus is due to the influence of business academics, primarily the textbook writers, and bankers. I agree that business plans are important, but the issue is "Who prepares them?" Business plans are moderately sophisticated documents. The business plan–oriented programs require students to prepare the business plan themselves usually after classroom training and with consultation by advisors. Generally, business plans require fairly good writing and arithmetic skills along with systematic analytical thinking. The business plan requirement acts as a screening mechanism to eliminate those who don't possess those skills or don't have the wherewithal to obtain them. If the business is moderately sophisticated and the owner will initially be going to a bank for a loan, a business plan is a necessity and substantial authorship of it by the client is essential. If the business is simple and bank financing won't be used, a formal business plan prepared by the client him/herself is, I believe, unnecessary. Someone should make sure the business makes sense in terms of a market being there, income likely to be generated, adequate cash flow, and reasonable longevity. But that can be done by the program, or the program in concert with the client, without a formal self-prepared business plan document and a lot of formal classroom instruction. Once the business is started, the client may see a necessity for obtaining additional education. That practical motivation can result in greater diligence toward acquiring business skill competence and will likely result in a more worthwhile experience for the client.[4] "Once abstract concepts are anchored in specific applications, the learning often comes more easily."[5]

Twenty-two percent of the programs did *not* focus their assistance on clients preparing business plans. Of the 11 programs that did not focus on client preparation of business plans, seven were industry linked. Essentially, these seven programs specialized in learning the essentials for operating and choosing a business in a certain industry and therefore could provide validated rules-of-thumb for business operations. Basically they operate like a franchise. I am very impressed with the franchise notion as a way to assist people into business ownership and feel this area should be further explored to develop self-employment programs.[6] See Chapter 8 and Balkin (1988d).

CASES

This section provides an example of each of the eight types of programs from the typology above. The programs chosen for example were not necessarily the best of their type but were merely the ones that I had the most information on. Where possible, evaluation results are presented. However, none of the evaluations found so far used long-term follow-up or resembled the rigors of an experimental design necessary for measuring impact. Industry-Linked programs (Types 1–4) will be presented first, followed by general Self-Employment programs (Types 5–8).

Industry-Linked Programs

Type 1—Business plan important and serves a particular target population: Intensive Horticultural Older Worker Training Program.

This program was funded by JTPA and existed in 1985–86, operating through the Governor's Office of Job Training and the State of Michigan Offices of Services to the Aging.[7] The objective of this program was to train participants to become self-employed in greenhouse/truck garden–related enterprises. All participants had to be JTPA eligible and also be 55 years of age or older.

The program operated in five Michigan sites—two urban and three rural counties. In two of the counties, the program had substantial start-up problems. Therefore, the project fully operated in only three sites.

Participants took horticulture and business training classes at their local community college. Locations were chosen where horticulture or greenhouse education programs already existed. The business training part of the program used a set of texts and exercises named "PACE," which was developed by the National Center for Research in Vocational Education. As part of the PACE system, all students are required to prepare a business plan.

The training period was six months with about 20 hours a week of instruction. Eight to ten hours a week involved entrepreneurship education, and ten to 12 hours a week focused on horticulture classroom instruction, greenhouse/outdoor activity, and field trips. Some of the horticulture projects were sophisticated, growing high revenue crops such as herbs, dried flowers, and hydroponic off-season vegetables to be marketed to restaurants and institutions. Some were simple and traditional, raising tomatoes, dill, sweet corn, cabbage, and squash, and selling them at an outdoor stand.

The program fell short of its process goals. The goals were 62 enrollees, 62 completions, and 41 placements or a 66 percent placement rate. Actual enrollment was 42, but all completed the program. However, actual placements were only ten for a placement rate of 24 percent, and some of these placements were for people obtaining wage jobs. No details were provided on the characteristics of the few businesses started.

An estimate of the total cost of the program was $116,000, which was 77 percent of its JTPA allocated budget. Even though all the JTPA funds were not spent, the amount above is an underestimate of the actual cost since it does not include stipend expenditures, in-kind contributions, and a small state grant.

On an average cost basis (as an underestimate), the cost per person completing the program was $2,762 and the cost per placement was $11,600. Since this program was set up to be experimental in nature, it is likely that a replication of it, working in fewer sites, would have lower costs.

The following were problems of the program: Participants were eligible for continued transfer payments (Title V of the Older Americans Act) which weakened the incentive to become self-employed; there were coordination difficulties among agencies; and resources were dispersed among too many sites.[8] The program was discontinued in 1986.

Type 2—Business plan unimportant and serves a particular target population: Lady Slipper Design (a nonprofit cottage industry)

This business was organized in 1973 by Northwest Economic Development Inc., a private nonprofit corporation whose mission is to improve the quality of life for residents of northwest Minnesota.[9] They serve a ten-county rural region from their central warehouse. Residents in this area face inadequate job opportunities, long winters, and long travel time to large cities. Lady Slipper provides a way for rural women to remain in the area rather than be forced to work in cities.

Lady Slipper (named after the state flower) is a nonprofit cottage industry wholesaler of crafts, such as stuffed loons, Ojibwe Indian crafts, and Paul Bunyan items.[10] They produce high-value items for the carriage trade. It has two sources of the products that it sells—an Ojibwe handcraft group, and a sewing program. Many rural Minnesota women have sewing skills and sewing machines. Lady Slipper provides the missing linkages that allow local residents to reach the national market. It provides designs to the clients that have been developed by a full-time product design staff, a network of sales representatives, and test marketing. Purchase orders are placed with its self-employed clients, material to make the products is delivered, and the clients receive a bill for the raw materials. The price for the materials is set at cost plus a small amount for administrative overhead. The price that the producers receive for each item is based on the time it takes a typical sewer or craftsperson to make the item, evaluated at the minimum wage rate. It is a principle of this organization that no one is allowed to earn on net below the minimum wage.[11] If someone is earning below the minimum wage, he or she is given assistance to improve technique or a different design to work on. Many of its clients improve their technique over time, and thus earn more than the minimum wage. All workers sign the labels of the items they produce. This instills pride in workmanship and assists in quality control.

Lady Slipper has contract sales representatives around the country that sell to retail stores and has representatives at the major gift shows. Feedback between sales representatives and product design staff is a key ingredient to its growth in sales.

Residents of northwest Minnesota, interested in supplementing their income, hear about Lady Slipper Design by word of mouth and apply. If there are purchase orders to fill that the present clients can't fill, applicants are given an introductory training session of about four hours after which they receive a design with which to complete just one item. They bring it back in a couple of days and work with a trainer to discuss quality, technique, and the time it took to complete. If that meeting is satisfactory they are in business and receive a purchase order.

In 1986, Lady Slipper provided self-employment activity for about 150 people—50 from its Ojibwe handcrafts project and 100 from its sewing program. Almost all clients are low-income women. They expected to have about 180 people in the sewing program by 1987. They receive supplemental funding from church groups, private foundations, business groups, and agricultural associations. In the past, they received technical assistance from the United States Department of Agriculture Cooperative Service.

Sales have been approximately $500,000 for the three years (1983–86). They expect to be self-supporting by about 1989 when they project sales to be about 1 million dollars per year. The typical self-employed client earns about $1000 per year from Lady Slipper. This is a considerable supplement to income, which can be very low in the counties it serves. Average income in some of the Indian reservations is about $1200 to $1500 per year. The average family income of applicants is $8000. This approach, therefore, does not seem at present to be capable of generating above-poverty full-time incomes, but it does provide a supplementary income to poor people in a structured way that removes risk and instills pride. It allows for obtaining extra income in a way that saves the expense of commuting and child care and allows the coordination of gardening and meal preparation with work. Many of the women have never contributed to the family income previously, and the sense of self-worth, confidence, and independence has been significant. Fifty percent of present self-employed clients have been involved with Lady Slipper for five years or more.

*Type 3—Business plan important and serves a general low
income population: Maryland Equity Participation Project
(EPIP).*

Initiated in 1986 and financed by a 1 million dollar fund, the goal is
to "increase small business ownership through franchising for socially
or economically disadvantaged persons in the State of Maryland"
(Maryland Small Business Development Financing Authority 1986).[12]
However, this program does not seem geared to people at the very bottom. There is a nonrefundable $150 application fee which includes a
kit. The kit provides information about franchises and requires the
client to fill out an application along with a business plan.[13] Further,
the applicant must have a "reputation for financial responsibility. . . ."
Its evaluation criteria of whether to fund or not include "that the
management team include dedicated and experienced individuals with
outstanding track records. . . . [and] have a strategy for the development
and growth of the franchise" (McDermott 1986, p. 43).

Technical assistance is provided upon request. Once approved, participants may receive "assistance totaling no more than 45% of their
total capital need or $100,000, whichever is less. The principals in-
volved must provide a minimum equity investment of 10% of the total
investment" (McDermott 1986, p. 43). Instruments for financial assistance include notes, subordinated debt with and without equity options,
preferred stock, and investment guarantees. The program expects to
recover its initial investment within five years. It is also allowed to
supplement with loan guarantees from other state programs.

A very important part of the program is the staff evaluation of the
franchisor. This includes visiting some existing operations, reviewing
disclosure documents, and requesting to see the franchisor's market
research for the recommended site.

This program has substantial merit. It uses the private sector to
enable purchase of an existing business set-up and support services.
However, I would like to see it streamlined on the application side and
made much simpler so applicants with very modest economic and educational backgrounds could participate. The program was too new to
have evaluation data yet.

*Type 4—Business plan unimportant and serves a general
low-income population: The Jane Addams Center Day-Care
Provider Training Program.*

The Jane Addams Center is a community center that is run by the
Hull House Association.[14] Its roots go back to the settlement houses
run by Jane Addams in Chicago in the early part of the twentieth
century. The Jane Addams Center offers many services to the com-

munity, including a referral service for child care. Thus, it has excellent industry linkage to train child care workers.[15]

In June 1982, the Jane Addams Center and Northside Family Day-Care Association established Chicago's first day-care home training program. This eight-week program trains individuals as licensed day-care home providers, in-home providers, and day-care wage workers in day-care centers. The first two are self-employment activities. Additional assistance is offered to providers once they are established in business.

The program started as a CETA program and is now funded from JTPA. This requires them to train people who are low income or receiving welfare or unemployment compensation. The training consists of an initial screening session, and if suitable, the client attends an eight-week session of 12 hours per week in classroom training and 16 hours per week in on-the-job experience in a day-care home. Topics in the classroom training include child development, nutrition, health, safety, first aid, activity planning, guidance and discipline, parent-provider relations, home day-care business skills, and state licensing procedures. Following completion of the course, trainees can enter into one of three types of job activity: operating their own day-care home, working in people's homes as a sitter, and wage employment for a day-care center. The most difficult of these is opening one's own day-care home. Support services offered to day-care homes include a once-a-week meeting to share problems among themselves and with a Jane Addams Center staffperson, a bi-monthly newsletter, quarterly workshops, social service consultations, substitute provider assistance, technical assistance with contracts, and 18-hour emergency phone availability to project staff.

Each eight-week training session enrolls 25 trainees, and two sessions are operated each year for a total of 50 trainees per year. The program also provides support services to over 250 day-care homes.

For 33 months of the program, from July 1982 to September 1985, 197 people were trained, and 143 were placed. Of the 143 placements, 47 (33%) opened homes; 34 (24%) worked independently as in-home providers; 52 (36%) worked as wage employees in day-care centers; and ten (7%) went to school or did other jobs. Cost per placement was about $1250. At a two and a half–year evaluation, it was reported that of 105 people placed in jobs, 72 (69%) went off welfare.

For the first six years of the program, 1982 to 1988, the program graduated 280 participants. In 1987, a questionnaire was mailed to the 152 graduates of the program for whom they had current addresses. Of the 73 respondents, 37 percent opened up their own home day-care center; 21 percent were in-home providers; 14 percent were wage employees in day-care centers; 20 percent were employed in unrelated work, and 10 percent were unemployed. The average monthly net earnings, for those who opened day-care homes, was $956.

Of the 60 percent of respondents who were receiving public assistance at the beginning of training, half no longer receive it. It took, on average, 8.5 months to get off aid. When on aid, they received an average total of $349 comprised of a monthly check of $235, plus $114 in food stamps. This was less than their present average earnings of $856 monthly for home care providers and $680 monthly for in-home providers. Those 40 percent of respondents, who were off public assistance at the start of training, have stayed off.

Seventy-five percent of respondents who opened up their own home reported difficulty in doing so. The problems encountered most were lack of start-up funds, fee collection, establishing a home, obtaining supplies, landlord difficulties, family cooperation, and organizing a home. Based on their write-in list, the problems most encountered were (in order of frequency): trouble obtaining children, problems with mothers, Title XX being closed to mothers, waiting for license, lack of support from the AFDC Workfare Project, and trouble with the licensing representative. Suggestions to improve training included a longer class, follow-up training, field trips, and a party—as well as new or expanded coverage of advertising, contracts, nonpaying clients, salary guidelines, budgeting, insurance issues, positive thinking, hygiene and licensing.

In June 1986, the program was awarded a two-year Federal Demonstration Project Grant from the U.S. Department of Health and Human Services to teach its unique model of services to seven other agencies in the Chicago metropolitan area. The purpose of the grant is to expand the quality, quantity, and access to family home day-care.

General Self-Employment Training Programs

Type 5—Business plan important and serves a particular target population: Women's Economic Development Corporation (WEDCO).

WEDCO was founded in 1982 by Arvonne Fraser of the Humphrey Institute of Public Affairs (at the University of Minnesota) and Kathryn Keely of Chrysalis, a Center for Women.[16] Its purpose is to increase the chances of business survival and success for women business owners. The primary focus is on women who are unemployed or underemployed. Its efforts are designed to provide access to business development skills, financial resources, and a business network. Women are provided assistance in understanding business folkways and breaking into the male-dominated business world.

The WEDCO process begins with a "Starting a Business Orientation Workshop" held twice a month. It describes the risks, hurdles, and work involved to succeed. Only about 50 percent of the attendees pursue the next step—an individual assessment appointment. At this stage, the nascent business owner presents her ideas and WEDCO responds with a proposal of assistance and the work required of her. Homework is assigned. Many leave at this point, when they realize the amount of work involved.

WEDCO does not judge the potential success of a business idea. They structure assignments so that clients can assess their own ideas. Payment for WEDCO's services are required on a sliding fee basis—$50 to $5 a consulting hour. This establishes a responsible business relationship.

The next steps are tailored to the client. The focus, though, is on preparing a business plan with a two-year cash flow projection, usually in preparation for trying to obtain a bank loan. Most start-up businesses seek between $10,000 and $15,000 of capital, and existing businesses seek between $20,000 and $30,000 of expansion capital. WEDCO serves as a conduit and screener for local banks it has developed ties to. Banks are more likely to approve a business loan, knowing the prospective borrower has gone through the rigors of WEDCO training. If a client can't obtain a loan from a bank, he or she is eligible to apply for a loan directly from WEDCO. It operates three of its own loan funds: WEDCO Seed Fund, SETO Seed Fund, and WEDCO Growth Fund.[17]

WEDCO is currently operating a two-year demonstration project exclusively for women on AFDC welfare, the Self-Employment Training Opportunities (SETO) program. This will utilize a somewhat different type of training and consulting approach.[18] The project includes 80 hours of training in business areas and 20 hours of training in personal effectiveness. There are to be four phases: a series of personal effectiveness courses to enhance self-esteem and build individual support systems; business training with marketing, business planning, management, and financial assistance; completion of a business plan and approaching a loan committee for start-up funds; and ongoing management assistance. An interesting component added to the program is requiring that participants produce their product or service and make a sale before going on to the business training phases.

An important part of what the program does is arranging with the welfare department to obtain a waiver of rules to eliminate a source of disincentives. In addition, WEDCO has been diligently working to clarify welfare rules for both SETO clients and welfare caseworkers. WEDCO has worked with the Appeals Division of the State Welfare Office to rewrite regulations for self-employment income and expenses that will apply to all welfare clients in the state.[19] Forty-five women are expected to complete the program.

For the first four years of operation the WEDCO main program has had an average of 23 new clients every month and 644 businesses have been started. For the three-year period, 1984–1987, 3000 women were provided assistance, 125 women obtained financing, and 110 direct loans were made. Of the 3000 women assisted, 67 percent had incomes below $15,000, and 63 percent were single heads of households.[20] For the businesses started, two-thirds created a job just for the owner, and the other third created an average of three full-time and five part-time jobs.

Between 1984 and 1987, WEDCO made 110 loans to 67 individuals from its own seed capital fund. Eighty percent were direct loans, and the remainder were in the form of guarantees. The average loan size was $6500. A 2 percent loss rate was experienced.

WEDCO also has been heavily involved in technology transfer and developing new training methods. They assisted groups in other cities (e.g., Flint, Michigan, and Chicago, Illinois) to replicate WEDCO, published workbooks, and developed peer marketing counseling work groups.

For the SETO program, as of October 1987, 155 women applied and attended an orientation session. Thirty-four percent of these applicants self-selected themselves out of continuing the program at the orientation stage; 21 percent have discontinued after attending some training sessions; 19 percent have not started the program for a variety of reasons. Therefore, 41, or 26 percent, of the applicants have been accepted and regularly attend sessions.

Eighty-seven percent of program participants are heads of households with an average length of time on welfare of a little over four years, 28 percent are black, and 8 percent are Native American. Their average monthly income, including welfare food stamps and housing assistance, is $693.[21] A third have been involved in running a business prior to coming to SETO.

One of the lessons from the early SETO program is that the longer a client is on welfare, the less tolerant they are about the additional regulations and red tape resulting from having a business while continuing to draw welfare benefits. Therefore, clients who have been on welfare longer are more likely to give up on a business.

Type 6—Business plan unimportant and serves a particular target population: Project C.U.R.E. (Curative Ultimate Rehabilitative Effort).

Project C.U.R.E. was started as a storefront drug rehabilitation center in the early 1970s.[22] It was eventually funded by the state of

Ohio and the federal government. They provide a detox program, methadone dispensing, and supportive services. The core of the staff consists of six counselors, a recreational therapist, a group therapist, and two supervisors. Clients come from referrals from court and lawyers.

It is in the area of supportive services that Project C.U.R.E. provides vocational counseling, and it is in the area of vocational counselng that C.U.R.E.'s staff developed an entrepreneurial development program. Drug clients have many work-related problems that inhibit their obtaining legitimate jobs. These include having prison records, limited formal education, and distaste for authority. Foremost is the problem that illegal activities pay well. The idea of C.U.R.E.'s vocational counseling effort is to examine the client's background to discover transferable skills found in illegal activities. They look to the client's criminal activities as a source of job skills. Besides being an overlooked resource, it enhances the clients' self-esteem to realize that they have valuable skills to make a legal living. Often this job skill analysis results in the client being directed to some type of legal self-employment activity.

In 1986, Project C.U.R.E. served about 200 clients. All are adults, mostly in their twenties; most are minorities. No hard evaluation data exist, though the developer, Leon Segal, feels a carefully controlled evaluation could be done. The following are examples of crossover (from illegal to legal) self-employment activities. Several clients who have run confidence games have become successful in "nothing down" real estate deals. A drug peddler converted his skills for organizing and networking to selling home-delivered fruit baskets. It was suggested to a prostitute that she become a legitimate masseuse. A good professional massage therapist can make a per-hour rate similar to that of a prostitute.

Segal has developed an extensive set of counseling exercises and materials. His techniques can be used in many types of self-employment programs. While little can be conclusively established about the impact of this program, the approach seems very promising for a formal demonstration project.[23]

Type 7—Business plan important and serves a general low-income population: Hawaii Entrepreneurship Training and Development Institute (HETADI)

HETADI was established as a nonprofit organization in Honolulu, Hawaii, in 1977. It was an outgrowth of the U.S. State Department's East-West Center program for International Entrepreneurial Development. Its mission was to promote small business development in the United States and overseas through training and consulting programs.

HETADI, as of 1986, provided technical assistance and management services to over 2000 small businesses and potential entrepreneurs in six countries. An underlying philosophy of HETADI is that entrepreneurs are not born, but people with high entrepreneurial potential can become an entrepreneur through a rigorous training process. High entrepreneurial potential concerns the motivation of the entrepreneur: not money assets.

The Institute offered two types of training, correspondence and classroom, that could be customized to fit local circumstances. The typical classroom program size was 25 to 30 clients and consisted of the following four phases: (1) recruitment and selection, (2) entrepreneurial training workshops, (3) implementation, and (4) evaluation. The recruitment phase involved advertising, interviewing and screening applicants, and general organizing. The training phase lasted three to four months, four hours a day, for a total of 156 hours. Topics included business plan objectives, entrepreneurial (motivational) development, and basic skills enhancement. Teaching media included lectures, seminars with outside guests, class exercises, case studies, audiovisual presentations, and business plan presentations. The implementation phase involved fine-tuning the client's business plan and providing concentrated start-up assistance. The last phase, evaluation, involved post-program follow-up to obtain data on costs and performance. There were six performance objectives for the program: completion rate of 85 percent; 50 percent start-up rate by the end of the program. Of those completing the program, 85 percent will complete a full-scale business plan; 60 percent will have their loan applications approved. Within one year of program completion, there will be one additional employee for each business started; and the unemployment rate for those completing the program will be 10 percent or less by the end of the program.

HETADI also developed its own instructional materials including "How to Prepare a Business Plan" and "How to Start Your Own Business." The first text was applicable for use whether the client was starting a business or expanding an existing business. It focused on making mistakes on paper instead of in the marketplace. The three sections of this text are Data Collection, Strategy Formation, and Forecasting Results. The second manual focused on basic skills. Its sections are Goal Setting and Time Management, Distribution, Budgeting and Control, and Leadership. Advice given includes: plan your business and start small; effective marketing is critical; substitute sweat equity for capital and be realistic about financing; know customs and traditional practices of your industry; be careful of starting a new business that requires breaking new ground or educating the public; and analyze the costs and benefits of everything.

The accounting firm of Arthur Young and Company (1982) conducted an evaluation of HETADI for the period 1978 to 1980. Through questionnaires, telephone interviews, and program records, they obtained information on 105 clients who graduated HETADI and on a control group of one hundred clients who applied for the program were CETA eligible but were rejected. This is the only program found to have used a control group for an evaluation.[24]

Methodological problems aside, the results indicate that the program was very effective. The start-up rate was 55 percent for HETADI as opposed to only 10 percent for the control group. Additional employment in the new businesses of the HETADI graduates amounted to 94 as against only 20 new employees in the new businesses of the control group.

Type 8—Business plan unimportant and serves a general low-income population: Institute for Self-Employment Enterprises (I-SEE).

This project is affiliated with the Community Renewal Society (CRS), the urban mission arm of the United Church of Christ, and receives funding from CRS and various government agencies.[25] The creation of I-SEE grew out of ten years of study by the Community Renewal Society's special committee on "Unemployment and the Future of Work." The principal director of the program is Sam Sains, a former program officer of the Woodlawn Organization. The objective of I-SEE is to encourage self-employment and cooperative enterprises among the poorest and most disadvantaged groups in Chicago, which includes public housing residents, welfare recipients, ex-offenders, and the homeless. I-SEE adheres to the notion that traditional (i.e. business plan and screening-oriented) entrepreneur development programs are the least likely to identify potential entrepreneurship opportunities within this most disadvantaged group.

The I-SEE model has three phases: introducing self-employment possibilities, developing a network of community-based support, and technical assistance follow-up. Through neighborhood groups, I-SEE holds workshops and presentations to explore the idea that residents can become self-employed. In this peer group setting, individuals examine their potential and decide whether their personal interest lies in self-employment. After individuals declare that they want to pursue self-employment and their business ideas, community-based support is developed to assist them to pursue their business idea. Community-based support includes a local program leader, community-based organizations, and local businessmen. The local program leader serves as an on-site coach and encourages group interaction. Community-based organizations include churches, block clubs, PTAs, and local government agencies. As part of their function, they identify the need for goods and services in the community. These groups not only provide market feasibility information but may eventually become a targeted market. Local businessmen serve as mentors who provide direct technical assistance. These mentors often become "silent partners" through the investment of resources and capital in the newly formed ventures. I-SEE provides follow-up help and continues to be a broker of services so their clients can obtain technical assistance when they need it. They also work with clients to prepare a short operating procedure document which sets out some rules of thumb and expectations for the business. This is in the spirit of a business plan, but it is not a big sophisticated formal document and is prepared jointly. Clients are not required to do this on their own. Requirements for start-up capital are intended to be modest, and repayment begins after a few weeks of operation. Access to capital is through funds of religious orders, church congregations, foundations, mentor businessmen, and community banks and lending institutions. Part of the start-up capital is donated in the form of free or low-cost business services.

The process sometimes involves stops and starts as clients drop out and then later drop back in. This is an aspect of the I-SEE project that few other programs have: being patient with clients, helping them build their confidence, tolerating and acknowledging that they have other demands on their life, and working with clients who have poor literacy skills. In terms of the latter problem, they encourage and provide remedial literacy tutorial education but do not require clients to take the added educational work if they can operate their business without it.

The program was formally initiated in 1987. No hard evaluation of the program was available. The types of businesses started include both individual small businesses as well as small worker cooperatives. These include a home maintenance co-op, resale shop, ceramics manufacturer, building maintenance company, clown for parties, crafts/jewelry business, and a modeling co-op.

I-SEE has had disagreements in obtaining funding from the local JTPA government agency which attaches performance criteria to grants that are inconsistent with the I-SEE model. The inconsistency is that I-SEE does not screen for the most job ready individuals, so that it works with extremely disadvantaged people. Therefore, it requires more time to develop start-ups by patiently coaching clients and providing technical assistance after start-up. Typically the JTPA grants are for short-term projects with performance criteria involving a certain number of start-ups after a specified number of months. I-SEE has turned down JTPA funds rather than try to work within its constraints.

PROGRAMS TO WATCH

Two very visible projects are currently underway which should provide substantial information on the viability of self-employment assistance for low-income people on a large scale.[26] One is an attempt to provide a U.S. version of the British and French transfer payment diversion programs (see Chapter 6). The other is to assist women on welfare to become self-employed, removing the impediment of welfare disincentives.

The Unemployment Insurance Self-Employment Demonstration[27]

As of 1988, unemployed people eligible for unemployment insurance benefits can not collect those benefits while devoted full-time to organizing a new business. This project will test the usefulness of changing that rule and actively supporting unemployed individuals in their efforts to start businesses. This project will attempt to measure the costs and benefits of early intervention strategies to assist unemployment insurance claimants to become self-employed.[28] The approach is to develop programs made up from existing services and then to test their effectiveness by using randomly assigned control groups. Unemployment insurance claimants who apply to participate in the Self-Employment Program will form a pool, out of which some will be randomly assigned to participate and some will just receive the usual services available for unemployed persons. Plans are for this project to start in 1988 and last two years with a two-year follow-up period for evaluation.

Two subprojects will be operated, differentiated by target groups. The first project will occur in the state of Washington to assist a broad array of unemployment insurance claimants. The second subproject will be located in three states (Massachusetts, Oregon, and Minnesota) and will target structurally unemployed persons—operationally defined as those likely to exhaust their unemployment insurance benefits and have difficulty finding a similar job.

The allowances can take three forms: a one-time, lump sum payment, a series of periodic payments over a period of time, or some combination of the two forms. The project will test which method of allowances is the most effective. Along with the allowances, supportive business services and training will be provided. Supportive services will include an assessment of client needs, help in making the psychological transition from being an employee to being an employer, and assistance in preparing a business plan.

Self-Employment Investment Demonstration (SEID)[29]

As of 1988, there are many rules attached to Aid to Dependent Children which inhibit recipients from starting a small business as a way to create a job and get off welfare. These impediments are in addition to the usual ones (i.e., loss of Medicaid; high marginal benefit reduction rate; limited access to child care) which inhibit the movement from welfare to work. Notable business-oriented impediments include the limitation on the amount of business assets one can own, monthly reporting requirements, and the inability of welfare payments to adjust rapidly to instabilities in the flow of income that often results in the start-up of a new business (see Anderson & Lehman 1985; Christopher 1986). This project will test the degree to which people on welfare are willing and able to engage in self-employment work activity and the usefulness of changing welfare rules to more easily enable the self-employment option. A key element in the program is obtaining waivers from the Department of Health and Human Services to set aside certain rules for the period of the demonstration project.

The project will be administered by the Corporation for Enterprise Development, last about 3 and a half years, and occur in eight sites in five states: two in Minnesota (St. Paul and Little Falls), two in Mississippi (Meridian, and Canton County), two in Iowa (Waterloo and Cedar Rapids), and one each in Michigan (Detroit) and New Jersey. The programs will be variations of two notable self-employment projects that already specialize in working with women on welfare: the Self-Employment Training Opportunities Program operated by WEDCO in Minneapolis (described earlier, in the case studies section of this chapter) and the Women's Self-Employment Project in Chicago. Both are Type 5 programs and have similar structures. They also have a keen sensitivity to the self-esteem issues that need to be addressed when working with welfare women. A process evaluation will be conducted to determine if this approach can be a workable option for a substantial number of welfare recipients.

SUMMARY

A review of entrepreneurial training programs during the CETA era revealed the programs were helping low-income people start businesses but the costs were high. Improvements in programs have occurred since then.

Eight types of contemporary self-employment training programs were described, and a national enumeration of them was made. The most common type targeted a specific population group, provided general self-employment training, and emphasized business plan preparation. Variety in self-employment programs ought to be encouraged because there are a variety of clients. There needs to be greater exploration and experimentation with Type 2 and Type 4 programs—industry-linked training where preparing a business plan is not a central component.

Four industry-linked programs were briefly examined. The Horticulture Program was innovative in addressing the needs of older persons but was too dispersed among sites and needed better interagency coordination. Lady Slipper Design is very systematic, has developed a good marketing process, and has helped a large number of rural low-income women supplement their income. They need to develop ways to increase their clients' earnings. The Maryland Equity Participation Project (EPIP) is innovative in using franchises to assist people into business but their program needs to become more streamlined to permit participation by less-educated people. The Jane Addams day-care program has been thorough at mapping out a training process. They picked a market with great potential and have established good industry linkages.

Four general self-employment training programs were also examined. WEDCO is very systematic, encourages self-direction, and has good ties to local financial institutions. WEDCO's SETO progam holds promise for translating the WEDCO model to women on welfare. Project C.U.R.E. is imaginative and works with very disadvantaged clients, ex-offenders, and drug addicts. It is still at the formulation stage, but its use of uncovering skills that clients thought they did not have can be applied in other programs. HETADI provides a well designed classroom-based program that seems capable of assisting motivated but latent entrepreneurs into business ownership. It has yet to prove its capability of assisting those with less savvy, meager skills, and a poor work history. I-SEE works with very disadvantaged clients. It is good at brokering services and very patient with clients in developing their potential.

All the programs in the case descriptions show promise of becoming effective at assisting low-income people into self-employment activities. However, that effectiveness has yet to be rigorously demonstrated. It is important to have many different approaches tried and tested to find out what works. When something doesn't work, it may just need to be reformulated rather than abandoned.

Substantial evaluation effort of self-employment programs is occurring through the Unemployment Insurance Self-Employment Demonstration and the Self-Employment Investment Demonstration. We need to know what works, for whom, and at what cost. While there is reason to think that self-employment training belongs in the manpower training program mix, just how much of it should be there will

Table 7.2
Currently or Recently Operating Self-Employment Assistance Programs in the United States

Name of Program Training Organization	Place of Operation	Program Type
Black Hawk College Entrepreneurship Series	Moline, IL	7
Business Enterprise Program for the Handicapped operated by State Vocational Rehabilitation Agencies	Most States	5
BYOB (Be Your Own Boss) Program of Florida Atlantic University and T.M. Corporation	Broward Co. FL	7
Cabrini Green Legal Aid Clinic Youth Entrepreneurship Project	Chicago	5
Community and Economic Development Association of Cook County - Entrepreneurship Program	Chicago	7
Community Economic Development Program of the Vietnamese Association of Illinois	Chicago	6
Community and Economic Development Association of Cook County - Community Basic Business Education Program	Evanston, IL	7
Dislocated Farmers Self-employment Training Program, of the Human Enterprises Development Group, Inc.	Bloomington, IN	5
EARN, Inc. Street Vendor	Philadelphia	2
Economic Development Resources, Inc.	Washington, DC	7
Entrepreneurial Training Pilot Program of the Entrepreneurial Development Institute for Training, Inc.	Brice, OH	5
Entrepreneurial Training Pilot Program of the National Center for Research in Vocational Education	Columbus, OH	5

Table 7.2 (continued)

Name of Program or Training Organization	Place of Operation	Program Type
Entrepreneurial Training Pilot Program of the Bowling Green State University Management Center	Bowling Green, OH	5
Entrepreneurial Training Pilot Program of the Upper Valley Joint Vocational School	Piqua, OH	5
Entrepreneurial Training Pilot Program of the Highland County Community Action Organization	Hillsboro, OH	5
Entrepreneurial Training Pilot Program of the Mid-East Ohio Vocational School District	Zanesville, OH	5
Entrepreneurial Training and Guaranteed Placement Program of STIA Systems and Associates	Oakton, VA	7
Equity Participation Investment Program	Maryland	3
Ex-offender Entrepreneurial Training Program	Springfield, IL	5
Gandos Del Valle Tierra Wools	Los Ojos, NM	2
Hawaii Entrepreneurship Training and Development Institute	Honolulu	7
Hispanic Entrepreneurial Training and Support Institute of the Latin American Chamber of Commerce	Chicago	5
Home Chore Referral Program of the Howard Community Center	Chicago	2
Illinois Central College Entrepreneurship Program	Peoria, IL	7
Institute for Self-employment Enterprises of the Community Renewal Society	Chicago	8

Table 7.2 (continued)

Name of Program or Training Organization	Place of Operation	Program Type
Intensive Horticulture Older Workers Training Program of the State of Michigan Office of Services to the Aging	Kalamazoo, Oscoda and Wayne Co., MI	1
Jane Addams Center Child Care Initiatives	Chicago	4
Lady Slipper Design	Bemidji, MN	2
Lake County Small Business Development Program	Waukegan, IL	7
Lane Community College Entrepreneurship Training Program	Eugene, OR	7
Neighborhood Entrepreneurial Training Program of South Austin Madison Development Corporation	Chicago	7
The Neighborhood Institute Entrepreneurship Training Program	Chicago	7
New Jobs, Inc.	Philadelphia	7
Project CURE	Dayton, OH	6
Project RISE (Readying Individuals for Successful Entrepreneurship)	Daytona, FL	7
Randolph-Sheppard Vending Stand Program for the Blind operated by State Vocational Rehabilitation Agencies	Most States	2
Rural Economic Development Project of Women and Employment, Inc.	Charleston, WV	5

Table 7.2 (continued)

Name of Program or Training Organization	Place of Operation	Program Type
San Francisco Renaissance Entrepreneurship Center	San Francisco	7
Self-employment Assistance Project of the Uptown Hull House Association	Chicago	8
Self-employment Project of the Women's Association for Women's Alternatives	Philadelphia	5
Self-employment Training Opportunities for AFDC Women of the Women's Economic Development Corporation	Minneapolis	5
Self-employment Training Program for Dislocated Workers of the Human Enterprise Development Group, Inc.	Bloomington, IN	5
Self-employment Training Program of Institute of Economic Technology, Joliet Junior College	Joliet, IL	7
Small Business Survival Training, Niagara College	Sanborn, NY	5
Threads	Chicago	2
Venture Concepts of the Pittsburgh YWCA	Pittsburgh	5
Wasatch Front Enterprise Center	Salt Lake County, Utah	5
Women's Economic Development Corporation (Main Program)	Minneapolis	5
Women's Self-employment Project	Chicago	5
Youth Business Initiative of Jobs for Youth	Boston	5

depend on thDdegree of demonstrated program impact, and the rate of social investment return compared to alternative programs. If programs can pass a cost-benefit test, there is reason to be optimistic about their growth.

NOTES

1. Many small business programs are run by community colleges, universities, and government agencies and are geared to provide either general business education or how-to workshops for particular types of business. However, it is usually not expected that the student or client will initiate the business immediately after the course, and post-program assistance is usually not provided. For a survey of community college and university programs in entrepreneurial education, see Solomon (1986). Many local private nonprofit agencies and community organizations provide technical assistance, networking, and referral services for low- and moderate-income people who are interested in starting a business. For a directory of such organizations in Chicago, see Balkin (1987). There are also myriad forms of for-profit private sector assistance to assist someone into self-employment. These mostly consist of professionals such as lawyers, accountants, real estate brokers and business brokers. In addition, there are franchises. The most common form of assistance into self-employment is through informal networks of family, friends, and associates. In a sense, a self-employment training program can be thought of as a substitute for the business-minded relative (e.g., Uncle Max) that low-income people never had, who could have taken them into the business.

2. I heard a version of this applied to Great Britain by Professor Sue Birley.

3. My list constitutes neither the population nor a representative sample of self-employment training programs in the United States. It is, instead, a listing of all the programs I knew about through various sources as of November 1987. Without doubt, I have missed several. My apologies to programs missed. The author encourages readers to send him information about missed programs.

Descriptions of most of the programs in this list can be found in Balkin 1987, Feit 1987, Gould and Lyman 1987, Puls 1988, Corporation for Enterprise Development (June) 1986, Illinois Department of Commerce and Community Affairs 1987, Mangum and Keyton 1986, and McDermott 1986. I tried not to include programs in the list that do not predominantly serve low-income people. There are many programs that serve minorities and women but do not serve very many low-income people, or intentionally screen them out. I also used discretion on how to enumerate programs with multiple locations.

Other lists of self-employment training programs for low-income people can be obtained from Rona Feit of the Corporation for Enterprise Development in Washington, DC, and Barbara Puls of the National Conference of State Legislatures in Denver, CO.

4. Another view is that once a business starts, the owner-manager gets extremely busy and won't have the time for business skills education. Knowledge of the relationship between the possession of specific business skills and

reductions in risk is needed to determine which skills must be learned before starting a business and which can be acquired afterwards, perhaps much later.

5. This quote is from Linda Stoker, a director of a literacy training program for the Polaroid Corporation. She was referring to the effectiveness of literacy training in the workplace.

6. In her evaluation of Ford Foundation–funded Third World income generation programs, Tendler (1987, pp. 9-14) found the better performing programs to be the ones with a narrow industry focus compared to the more general programs. She also notes similar findings from other researchers on microenterprise programs in Africa and on minority business enterprise programs in the United States (Kilby 1979; Barclay et al. 1979; Rial & Howell 1986).

7. The information for this program was obtained from Czuchna (1986), the Project Completion Report to JTPA, and an interview with the project director David Houseman.

8. Under Title V of the Older Americans Act, participants in the program could receive a guaranteed half-time minimum wage job in subsidized employment. For most clients this seemed preferable to the type of self-employment they were trained for.

9. Information about Lady Slipper Design came from Bruns (1986), and Castle (1985), an internal memo on participants' profile, and a phone interview with Jim Shortridge of Northwest Economic Development, Inc.

10. Lady Slipper is in the form of a classical cottage industry organized along the lines of a "putting out" system. This is an arrangement where a parent organization supplies materials and pays its subcontractors on a piece rate basis. It is one type of home-based business industry. See Balkin (1988c). It is used heavily in Switzerland in watchmaking, Germany in toy manufacturing, and India and Denmark.

11. One of the problems historical to cottage industries is the opportunity to exploit workers because they have few alternatives. There are at least three ways to avoid this. The first is to enforce Department of Labor rules that prohibit rates of pay less than the minimum wage. The second approach is to have, like Lady Slipper, the parent company be a nonprofit organization with strong ties to the community. The third approach is to have the parent company be a for-profit worker cooperative.

12. The Maryland definition of "socially or economically disadvantaged" is being unable to obtain financing because the applicant belongs to a group that historically has been deprived of access to resources, has a physical handicap, or has any other social or economic impediment that is beyond the personal control of the applicant.

13. The business plan must include, at a minimum, summary of financial requirements; description of the business; analysis of the market, marketing strategy, key personnel, and financial data including projections (Maryland Department of Economic and Community Development 1986, p. 5).

14. Information about the Jane Addams Center Day-Care Provider Training Program was obtained from interviews with staff, internal memos and reports, and Jane Addams Center (1987; 1988).

15. The staff at the project indicated the purpose of the training program

was not job creation, but assistance in providing high quality child care, which was and is in great demand in the community.

16. Information about WEDCO was obtained from Women's Economic Development Corporation (1985a; 1985b), Kleiman (1985), numerous internal reports and memos, and interviews with Kathryn Keely and Winifred Brown.

17. For the Seed funds, four types of loans are made: direct loans with fixed terms for repayment, a line of credit with either fixed or variable terms of repayment, a line of credit tied to specific sales, and factoring. Terms ranged from five days to three years. Interest was below market. Nontraditional collateral and personal guarantees were taken on loans. All applications are reviewed by a committee, and at the closing, a loan agreement, management letter, and security agreements are signed. An attempt was made to meet with borrowers on a quarterly basis.

18. The program was initiated with a leasing subsidiary to hold the assets of AFDC women clients so welfare reductions would not affect clients while they tried to start a business. When net revenues of the client business start to flow, those monies are used to pay back WEDCO for the loans it made for the business assets. No "income" was generated and clients do not formally own the assets. Therefore, welfare benefits were not reduced. When the business grows to a point at which it can replace welfare, the tie to welfare is severed. This process has become too difficult to manage and was discontinued. I think more experimentation is needed with this leasing concept.

19. A welfare recipient in Minnesota is now allowed to set up a separate business bank account, own some supplies and inventory separate from equipment, and accumulate money for payment of payroll and sales taxes without penalizing the welfare grant. To deal with reporting requirements, the SETO program has set up a system whereby clients bring their business financial information to a staff member who helps him or her input the data into a personal computer that automatically generates all the financial statements she will need to show the welfare department.

20. It would be helpful to know the educational background of clients served as well as the background of clients who actually started businesses. I suspect the background of clients who started businesses was more middle class than the ones who just received assistance.

21. For the 155 applicants, 81 percent have attended a proprietary school and have student loans outstanding; 75 percent own a car the average age of which is ten.

22. Information about Project C.U.R.E. was obtained from attending a workshop they gave at the 1982 annual meetings of the Academy of Criminal Justice Sciences in Louisville, and from interviews and correspondence with Leon Segal, one of its developers.

23. There have been other entrepreneurial projects working with offenders in prison and ex-offenders out of prison. Many prisons have craft programs where offenders make things inside and sell on consignment to an outside prison store. There was a notable New Jersey experimental entrepreneurial program working with ex-offenders that was well documented (Toby et al. 1969). Of the 22 clients, there was only one clear failure at self-employment. Five cases were considered near failure, reporting earnings less than $6000

(in 1969 dollars). Ten were considered well established but earning between $6000 and $10,000. Six were considered clearly successful, earning from $12,000 to $20,000. Offenders in prison and ex-offenders seem to be groups for which self-employment has great potential. It would seem worthwhile to try to provide self-employment training inside prison to be used as a basis for a legal job upon release.

24. This is a step forward, but there is a serious problem with the particular methodology used in this evaluation. Using rejected applicants introduces the possibility for selection bias. There is reason to think that applicants previously rejected by HETADI are different (i.e., less motivated) than the clients selected in the program, and therefore may not represent what would have happened to the HETADI clients in absence of the program.

25. The information for this section is based on two grant proposals that I-SEE has prepared and interviews with its director, Sam Sains.

26. Many self-employment projects are locally based and will not be noticed by researchers or policymakers. People in the field should be vigilant for new and innovative programs. It is hoped that a self-employment program clearinghouse will be set-up to actively search for and monitor programs across the United States.

27. The information for this section is based on the Request for Proposal by the U.S. Department of Labor to seek bids to do the evaluation of the project and from interviews with Washington State Department of Labor researchers. The law which authorizes this project is Section 9152 of the Omnibus Budget and Reconciliation Act of 1987.

28. Alternative uses of unemployment insurance to promote rapid reemployment include retraining, relocation assistance, job search assistance, and cash bonuses for early reemployment.

29. The information from this section is from Iowa Department of Economic Development (1988) and interviews with people at the Corporation for Enterprise Development who have been the prime organizers for this project.

III.

Policy and Evaluation

8

Policies to Encourage Self-Employment for Low-Income Persons: Modest Goals and Supportive Linkages

INTRODUCTION

Four policies for expanding low-income peoples' participation in self-employment activity are considered: do nothing, remove government impediments, develop programs, and create supportive institutions. One could choose any one of the four alone as a self-employment policy, or choose some combination.[1] This chapter discusses the first three self-employment policies. Creating supportive institutions is presented as a continuation of the policy discussion in the next chapter. Three themes run throughout many of these policies: goals should be modest to ensure attainment, clients should be linked to supports that can ensure success, and focus should be on people at the very bottom of the income distribution.

DO NOTHING

We know from Chapter 3, that low-income people do engage in self-employment activity on their own. Perhaps there is a natural rate of self-employment for low-income people and any interference, no matter what the intentions, will cause economic harm to them. Three situations come to mind where interventionist efforts to actively expand self-employment activity of low-income people may harm them: overcrowding, ignoring the side benefits of informal capital acquisition, and inadequate substitution for transfer payments.

Assisting a large number of persons to start small businesses in a particular sector increases the supply of goods and services in that sector and may depress prices. This is good for the consumer but the decrease in prices can lead to decreased profits and earnings. More businesses may operate, increasing job slots, but each business may have decreased earnings eating into normal profits. The existence or strength of this overcrowding effect would depend on the particular market that the new businesses entered. Perhaps there is a disequilibrium (gap) in a market (i.e., unfilled niche) and that market gap wouldn't be filled or might get filled but only after a long period of time. In that case, an increase in the number of new businesses in that market is absorbed with little or no decrease in the earnings of existing businesses. This suggests that low-income people interested in self-employment should be steered to sectors that can best absorb them. On the other hand, "Do nothing" is implied by the notion that low-income people will choose to go into certain businesses based on their perceived earnings. If the perceived earnings are too low, that is evidence of overcrowding, and they will choose by themselves not to start those types of businesses. However, they may not have the full information to make that choice, or have no alternative earning activity. In such a case steering, or information so they can steer themselves, seems recommended.

A second example of possible harm from active intervention involves providing subsidized bank financing which may substitute for informal financing from one's family, friends, and acquaintances. The latter groups may be more patient financiers than banks and may have a personal interest in the borrower. That personal interest could result in the provision of advice and networking contacts which may be lost if someone goes it alone just with a banker. Subsidized bank financing is likely to help solve the common problem of new businesses being undercapitalized but the mechanism for providing formal financing should be one that adds to the total capital pool for the client and is not merely substitutive.

A third way intervention may harm low-income people is if it fosters the perception that it is easy to get out of poverty through self-employment, thus reinforcing the belief that poverty is entirely one's own fault. This thinking, if widespread, may politically encourage the elimination of transfer payment safety nets. Engaging in self-employment, when one is without a job, can improve earning capacity and be a route out of poverty for some. However, the self-employment strategy is certainly not applicable to every poor person, and even if it were, it is unlikely to generate sufficient income to get most poverty-stricken people out of poverty entirely. Welfare reform is certainly needed but the services to assist people into self-employment are not sufficiently developed to infer that transfer payment programs should be reduced or eliminated.

REMOVING GOVERNMENTAL IMPEDIMENTS

Government creates impediments that block and frustrate attempts by individuals to better themselves through the avenue of self-employment. The governmental impediments, which should be considered for removal, concern some of the laws that regulate where and how very small businesses are to be conducted and some of the restrictions imposed by the welfare system. The first impediment mainly comes from local and state governmental regulation; the second is imposed at the federal level.

Deregulation

Regulations affecting micro-enterprises involve zoning, health and safety, registration, and business taxes. These regulations have the effect of discouraging formal businesses either from starting at all or from emerging out of the underground.

An important source of formal business start-ups is the informal or extra-legal sector of the underground economy. If there were less regulation, more of these underground businesses would emerge aboveground. The term, extra-legal businesses, refers to businesses that engage in moral activities similar to those in the aboveground economy but fail to follow or fully follow business regulations.[2] Many formal aboveground businesses first began as underground businesses—a true incubator. This sector is most often viewed by governmental authorities as a nuisance. Whether it is a nuisance or not is a matter of taste and point of view. For some, it is unpleasant to observe the ragged way in which some earn their living. For others, it is excitement, the enhancement of public life, and a source of inexpensive goods.[3] For some, it frustrates attempts at running a tidy transfer payment and tax system.[4] For others, it creates additions to gross national product. For some, it provides competition with existing formal businesses, many of which are contributors to political campaigns.[5] For others, it is a source of jobs and a force for downward pressure on prices. While suggestions are provided below to remove regulatory impediments, the tough issues remain of how to resolve the conflicts presented above.

Zoning

Zoning laws partially determine where economic activity takes place. This has adverse impact on micro-businesses. They do not have the resources either to adjust to the zoning system through relocation or to hire an attorney to seek an exception to existing zoning. It is currently unlawful in many localities to run a business from the home, operate from a vending cart, sell in a certain proximity to an existing business, sell in certain neighborhoods, manufacture goods in certain sections of town, have a store of less than a certain dimension, be stationary if the business is operated in one way, or be moving if it is operated in another way. Some of these zoning regulations have reasonable rationales such as separating toxic industrial activity from where people eat and sleep, promoting smooth traffic flow, and encouraging a tidy environment. Some rationales are questionable: such as inhibiting business competition, appealing to the aesthetics of suburban middle classes, and carrying on "tradition." While regulations for critical safety purposes should remain, the other zoning rationales may need to be overlooked for a greater social good. If our society were capable of providing decent jobs for all who want them, then all questionable zoning practices may be affordable. If our society cannot provide these jobs, then certain superficial discomforts may have to be tolerated. I suggest that many of the existing zoning regulations be waived for those who are poor and are operating or attempting to start a very small business. Wholesale abandonment of local zoning laws need not occur as applied to all businesses. Only those zoning regulations that are not critical for the management of localities, but are critical for the establishment of very small businesses by low-income people, need be modified. This is an example of what is called tiered regulation, that is, regulation applicable to one size of business but not to other businesses.[6] For a discussion of tiered regulation see Brock and Evans (1986).

Further, it is important that whatever minimal zoning regulations are left in place be communicated succinctly and simply. Eastwood (1988) describes the enforcement hassles that befall Chicago street vendors because they cannot get clear answers on where they can work. Vague business laws can be quite a deterrent to people considering starting a business. Wanting to follow the business laws, but not knowing how to, can inhibit business formation. I suggest that a cartoon-style book of regulations concerning micro-businesses be developed so that people who are illiterate can understand their legal responsibilities.

Health and Safety

Similar to zoning laws, many localities have health and safety regulations that protect the public from probable harms. Many health and safety regulations without strong substantive rationales should be waived for fledgling low-income businesses. Basic laws such as those relating to preventing harmful bacteria from entering foods, disease transmission, ventilation, accident prevention, and exploitation of children should still be kept and vigorously enforced. However, health and safety regulation without compelling purpose ought to be waived in the low-income self-employment sector. Examples of health and safety laws (occurring in Chicago, at least) that can be waived without dire consequence concern: requirements that food-vending businesses have running water, prohibition of the operation of beauty parlor equipment in the home, prohibition of the use of nonmetal pipes in plumbing systems, and requirements that certain vended foods be wrapped.[7]

Registration

It is not compelling that micro-businesses ought to be registered. Yet every business operating in certain localities is required to register in some form. Often these are minimal procedures that are not difficult for a college-trained business person to understand and implement. However, for someone with a poor educational background and meager capital, this can be a formidable obstacle. Someone may be at the margin of deciding to engage in self-employment, perhaps wanting to initiate the business on a trial basis. Requiring business registration may tip the decision in favor of not doing it.

Registration may be providing government revenue and statistics that are rarely analyzed, which seem a small benefit. It does, however, seem a barrier to business formation of very small businesses and its corollary costs of increased welfare dependence. By definition, businesses that go unregistered are part of the underground economy. Either we should tolerate this with benign neglect to accomplish a greater social good or we should enable the low-income self-employed to more easily become part of the regular economy. If business registration should still be required, it should be kept as simple as possible for micro-businesses.[8]

Business Taxes

Requirements to pay business taxes (e.g., sales tax, social security) also present an obstacle to the low-income, would-be self-employed. The obstacle is not so much that their after tax incomes would be reduced but that paying these taxes involves paperwork and procedures that may be beyond their skills. I suggest that payment of business taxes be waived for this group and reinstated only when their businesses reach a certain size in terms of number of employees or revenues. For example, the business size limit could be based on a criterion of having three or more nonfamily employees or sales of at least $30,000. This would not waive federal income tax obligations. Government revenues lost would likely be minimal. It may even be possible that government revenues could increase if this policy brings enough of the low-income self-employed out of the underground sector. It may increase tax compliance rates, additionally, as this group perceives enhanced fairness of the tax system.

If business taxes are to be imposed on micro-enterprises, the Korean practice of imposing only a small uniform yearly lump sum tax on micro-enterprises should be considered. The tax should be minimal, for example, ten dollars a month, and gathered by a visiting tax collector. This would eliminate one need for the business to keep records and fill out forms.

Welfare Reform

A major deterrent to starting a business or obtaining legal earned income of any kind for low-income people is the high marginal tax rates (benefit reduction rates) imposed by the welfare system. Much has been written by economists connected with the Reagan administration regarding the impediment to economic growth caused by high marginal tax rates creating a disincentive to produce (Laffer 1979; Roberts 1984). Even though the nonworking or minimally working poor face zero or low marginal tax rates of the federal income tax system, they do face severely high marginal tax rates of the welfare system. These benefit reduction rates are often higher than the marginal tax rates that the rich face. Recent tax reform proposals do not remedy this. These confiscatory high rates impose a barrier to the search for economic activity for the poor, no less than they would for the rich.

In some instances, the marginal tax rates can go above 100 percent— an extra dollar of earnings results in a reduction of more than a dollar's worth of benefits (Joe 1982). Reducing the marginal tax rate would do two things. It would induce some welfare recipients to increase their hours of work or to join the labor force, and it would increase the income level at which persons can initially be eligible for welfare. This latter effect may cause some to reduce their hours of work to become a new entrant into the welfare system. The net effect on work effort by reducing the welfare benefit reduction rate depends on the relative magnitudes of these two effects. A reanalysis of a myriad of empirical studies on the work effect of reducing the marginal benefit reduction rates of welfare leads Moffit (1986) to conclude that for female heads of households (the primary group affected by AFDC), there is an overall inverse relationship between hours of work and the welfare marginal benefit reduction rates—reducing the marginal rates will increase hours of work.

Reducing the marginal benefit reduction rates of welfare would lead to increases in work effort for both wage labor and self-employment. Thus, this is a general policy to help low-income people obtain upward economic mobility. An advantage to low-income people, who try self-employment as a mode for earning income, is that since many of the transactions involve cash, they can hide their earnings from welfare caseworkers. This amounts to a reduction in the marginal benefit reduction rates. Rather than discourage this as welfare cheating, this can be encouraged by either building in more generous disregard for rules or benign neglect in enforcement. Middle- and upper-income people, who manipulate the welfare system, should have the full enforcement of the law brought to bear to discourage such activity, but a different set of rules or enforcement policy should be in effect for those at the bottom of the income distribution who try to work and eke out small incomes. A less than tidy welfare system may be worth the increases in real gross national product, upward mobility, reduced social pathology, and enhanced self-esteem for underclass people.

A welfare rule that particularly discourages self-employment is the regulation that considers capital equipment purchases as earned income. This higher earned income could make a person ineligible for welfare. To avoid this, a person would have to lease the equipment to count it as a deductible business expense (Anderson & Lehman 1985).[9] A related problem is that there is a limitation on dollar value of the assets that one can own. If one saves to buy equipment for a new business, and it is over the limit (in most places this limit is $1000), that will make one ineligible for welfare.

The reporting and record keeping requirements of both the IRS and AFDC can be overwhelming to those with poor literacy skills and limited capacity to deal with bureaucracy. Of the two, AFDC involves greater reporting efforts. If one declares that they are starting a business, they must report their net business income to the AFDC caseworker every month. This involves keeping records to substantiate gross business income and current business expenses. Someone running a business should keep accurate business records, but for very small businesss it is not crucial.[10] One just has to operate in a rule-of-thumb manner that ensures profit. Welfare clients may be willing to give up some benefits to earn higher business income, but the reporting requirements may discourage them entirely, or force them to operate their businesses in the underground economy.

A possible way to encourage self-employment activity within these constraints is for community groups or private foundations to set up holding companies. No income would technically be earned until the business is solid enough so the client can afford to go off welfare. The organization can also hold title to the assets. As described in Chapter 7, WEDCO has attempted something like this in its SETO program.

Another severe inhibition to business formation is the loss of Medicaid benefits (the green card). Even if the business gets off the ground, earning enough income to live adequately without welfare cash benefits, many would still have insufficient income to replace the Medicaid benefit with private nongroup insurance. One can take a chance living with diminished welfare cash income, but people don't want to take a chance at not being able to provide for the health care needs of their children. A strong recommendation is that people on welfare, trying to start a business (or get a job), should be allowed to keep their Medicaid benefits until they earn substantially higher incomes for a long period of time (e.g., 24 months). Encouraging people to leave welfare and start a small business can be considered a joint venture between individual welfare recipients and society. Society can provide support for the venture by removing impediments and supplying the missing links. One of the most crucial missing links is basic health care benefits.

Tied to the above is the necessity that actual payments for child care be a deductible expense for determining the welfare grant and that the nascent self-employed welfare client be assisted to find a convenient place for child care. Another approach to providing child care is some type of National Child Care system. For example, low-income people could receive vouchers for child care services. This has been proposed by Representative Nancy L. Johnson. It would have the further impact of stimulating the child care self-employment sector.

PROGRAM DESIGN

This section suggests designs for programs to encourage and assist low-income people to start micro-enterprises. To stimulate discussion, these design suggestions are based on the notion that vigorous effort be applied to ensure that people succeed as opposed to the notion of making the training difficult so only the best will succeed.[11] A self-employment training program is only one policy approach among others to encourage self-employment, and it is probably the most expensive. One strategy to consider is that training programs be upgraded and used only for the most disadvantaged persons, educationally and in terms of income.

The design characteristics discussed are client selection, networking, market research, training, mentor matching, business goals, franchises, an integrated program with three tracks, and follow-up. Financing client businesses is discussed in the next chapter.

Client Selection

A first principle here is that people considering entering a self-employment training program should be politely assisted to consider all their career/job options. Counseling should be biased in favor of obtaining higher levels of formal education or vocational skill training. Entrepreneurial endeavors are likely more effective after one has had extensive job experience, a good general education, and possession of a skill. A business owner has to perform varied tasks, so a good background is having knowledge in many areas. There is no "Halsted Street to Easy Street." One will probably have limited success as a business owner if one has very limited education and experience.

For many low-income people this option is not possible. Then they should be seriously encouraged to consider the micro-enterprise avenue. The potential client pool can then be placed into one of three groups and the principles of triage applied.[12] There are three groups to consider. The first group includes those who possess enough business background, experience, and intellectual skills that they could likely start a business and succeed on their own. The second group consists of those who have extreme deficits such that they cannot minimally read or write and may be borderline mentally competent. The third group consists of those who have a low-level background but who could start a business if provided with assistance. Programs should be directed to the third group. If all in this last group are helped, the next priority should be directed to the second group with, perhaps, a remedial education component added. Only if there are still resources remaining should the first, most sophisticated group, be brought into the program. Currently, this is the opposite of how most self-employment training programs in the United States pick their clients. Since most programs do not use control groups to calibrate impact, they are likely to show the highest rates of start-up and success by selectively cream skimming to pick the brightest, most promising candidates, the first group. This behavior makes sense for a private sector banker, but for a social and economic program, it is likely to cause the least impact. Impact is an outcome different than that which would have occurred without the program. Program operators often counter this notion with the view that they select the best clients to demonstrate to their community that the program can succeed. In addition, they claim that these successes act as role models to encourage others to try self-employment.

Many programs claim that they do not screen because they let clients choose for themselves whether to leave the program or continue. This is called "self-selection." The program will often include difficult assignments, and those that can't keep up leave on their own accord. This is, however, a form of screening because only those with the best backgrounds and most determination are likely to do the assignments. From a banker's perspective of weeding out losers, this makes sense, but from the point of view of assisting extremely disadvantaged people into upward economic mobility, self-selection, as usually practiced, defeats that purpose. Self-selection is better than preprogram screening, but it is a form of screening nonetheless.

If programs were to heavily select clients from the low end of the abilities/income spectrum, they may still want to select some sure winners to mingle with the more disadvantaged clients. This would provide success examples, some high-end peer support, and additional networking opportunities for the more disadvantaged clients in the program.

Networking

It is not entirely clear how to develop one's social network or networking skills short of advising a client to obtain work experience in the industry they want to start their business in. Several programs encourage mutual peer support from other members in their training class. Mentor matching, discussed in a section that follows, should lead to enhanced networking. I often hear of clients in self-employment training programs being told to join trade associations. That expands the reach of one's network through acquiring additional weak ties and it is a worthwhile activity. But I think one also has to augment their strong ties to obtain valuable "insider" information and support. Marriage to the boss's son or daughter would seem to work. Joining and being active in certain private clubs might work also. Clients could be made more aware of the importance of family and friends in starting businesses. As an assignment, they could list all the people close to them with a brief description of their skills, resources, and business background. This would make clients more aware of resources near to them. Perhaps programs should work more on the networking dimension of self-employment and less on the acquisition of formal business skills. This will emulate more closely what goes on in the real world of business.

Market Research

A way to design a micro-enterprise program to enhance client success is encouraging clients to enter one of a limited set of businesses that show a high likelihood of success. This can be accomplished by extensive market research to uncover the best micro-enterprise ventures in a metropolitan area. Then clients would be steered or trained for those businesses. It is not necessary for clients to already have an idea for a business. Most current self-employment training programs work with clients to develop business plans based on the client's idea for a business. Instead clients can be encouraged to enter a business similar to the one they were interested in that market research shows is likely to generate good earnings and be absorbed by the market. I don't want to presume that systematic market research is always better than informal knowledge which local people have of local markets. Those that have already operated their business casually and uncovered a genuine market gap should, of course, be encouraged to continue. However, one should be cautious about encouraging people with fantasy business ideas such as boutiques and nightclubs.

Market research is expensive and difficult. One cannot expect a would-be business owner with meager resources and a low level of education to conduct sophisticated market research. An assistance institution could perform market research for a whole metropolitan area applicable to many micro-enterprise programs and for a large number of clients. This can be economically feasible when costs are spread across a large number of clients. For example, $500,000 worth of market research to enable 5000 clients to start small businesses amounts to only $100 per client.

There are various analytical techniques to uncover market gaps where new businesses are more likely to succeed. Some approaches use primary data (surveys), some use secondary data (published statistics) and some use a combination of the two. One technique uses census-type industry data that compare the area in question to similar areas elsewhere. One then looks for differences in their industry distributions indicating what types of businesses could exist but are not presently operating to their usual extent.[13] Another technique utilizes surveys to find out what people want that they are not getting or are not able to obtain adequately. These techniques are complementary and can be supplemented by a panel of business experts to pick the best micro-business types. Further, interviews can be performed with existing business owners of a certain type to determine their plans for expansion to confirm a growing market, and interviews can be performed with target consumers to determine their sentiments. Once a set of businesses has been determined, additional research should be performed (e.g., traffic counts) to determine the best locations.

These "best" businesses should be those which low-income people with little education can operate, can generate profits and positive cash flow soon, and be forgiving (a sailing term referring to a boat's ability not to capsize even if mistakes are made). A key issue is the ability of a market to absorb a large number of businesses. This is to prevent overcompetition such that earnings drop below an acceptable level. An assistance institution could keep track of starts for particular types of businesses and advise programs when markets are becoming too saturated.

Even better than research to uncover market gaps is research to find and arrange for sheltered markets that clients can exclusively serve. This will involve negotiation with large corporations and government agencies for subcontracting or exclusive licensing deals. An example of this is the Randolph Sheppard Vending Program for the Blind. In this program, blind persons are granted an exclusive right to operate small convenience stores in large government office buildings. Competition is strictly limited, and they have a built-in market. This could be extended to subcontracted services with private corporations (e.g., evening maintenance service), where the program acts as the negotiator for the contract to make sure clients obtain a good deal. Clients should participate and have veto power in negotiation for deals but with advice and counsel from the program rather than, initially, as a do-it-yourself project. Eventually clients should be able to do-it-themselves.

Training

Most manpower development programs begin by providing training for clients, and then it is hoped that clients will be able to find employment. First comes training and then maybe a job. However, for low-income people with modest capacity for formal training, the opposite seems preferable. First provide the job at which effort can be applied and income can be received. Then the client has an incentive to acquire further skills and discipline. This approach is usually not possible. If the upfront training can't be eliminated, maybe it can be minimized.

In contrast to the usual approach of providing general entrepreneurial training for a wide range of businesses, I suggest that programs specialize in becoming "expert" in only a few types of business. If there are enough programs specializing in different businesses, clients would be able to choose among a variety of programs to start the type of business of the client's choice.

After market research is obtained to find the best ten or 20 types of businesses to start in a particular area, a program specializes in acquiring the know-how to start and run these business types. Included in this assistance is advice on where to locate. Much of this information can come from people already running these businesses who can be paid for this. A related approach to determine a program's business specialities is from past experience with clients. General entrepreneurial training programs can systematically monitor client outcomes to learn which types of businesses their clients had the most success in. The program can then try to train others to follow the same path.

Perhaps the training process can be shortened to a week—classroom training no longer than two days, followed by two days working at someone's else's business of the same type. At the end of the fourth day, the client is told that the business will be set up tomorrow and start generating income. Someone from the program meets them at their home and escorts them to a business location and works with them that first day, "holding their hand." Someone is then on call every day to answer their questions or to come to their business site and assist them. If the upfront training could be shortened, that would be an improvement.[14]

The process described above is the opposite of what most small business training programs do. Most programs try to portray the high hurdles that one has to jump over to start and run a small business. They emphasize all the formidable skills one has to possess. After a workshop is provided, clients are on their own to jump the hurdles and make up their skill deficits. This is sometimes referred to as a "scare-off" session. Some of the better programs actively assist the client to prepare a business plan which includes a marketing plan and a two-year projection of cash flows. This makes sense for middle-class people trying to start businesses to earn middle-class incomes, but this rather sophisticated preparation is, I believe, beyond the grasp of the target group I have in mind. In contrast, the approach I am suggesting is to lower the hurdles. After clients have established their businesses, they can then be encouraged to take additional training from traditional small business assistance programs to improve business profitability.

In sum, I offer the idea that the usual training time for assisted self-employment may not be optimal. Either clients should be encouraged to postpone entrance into self-employment for more extensive preparation (e.g., industry experience, a college degree) or clients should be taught the rudiments of a particular type of business so they can begin quickly and simply. The first approach steers the brightest to the big time, and the second approach helps those at the very bottom concretely achieve a limited but highly probable business success.

Mentor Matching

A key element in starting a business is linkage to a social network that can provide opportunities, information, services, and capital. If one has an undeveloped network, they may be able to quickly acquire access to a well developed network by linkage to someone who does have one. A very useful element in many of the programs surveyed was internships in existing businesses or the appointment of an advisor who owned a local business. If the local business owner-helper should become committed to the client and become the client's mentor, a whole range of support opens up. Business owners who mentor fledgling entrepreneurs may approach the task as a challenge similar to what they face in operating their own businesses; they will do whatever it takes to succeed. This resource is difficult to emulate in a classroom. It may be possible to skip the classroom training and just match clients to mentors, or the classroom training could stress how to socialize with business owners rather than provide exercises in accounting and economics.

Business Goals

Businesses to steer people to should be capable of being started easily and have a high rate of success. The basic criteria of success can be that the participant, with the business, earns more income and has a better quality of life than without it. Adequacy of earnings for a business should be judged after a period of time after its start since most businesses don't generate profits or positive cash flow immediately. Clients don't have to earn $20,000 a year for their businesses to be successful. They just have to earn more than their next best alternative. For people with low incomes and modest educational backgrounds, that (legal) alternative is likely to be very low.[15] Further, these businesses don't have to be operated on a full-time basis. They can be run on a part-time basis to supplement income and then expand as the improvements in earnings are made. Many full-time businesses started as moonlighting activity.

All businesses don't have to provide enough income to leave welfare entirely. It can be considered an accomplishment if people use less welfare and still have higher incomes. Some welfare benefits, such as Medicaid, may still have to be extended. Of course, it would be hoped that middle-class incomes are generated, sophisticated skills are acquired, and welfare is left entirely. However, this is unlikely to occur for all of the target group. Nevertheless, if the program accomplishes the former more modest objectives, it should still be considered worth doing. In any case programs should provide a way for clients to have knowledge of the likely range of expected incomes from their enterprises so they can make informed decisions.

Franchises

An alternative to searching for the "top ten" businesses is to link the low-income client to a business format franchise company (Balkin 1988d). A franchisor (parent company) has a vested interest in the continuing financial success of its franchisee. Franchisors experience a diminishment of profits if their franchisees fail since franchisors receive a percent of the franchisees' revenues. This makes them a type of private sector business ownership program that has potential to be very effective for people with modest abilities who can use practical guidance from an experienced source.

Vouchers, representing partial financial assistance, can be made available to low-income people interested in self-employment to choose the type of modest franchise business they would like to own and run. However, research is needed to screen franchisors who operate the downscale end of their franchise industry to find out what works. In addition to using the existing franchise industry, community organizations can be encouraged to become franchisors if they have a well-developed system to assist low-income people to become a business owner. Community organizations are always looking for ways to generate revenues to support their efforts. Surely, from amongst their members, they can do at least one thing well enough to set up a small successful business that can, for a fee, be spun off to others. This can be stimulated by making community organizations aware of the market potential, particularly if there is outside financial intervention; reducing the legal information hurdles to become a franchisor; providing grants to potential franchisors to spur development of new prototypes; and encouraging the development of franchise-like arrangements.

Presently the downscale end of the franchise industry is limited. If it can be stimulated enough so that there were to exist large numbers of franchisors offering franchises for an initial cash outlay under $5000, many low-income people would be able to afford them on their own.

An Integrated Program with Three Tracks

The program ideas presented above suggest that clients should be linked to knowledgeable practical business people or institutions to reduce the probability of failure. These design suggestions would tend not to cater to the highly independent-minded client who wants to implement his or her idea. A way to deal with the highly independent minded low-income client should be available. If a client should reject the franchise option and the "top ten" micro-enterprise option, they should be provided a general entrepreneurial training option based on the more "successful" programs discussed in Chapter 7. This would require a much longer program training time than the other two options.

A three-track program is suggested: franchise vouchers, "top ten" micro-enterprises, and a fully independent business track. The total

Figure 8.1
Integrated Three Track Self-Employment Training Program

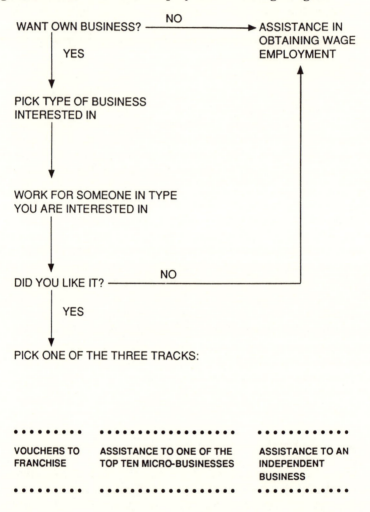

program can be promoted in low-income areas. The intake criteria ought to be very minimal. Routes to leave the program should be made available by providing assistance in obtaining wage employment if self-employment is not desired or reachable. Clients should be encouraged to work in someone else's business of the type they are interested in for a short period of time to determine if this is really what they want to do. A suggested outline of such a program is presented in Figure 8.1.

Follow-up

While it was suggested that training in general be short, it is suggested that follow-up be long, at least a year, and with many resources attached to it. Follow-up should include both technical assistance and emotional support. Help should be available from various sources including program counselors, peer helpers, and experienced business mentors. Someone should be designated as "master handholder" and be available for calls at odd hours to troubleshoot and help clients maintain relationships with their other advisors. Since training was short, numerous questions and difficulties will be revealed to the client as the business is operated in its early phase. Clients have to be encouraged to ask questions. They will likely do so only in an atmosphere where they feel acceptance and don't have to be defensive about their lack of ability. I am suggesting the coddling of entrepreneurs. Advisors will have to be on hand and be patient to help with immediate problems so obstacles, both real and imagined, can be removed. Some think that to be a successful business owner, some sense of insecurity is necessary to produce a do-or-die mentality. To the extent this is true, coddling should not try to eliminate insecurity. Good coddling should encourage a do–whatever–it–takes attitude and expand resourcefulness, not diminish it.

Some programs concern themselves about the motivation of clients by either screening only for the most motivated or trying to instill motivation by positive-thinking pep talks. Rather than exhort clients to will themselves to succeed, principles of behavioral modification can be applied. Clients can be shaped to succeed by assuring rewards for small incremental efforts directed to the goal of proper business operation. Training and follow-up should be designed so that clients, in preparing and initially operating their business, can meet with some degree of initial success. Those modest initial successes coupled with on-going counseling may be capable of motivating those with little confidence and belief in themselves to more diligently exert effort in their business.

SUMMARY

The following policy suggestions were made: tiered regulation for the low income self-employed sector in zoning, some health and safety realms, business registration, and tax reporting; welfare reform in terms of reducing benefit reduction rates, disregarding business asset purchases as income, and extending eligibility for Medicaid; welfare waivers freezing eligibility should be granted to persons trying to start a business; first priority for selection to programs should be those with low income and a low level of education where the program is likely to make a difference; a key to program success is market research performed by professionals, with the cost spread among a large number of clients; assistance should be provided to enhance social networks and match clients with a mentor, initial training to cause a business start-up should be as short as possible; providing vouchers to clients to purchase a franchise business seems likely to cause successful business start-ups as well as stimulating the downscale part of the franchise sector; a suggested model self-employment program has three tracks: vouchers to franchise, assistance to businesses discovered by market research, and assistance to independently created enterprises; intensive long-term follow-up is essential, particularly for a program that has a short training period.

A principle underlying these policies is that the self-employment option should not only be for natural entrepreneurs but also for low-income people who want to enhance their survival and have weak educational backgrounds. Self-employment can then be considered a serious alternative way to alleviate poverty.

NOTES

1. Not discussed is the notion that some types of self-employment should be actively discouraged. There is a continuum of policy stance toward self-employment activity:

Negative: Discourage	Zero: Laissez faire		Positive: Encourage
Add regulations inhibiting self-employment	Do nothing	Partially deregulate	Provide supportive institutions and programs

A thoughtful self-employment policy is likely to be a combination of all the elements above differing in its applicability based on the particular self-employment sector.

2. The term *extra-legal sector* of the underground economy is attributed to Dow (1977) and Ferman (1985). Portes and Sasseen-Koob (1987) similarly define the informal sector "as the total of income earning activities with the exclusion of those that involve contractual and legally regulated employment. ... the term is customarily reserved for such activity as those in the food, clothing, and housing industries that are not intrinsically illegal but in which production and exchange escape legal regulation." Reviews of issues of the informal sector as applied to developed countries can be found in Portes, Dewey,

Castells and Benton (1988), Ferman, Henry and Hoyman (1987), Portes and Sasseen-Koob (1987), Heinze and Olk (1982), and Gershuny (1979).

3. Smith (1987) interviewed a national probability sample of approximately 2100 U.S. families in 1981. He found that four out of every five families purchased something from an informal seller, totalling 42 billion dollars. He defined informal suppliers as individuals who had casual record-keeping systems, lacked a fixed place of business, and relied upon word of mouth and other casual means of advertising. The greater the income and education of the family, the more was purchased in the informal sector. The most frequently cited reason for making purchases in the informal sector was lower prices. The second most cited reason was better quality.

4. There is a larger amount of business tax evasion from the shadow economy than from the extra-legal sectors of the underground economy (Rabb 1986). The shadow economy refers to registered, licensed, generally fixed location businesses, that evade taxes, for example, the restaurant you ate at for lunch today that skims cash receipts.

5. From interviews with street vendors and government administrators, Eastwood (1988) found some evidence that the strong anti–street vendor ordinances and practices in Chicago were the result of political pressure from fixed-location businesses.

6. Another example of tiered regulation is that in Illinois a license is required to operate a day-care service only if the number of children being supervised is greater than three.

7. For a study on Chicago building regulations affecting small businesses, see Markle (1982).

8. The state of Illinois operates a "one-stop" permit center to provide information on busines start-up permits and requirements at the state and federal levels. It would be helpful to have such centers also cover city and county permits and requirements.

9. When one comes on welfare the business assets that one owns are excluded from determining eligibility. Income from those assets then has to be declared. If no income is declared, they are considered personal assets and that can affect eligibility. If "income" is earned from the assets, it is supposed to be allocated to current needs. Welfare benefits are reduced even if the client spends that "income" on business equipment.

10. Smith (1987, p. 87) claims that for very simple small businesses with no employees or only family employees, "record keeping may not be cost effective."

11. The design suggestions here are often contrary to what is currently being practiced in the field. However, this does not mean I am right and they are wrong. I have deep admiration and respect for those on the front lines actually operating programs.

12. *Triage* is a term used to describe the classification of patients in an emergency medical situation. The lowest priority goes to patients who have a minor illness and are likely to recover on their own. The middle priority goes to patients who are severely ill and will likely not recover even with intervention. The highest priority goes to patients who are seriously ill but could be helped to improve with intervention.

13. The Council for Economic Action in Boston uses this approach to identify markets for its Small Business Development Program.

14. Coaching clients to be persistent and to actively seek emotional and technical supports would seem useful to help them tolerate the early mistakes and rejections experienced in the early phases of the business. Peer support groups would also be very good at this.

15. An argument was made to me that low-level legal self-employment activity can not compete with high-pay criminal activities. This may be true if everything else is held constant, but it isn't. Legal self-employment activity is less risky. If you fail, you don't go to jail. You just start over. There is also more community respect for people who engage in legitimate enterprises than for those who commit crime. There are people who are at the margin of decision whether to commit crime or engage in legal income-earning activity. Many might prefer to "go straight" if an opportunity were available to earn income in a way compatible with their lifestyle and that generated adequate income. Self-employment may fit that need.

9

Policies to Encourage Self-Employment for Low-Income Persons: Creating Supportive Institutions and a Research Agenda

SUSTAINING MICRO-ENTERPRISES

Once an enterprise has been formed, it will need linkage with supports that can sustain it. The goal is to assist in the creation of enterprises that will endure and generate a maximum income stream for the owner, as well as additional jobs. Techniques for enhancing survival of micro-enterprises follow.

Advocate for Micro-Businesses

There are few organizations that advocate for micro-businesses in the United States.[1] Low-income self-employed people are usually very busy with the immediate needs of everyday survival. In addition, they lack the sophistication to understand the importance of trade associations and lobbying for government favoritism. Yet there are politically powerful groups that unilaterally impose policies and pass laws against the interests of the low-income self-employed.[2] These are regulatory committees of local government, small business trade groups, and commercial associations. Mainstream small businesses often view micro-enterprises as competition, so they use their influence to pass laws against the interests of the more marginal business sector. The interests of established small business can often be in direct opposition to the interests of *very* small business. The constituency of organizations such as the Small Business Administration and the White House Conference on Small Business, are mainstream moderately sized small business owners. Therefore, they don't seem to be effective advocates for micro-business owners.[3] Perhaps, there may be a convergence of interests with micro-enterprises at some time in the future. For now, I propose the creation of something like a Very Small Business Administration to serve the advocacy and informational needs of this sector.

Micro-Business Information Clearinghouse

An immediate need is for the establishment of a research center to monitor legislation around the country affecting low-income self-employed people, develop a nationwide listing of organizations that consider low-income self-employed people as part of their constituency (e.g., street vendor unions, community development credit unions), develop a data base and computer search system for existing self-employment training programs, and publish a *Consumer Reports*–type of magazine that will "scientifically" evaluate small business opportunities. Most advertisements selling a small business scheme provide a testimonial from someone who succeeded as evidence of a high rate of success. To estimate the probability of success, a random sample survey of people who attempted a particular type of business should be performed. In particular, this will reveal people who tried but failed, and the reasons why they failed can be determined. The Better Business Bureau currently exposes small business schemes that involve fraud and gross misrepresentation (Better Business Bureau 1983). This type of activity needs to be greatly expanded. It is important to provide the low-income nascent self-employed with easily understandable information on the likely difficulty, or ease, of successfully starting a myriad of businesses. Commercial business opportunity magazines, which take advertising, cannot do this because they have a vested interest in attracting advertisers, many of whom misrepresent business opportunities.

An important aspect of this clearinghouse would be to track government programs that relate to the micro-enterprise sector. Burton-Snell (1988), as part of the FIRMSTART research project, surveyed 70 programs in ten government agencies, which are part of the state of Michigan, to determine which programs had elements that related to self-employment. She found almost all of her sample programs did things that serve self-employed people. This ranged from financial assistance in the Department of Commerce to self-employment training for family members in the Department of Vocational Rehabilitation.[4] The U.S. Senate Committee on Small Business (1984) periodically surveys small business programs of the federal government across major departments and agencies and has produced a 228-page handbook. However, very few of the programs are applicable for micro-enterprises.

Producer Cooperatives

This book has focused on businesses for low-income people that are individualistic. However, it is desirable to encourage low-income business owners to cooperate, as was demonstrated in Chapter 5 by economically successful immigrant and ethnic groups. Cooperation can provide mutual support, exchange of market information, maintenance of prices, and possibilities for reaping economies of scale in various business functions. The trick is to get these advantages while at the same time maintaining a system whereby people who produce less earn less.[5] This can be achieved through producer cooperatives.

Producer co-ops are organizations setup by firms that produce similar products to achieve scale economies for limited functions. The realms of shared interest are usually marketing, processing, and purchasing.[6] Co-ops can also take on functions similar to trade associations, setting prices and restricting competition.

Efforts to organize these can be made by contacting all micro-businesses of a certain type in a particular area. The advantages of forming an organization can be explained, and names and phone numbers can be exchanged. Services of an attorney can be supplied to the organization free of charge. Examples of activities that the co-op can undertake include buying supplies together to obtain a quantity discount and better credit terms, producing for a common retail outlet, sharing a manufacturer's representative, jointly conducting an advertising campaign for the product or service they individually produce, and sharing an accounting service.

The U.S. Department of Agriculture actively promotes producer cooperatives for self-employed farmers through its Agricultural Cooperative Service. They perform research, provide technical assistance, publish a magazine, and make available numerous publications. Perhaps there is need for an urban micro-enterprise cooperative service.

Solidarity Groups

This form of mutual support was devised by micro-enterprise development programs in the Third World, such as those mentioned in Chapter 6. Financial assistance to self-employed people is not provided directly to an individual but through groups of five individuals who have voluntarily come together to co-sign each others' loans. Programs encourage formation of these groups by providing assistance only to individuals associated with a group. If a loan applicant is not a member of a solidarity group, he or she has to find four other people to form one. If the borrower does not pay back the loan, the other members of the group are liable. This takes the place of collateral and also creates a vested interest on the part of the other four members in the group. This interest in the success of others can take the form of business advice, supplemental labor, or access to additional networks. It also puts an additional burden of responsibility on the borrower not to let his fellow members down. Five members may be an ideal size for a group of this type because less than five may not provide sufficient breadth of resources, while more than five diminishes a sense of intimacy and loyalty to the group.[7] Further, solidarity groups can join together to form an association to pursue shared interests.

Jeffrey Ashe, who operated the PISCES Project for the U.S. Agency for International Development, also thinks that solidarity groups can be used for U.S. community economic development. His Solidarity Group–based strategy, applicable to the United States includes working directly in a community, simplifying credit applications for a quick response, avoiding complex accounting and business plans, avoiding requirements that eliminate most of the potential candidates, and using community knowledge of who is reliable and who is not (Ashe 1987, p. 2).

The formation of solidarity groups can be encouraged even if they are not tied to loan arrangements. Peer review and mutual support from a small group of people sharing the same experience can make a new, scary, and challenging effort bearable. These groups can partially fulfill the same function as the business networks that successful ethnic groups used. To further strengthen solidarity groups, they can be composed of people who share a common characteristic. This could be immigration from the same town, even if the migration was within the United States. For example, one could try to create solidarity groups for northern inner-city residents who originated from the same region in the southern United States. There could be Tupelo, Mississippi, *Landsmannschaften!* This should enhance mutual trust among the members, and trust is a precious attribute in the business world. If small groups within the *Landsmannschaften* also internally generated a small capital pool and individual members used it consecutively, it would have become a rotating credit association (discussed below under "Client Financing"). This is an effective technique for raising small business capital used by many immigrant groups.

Vertical Producer Cooperatives

This type of organization has been developed to assist small businesses of middle-income people. It can also be applied to the low-income self-employed. The term *vertical* comes from industrial organization theory in economics. It refers to a type of merger where a business combines with one of its suppliers.

The idea here is to form a moderately sized group of self-employed people where each member produces a good or service that the others could also use. Each business is totally independent, except that each is mandated to purchase from other members of the group if a particular good or service is available, thus providing a built-in level of demand. For example, such a group could include a day-care worker, caterer, window shade installer, bookkeeper, ice cream vendor, street musician, home health care worker, and beautician. Everyone in the group brings their children to the day-care worker; everyone gets their hair done by the beautician; everyone has their accounting done by the book-keeper; when they have parties, they hire the caterer for food and the street musician to entertain. One could experiment with the type of business mix that works best. While this cannot provide the entire customer base, it does provide some minimum number of customers and referrals that are helpful when starting a business.

Incubators

These are buildings that are accompanied by subsidized rents to small businesses that need help in starting up or expanding. Usually essential business services such as secretarial assistance and a loading dock are available on an affordable basis. Businesses leave as they become successful enough to obtain space and services on their own, thus creating an opening for another business in delicate newborn condition. Rarely do incubators provide services for the very marginal businesses that low-income, low-educated people would own. Incuba-tors often try to attract disadvantaged business owners, such as mi-norities and women (Temali & Campbell 1984), but they usually screen to pick bright responsible people who have had substantial business experience and education.

I suggest that incubators expand their role to include unsophisticated start-up micro-businesses of very low-income, low-skilled people.[8] Some incubators can specialize in that type of clientele. For some it may be better to integrate them among the more high-level businesses. Per-haps requirements for government funding of incubators can include setting aside a certain portion of space for micro-businesses whose owners, for example, have not graduated high school and have been on welfare or out of the labor force more than two years. An example of an incubator applied to micro-businesses of low-income owners could be a large building in the middle of an urban retail business district where small spaces are rented at very low rates to a multitude of business types grouped homogeneously by floor.[9] This would be a type of downscale shopping mall. Another kind of incubator could include a mix of business types such that a vertical producer cooperative could form.[10]

Incubators Without Walls

George Kaladonis, of the Chicagoland Enterprise Center, has suggested this new type of business creation mechanism. This is in the spirit of incubators but does not necessarily involve a building. In this arrangement, a knowledgeable person buys and operates a business with the purpose of creating micro-enterprises by subcontracting out very simple work to individuals from a target group. The parent business gradually increases the amount and complexity of the work that is subcontracted. Eventually, the entire business is sold to one or a group of the original small subcontractors. Deals can be structured so the parent business is a for-profit company and earns an appropriate rate of return given the risk it assumes, or it can be arranged where the originating owner is a nonprofit economic development corporation.

Religion and Charismatic Leadership

One characteristic of some large-scale small business programs or movements (see Chapters 4 and 5) was that they were connected with religion or had a charismatic leader. Low-income people were motivated most when opportunities for income improvement were reinforced by a sense of transcendental purpose or by a movement for the common good. This gives meaning to the present sacrifices in expectation of the economic (and spiritual) benefits of the future. Present consumption needs are also reduced when many vices are prohibited. This makes life easier in the early lean times of a new business and gives practice at self-discipline. Prohibitions against smoking, alcohol, and conspicuous consumption can go a long way toward building capital. They can also provide an ethical base on which the business gets a reputation for fairness with customers. A charismatic leader can motivate and set an example, as well as provide emotional support, when great personal sacrifices are required or when risks are faced.[11]

Efforts should be made to recognize religious and community organizations that instill motivation for self-improvement and that have a theology or ideology that supports this. These organizations can become a primary place to foster small business development programs for low-income people. In places where no such organizations exist, current groups can be encouraged to establish branches at target sites. The profit motive alone can be a powerful inducement for people to engage in gainful business activity, but when problems appear in operating a business, this extra emotional support can greatly help a person bridge difficulties.

On an earthly level, religious organizations that foster small businesses can also provide a built-in part of the market for the new businesses. Religious organizations can regularly make purchases from these new businesses and encourage their parishioners to patronize them also.

There should also be awareness of the negative aspect to religious involvement. An assisting religious organization may siphon off surplus earnings from low-income congregants to build church buildings instead of helping accumulate business capital. Another possible harm of religious involvement is that it may make clients dependent upon rituals to solve problems, rather than taking worldly constructive action. A self-employment trainer relayed an example to me where a client had difficulty making sales and lit candles rather than prepare a marketing plan. Only pragmatic capital augmenting religious involvement should be encouraged. Spiritual practices have to be consistent with economic development of the poor.

SOURCES OF FINANCING

This aspect of self-employment encouragement has received too much emphasis.[12] It is important but it is not the only major problem inhibiting self-employment of low-income people. The biggest problem seems to be how to establish a system whereby low-income people obtain information and ease of entry for sustainable self-employment activity.[13] Many businesses do not require a great deal of start-up capital, and many low-income persons could generate that small amount of capital on their own. These businesses require more time investment than money investment because, for the most part, they are labor- rather than capital-intensive operations. After a low-income person starts a business and wants to expand, access to institutional money capital can then be a big constraint to business growth.

Micro-businesses can be started with a small amount of money capital.[14] As of 1982, the majority of all business start-ups required less than $5000 in total initial capital (see Chapter 3). However, there may still be some need to provide a source of money capital, even though these requirements may be modest. The following are possible sources for this financing need: commercial banks, credit unions, state and community micro-loan funds, venture capital matchmaking, seller-supplier-customer financing, state education budgets, Job Training Partnership Act, transfer payment diversion, private foundations, churches, and client resources.

Commercial Banks

Most business owners did not use borrowed capital to start their businesses. Of those that did use borrowed capital, between 40 and 60 percent obtained part of their borrowed capital from commercial banks.[15] Commercial banks will make loans for start-up businesses if appropriate collateral is present, and they can expect to be paid back but the term of the loan is usually short. One can even obtain very small and unsecured loans as personal loans. The bank is interested in minimizing risk: They want to get paid back. If adequate collateral is present (e.g., a home, automobile, certificates of deposit), commercial banks are not too fussy about the purpose of the loan. If collateral is not present, they may still make a loan based on a good credit history and earning power of the applicant, that is, a steady good paying job. If a person has no collateral and no job other than the earning prospects from the new business, banks will not lend money unless some qualified person co-signs the loan. An exception sometimes occurs when there is a reputable organization that screens unconventional loan applicants for their ability and willingness to pay back a business loan. Several self-employment training programs serve this function.

Without a reference organization or a cosigner, most low-income nascent self-employed people are not likely to meet the banks' criteria for credit worthiness. Thus, while commercial banks are a good potential source of capital for start-up businesses, they are a source generally not accessible for low-income people. Experimentation and innovation are needed in the ways organizations can reduce risks for commercial banks, in order to encourage banks to provide start-up business loans for low-income people.[16]

Credit Unions

Credit unions are a potentially large source of loans for very small businesses. There are approximately 16,000 credit unions in the United States with about 57 million members (Credit Union National Association 1988, p. 20).[17] Credit unions have a different purpose than commercial banks. Their objective is to serve the financial needs of their members who deposit money with the credit union. They are either federally or state chartered and have to follow specific rules of operation. However, for small loans, the credit unions can set their own policy and make unsecured loans. Ninety-seven percent of all credit unions make unsecured loans (Credit Union National Association 1988, p. 7).

A business loan is defined, according to federal credit union regulations, as a loan which is for business purposes and is $25,000 or more. Credit unions have to follow formal guidelines to establish the credit worthiness of those loans. However, a loan less than $25,000, even though for business purposes, is considered a personal loan, and the credit union rules and procedures for granting that loan can be more liberal. This means that credit unions are a source of micro-enterprise loan money that can be experimentally developed. One active credit union in Chicago had 17 percent of its portfolio in personal "business" loans. Up to $2000 could be loaned to a member on an unsecured basis with the criterion being expectation of repayment. Expectation of repayment concerns past repayment history with the credit union, credit history elsewhere, and being employed. Normally, unsecured loans are not made for more than one month's income. This criterion implies that it is much easier to obtain a loan for starting a side-business while one is employed in a wage job, than for starting a full-time business while unemployed.[18]

State and Community Micro-Loan Funds

It is difficult and expensive to loan small amounts of money for business start-ups. It is difficult because most loan officers don't have the expertise to evaluate the soundness of micro-enterprises. Their experience and training relate to larger businesses, where the loans are mostly to existing businesses. One reason most self-employment programs require business plans is to provide a way for nascent self-employed individuals to communicate with bankers who are accustomed to evaluating big businesses that way. Loaning small amounts is expensive because of the high fixed cost in the approval, record keeping, and repayment process for providing the loan. A large loan requires nearly the same fixed cost to process as a small loan.

I think there is a large amount of potential institutional loan money for micro-enterprises but that it isn't loaned out because banks either don't know how to make loans without conventional collateral, or it is too costly for them to do so.[19] If financial intermediaries can be created that have the capability to successfully loan small amounts of money to new self-employed individuals at reasonable cost with a low default rate, capital will flow to them. Friedman (1988a) suggests that 1 percent of all economic development finance programs be targeted to financing self-employment ventures for low-income people.

While very new, several micro-loan funds do exist in the United States. One of the oldest micro-enterprise loan funds is Vermont Job Start, a state-funded organization operated by the state Office of Economic Opportunity.[20] It was started in 1970 with an initial capitalization of $477,000. The maximum loan available is $10,000, with the average being about $5000. For the last fiscal year, 1987/88, 48 loans were made. The loss rate was about 6 percent. Eligible applicants must be Vermont residents, at least 18 years old, have a household income between $14,000 and $24,000, and not have access to traditional sources of credit. A Job Start specialist does research on prospective enterprises and forwards the best proposals to the Regional Advisory Board, which votes whether to fund the project. Approximately 60 percent of the proposals referred to the board are approved.

The state of Iowa has implemented the Self-Employment Loan Fund (SELP) to provide start-up business loans of up to $5000. The SELP is administered through the Department of Economic Development Division of Job Training. Applicants must have a local sponsor, for example, someone from a local Small Business Development Center, who helps them prepare a business plan and fills out the 15-page application. Collateral is required, but the Fund is creative as to what they will accept. They fund only permanent full-time businesses. Interest is 5 percent, and the maximum length of a loan is five years. A committee reviews the loan applications. They have turned down about 70 percent of the applications and have made 32 loans as of 1988, being in operation one year.[21]

The state of Illinois, through local agencies, operates a Community Services Block Grant (CSBG) loan program where very small loans can be made. The CSBG began in 1981 funded from the Department of Health and Human Services, Office of Community Services.[22] Part of CSBG money is to be used for economic development. In the Illinois program, the typical loan is in the $25,000 to $50,000 range. A requirement is that the business employ one CSBG-(poverty) eligible person for every $5000 of money loaned. The loan money is not to be used for real estate or other permanent assets. A recent additional part of the program is for micro-enterprise loans to CSBG-eligible self-employed individuals who hire no one but themselves.[23] Without any bank participation, the maximum loan is $1000, and with bank participation, the CSBG loan fund will match 50 percent up to $2500. Interest is 3 percent, with repayment starting 30 to 45 days after closing. The maximum term of a loan is seven years, with most loans made for a much shorter time. An impetus for this loan program was to provide some seed capital for the use of clients of five entrepreneurial training programs in Illinois where the training itself was funded with CSBG funds.

The Small Business Venture Program operated by the Wamy Community Action Agency in Boone, North Carolina, also operates a micro-loan fund using CSBG money. Rather than provide direct loans, they deposit money in an escrow account with a local savings and loan bank to provide 100 percent loan guarantees for first-time entrepreneurs. The interest on the deposited funds is split between a loan-handling fee to the bank and a subsidization to lower loan interest rates. A local certified public accountant was hired to provide one-on-one technical assistance. In two years, 28 businesses were started with loans averaging $5000.[24]

The City of Chicago Department of Economic Development has set up a micro-loan fund for several of the self-employment training programs it finances. The funds are administered by the programs themselves. The programs are allowed to be experimental and can use up to 30 percent of the loan fund for administration. Feit (1987) lists 21 loan programs that provide business loans for $50,000 or under. Mt. Auburn Associates (1987) recently reviewed 116 revolving loan funds funded by the U.S. Economic Development Administration but operated by state and local government agencies and economic development districts.[25] Nearly half of the loans were for less than $50,000. Thirty-eight percent of the loans were for start-ups, and 61 percent of the borrowers had less than ten employees.

The National Association of Community Development Loan Funds was formed in 1986 and has 30 member organizations. All members act as financial intermediaries rather than depending solely on grants for loan capital. Their mission is to assist in community economic development. About half make business loans, and half of those have made micro-enterprise loans.[26]

Community loan funds have mostly concentrated their efforts on supplying low-income housing. Assisting businesses with start-up and expansion loans is a relatively small and new endeavor for them (U.S. House of Representatives 1988). It is important to experiment with different techniques and evaluate them to learn what works. The impact of these micro-loan funds on income improvement and the amount of business ownership for low-income people should be measured and compared to each other to discover what works best.

Venture Capital Matchmaking

Formal venture capitalists are not interested in micro-enterprises but informal venture capitalists might be. Informal venture capitalists, called "angels," are individuals with excess liquidity in their portfolios who want to earn a higher return than in the financial securities markets. Through informal information networks, they learn of entrepreneurs who need financial backing. Angels can provide patient money, and they often take a personal interest in the business and provide advice. Angels are the largest source of venture capital in the United States (Wetzel 1983).

Wetzel (1984) developed an angel-entrepreneur matching system that is operated by The Office of Small Business at the University of New Hampshire. The Venture Capital Network (VCN) operates by maintaining an investment opportunity list provided by entrepreneurs and investment interest profiles provided by investors. During the process, until a match is made, both parties remain anonymous. First, investors are given a list of investment opportunities in their area of interest. If a company looks promising, the investor can request a summary of his or her business plan. After a single company has been chosen, the investor and entrepreneur are introduced. The Network then ceases to participate in the relationship. Reasons investors reject opportunities are recorded, and the information is made available to entrepreneurs. As of 1988, replications of this model exist in nine states (U.S. Small Business Administration 1988).

The existing formal venture capital networks generally do not deal with micro-enterprises.[27] However, such an information system could be developed for the low-income self-employed. A clearinghouse could be targeted to socially concerned banks, foundations, churches, and individual investors who want to "adopt an entrepreneur."[28] An added incentive would be in the form of tax credits for loans to start up micro-enterprises of low-income people (Pryde 1987).

Seller-Supplier-Customer Financing

An important, though often overlooked, source of start-up financing is from firms linked to the new business. These include the former owner, suppliers, and customers. It is difficult to value existing businesses because much of their future profitability is tied to the skills and networks of the owner. If businesses are highly dependent upon the management skills of their owners and they leave it, the businesses may be difficult to sell. One way owners can sell their businesses is if they finance the sale. The business is financed by the new owner paying the old owner payments over time out of the cash flow of the business. In this way, a buyer of the business can obtain ownership for little or no initial investment. Further, the old owner has a vested interest in the success of the new owner because the old owner wants to get paid. Therefore, he/she may share expertise and networks with the new owner, which provides a valuable source of technical assistance. An important task for self-employment training programs could be to find the existing businesses for sale in an area and then try to make a match.

Another source of financing is from suppliers, who are apt to generate a large amount of revenue by selling things to a new business. They are often willing to provide some financing to the new business in addition to the usual trade credit. Suppliers want to see new businesses succeed if their income is tied to them. They may go to extraordinary lengths to help newcomers succeed.[29] Likewise, customer firms who are heavily dependent upon having a convenient and ready source of supply may be willing to financially help out the new firm.

State Education Budgets

State subsidies for public elementary and secondary education are substantial, in the realm of $1000 to $4000 per pupil per year. They are two to three times that for public higher education. It seems fair, for persons who did not obtain a high school diploma and a college education, that some state education funds be set aside for participation in a small business ownership program. The reasons cited for public spending on education are the same reasons one would want to spend on self-employment assistance. These reasons are: to assist in gaining skills that will increase productivity and hence economic growth, increase future tax revenues, create jobs, create an environment hospitable to business, foster citizenship, and enrich life and awareness for its own sake. The funds could even be administered through public institutions such as high schools, community colleges, and prisons. These institutions already use state and local tax money to provide education and job training. I am suggesting that part of those dollars be diverted to loan or grant funds to finance low-income individuals to start businesses. This could function as an alternative intermediate educational arrangement for the dropout, whereby business training is accompanied by a loan, or equity stake in the company. If a state were to enhance its revenues by returns from equity investments in state-assisted self-employment directly, it might take a keener interest in self-employment training.

Job Training Partnership Act (JTPA)

This Act is the federal legislation that establishes and funds our current nationwide system for job training, which is locally administered. It is the reincarnation of the Comprehensive Employment and Training Act System (CETA) which ended in 1982 when JTPA was newly implemented. Although CETA and JTPA provided training to assist low-income people to engage in self-employment activity, none of the programs provided any start-up capital. At best, participants had access to a friendly banker who might provide some loans after the program carefully screened ("creamed") applicants and assisted them in preparing a business plan.

Average cost per adult client who entered employment for the first 21 months (October 1983 to June 1985) of JTPA, for all Title 2 programs (economically disadvantaged), was $3319. Overall cost per participant was $1498 (U.S. Department of Labor 1985). This average cost could instead be reallocated in a new type of self-employment development program. Part of the cost would go for start-up training, part for start-up capital, and part for follow-up consulting. The optimal proportions for these three components have yet to be determined, but a reasonable first approximation might be one-third each. It would depend on their demonstrated relative effectiveness. These new type programs, with an amendment in legislation, could still be administered through JTPA.[30]

Transfer Payment Diversion

Transfer payment diversion is a mechanism whereby welfare or unemployment insurance payments are used to develop employment opportunities, rather than for mere maintenance. This is already in use where welfare cash benefits are converted into earned income through a wage subsidy. When a job is found by a welfare recipient, part of the wages are deducted from the welfare cash benefits. In welfare diversion, that amount is used as a wage subsidy to an employer to encourage hiring welfare recipients and providing on-the-job training. The assumption here is that the government, foregoing some amount of short-term welfare savings, will cause higher long-term savings if the funds are invested in programs that prepare recipients for stable employment. The federal Office of Family Assistance sponsored a demonstration of this approach in six states.

It has been suggested that this welfare fund be used not just for private sector wage subsidies but also for a whole range of programs that might improve the earning streams of welfare recipients (Jones 1985, Friedman 1987; 1988b). An important aspect of welfare diversion is that eligibility is frozen at the onset of participation. Thus, welfare disincentives are moderated. As of 1988, welfare diversion rules do not permit participation in self-employment. Just allowing self-employment participation in welfare diversion would go a long way to stimulate this activity. Welfare diversion can fit with self-employment programs in a number of ways. For example, wage subsidies from the fund can go to employers who are willing to train welfare recipients in starting and running a business like their own. This experience would be useful to determine if a welfare client is really interested in becoming a small business owner. These employer/mentors can be recent welfare recipients, now off welfare, who have been successful at starting and running a micro-enterprise. This could provide an additional cost break to these mentor/business owners that might help to further sustain their businesses. This also provides for peer counseling.

Two large scale demonstration projects are underway to modify Unemployment Insurance and Aid to Families with Dependent Children system rules to permit and encourage recipients to enter self-employment (see Chapter 7). Payments go directly to recipients either for start-up physical capital and/or for living expenses during the start-up phase.

Private Foundations

Private foundations can play a very significant role in acting as a catalyst to encourage self-employment experimentation. It is my view that the goal ought not to be to help just 10, 20, or 100 low-income people in a program. The goal instead ought to be to systematically develop successful micro-enterprise assistance approaches that can be replicated on a large scale. Evaluation and documentation are thus very important.

Foundations provide money for micro-loan funds as well as direct grants to programs for training and technical assistance. There should be expansion in both these activities.

Linked deposits and program related investments are two approaches that foundations use to allocate part of their asset portfolios in support of the funding of microenterprises. In the linked deposit strategy, foundations place part of their cash assets in bank accounts where funds from those accounts are designated for business loans to low-income people. Banks are willing to participate in order to acquire the other accounts of the foundation. In the program related investment approach, part of the foundation's assets are allocated to long term low interest friendly loans made directly to programs or other intermediaries who, in turn, make microbusiness loans to low-income borrowers. Under the leadership of the Ford Foundation, two workshops were held in 1988 to encourage the development of additional foundation and corporate support for business development and self-employment loan funds. One workshop was for the operators of loan funds to exchange information. All of the loan funds were recipients of Ford Foundation support in the form of program related investments. Most of these loan funds were also supported by other foundations as well (Henze, Nye and Schramm 1988). The other workshop was for 18 foundations and 2 government agencies that either were already involved in supporting these types of loan funds or were interested in doing so (Henze, Nye, Schramm, and Hoekman 1988).

Many private foundations provide funding for community development projects. Private foundation programming to community groups can also include a low income self-employment component. Many foundations also provide assistance for the homeless. Grants or loans to help homeless people obtain work through self-employment can be made part of aid to the homeless programs.[31]

Private foundations have played an important role in funding nongovernmental organizations (NGOs) and private and voluntary organizations (PVOs) that operate micro-enterprise projects in the Third World. They can do this also for the Fourth World—Third World–like sectors embedded in developed countries. As part of this program, providers in the Third World can be enlisted to develop programs in the Fourth World. The South Shore Bank of Chicago has developed a micro-enterprise loan project, funded in part by the Winthrop Rockefeller Foundation, that is modeled after the Grameen Bank of Bangladesh. Its name is the Good Faith Fund, and it is being implemented in Arkansas (Shorebank Corporation 1986). The Charles Stewart Mott Foundation, from 1985 to 1988, committed almost a million dollars to 16 seed-capital entrepreneurship projects in the United States. One of its projects, Micro Industry Credit Rural Organization (MICRO) provides small short-term loans to budding entrepreneurs on the Mexican border in Arizona and California. This was developed jointly with AC-CION, a provider of micro-enterprise programs in Latin America and PREP, a local social service organization (Rugg 1988).

Churches

Implementing self-employment programs on a wide scale will require some government assistance but does not necessarily have to imply greater government spending. In the immediate period, churches and private foundations can be experimenting with self-employment program designs, funded by their own coffers. A very successful program, documented by rigorous evaluation, can convince policymakers of the desirability of the self-employment approach to alleviate poverty.

Churches could, for example, set up a revolving loan fund, donated by their more affluent parishioners for the less well-off members of the congregation. Congregants who own businesses can also serve as mentors. There may be "Angels" (informal venture capitalists) in the church. The church can find out who they are and try to match them with low-income congregants who want to start a business. Affluent churches often adopt a church in a poor neighborhood as charitable assistance to people in hardship. Self-employment training, including a loan fund, could be part of that assistance.

Connecting tithing to a micro-enterprise loan fund for the poor could be an important source of financing. This need not involve substitution for other church needs. Many congregants do not contribute the full 10 percent tithing of income. If congregants could count investments in a micro-loan fund for the poor as part of tithing, parishioners who do not give their full tithing share might increase it in a relatively painless though socially beneficial way.

Another way to develop a loan fund is to institute a group cooperative purchasing program in a church with the condition that a portion of the savings from each congregant's budget be contributed to a micro-enterprise loan fund for the poor. This can most easily apply to groceries but also to health care, burials, insurance, and financial planning.[32] Many churches have emergency loan funds for congregants who suffer accidents and injuries. Perhaps, these can be expanded to assist in employment generation also.

The first two formal credit unions in the United States founded in 1908 and 1910, were associated with Catholic church parishes in New England (Moody and Fite 1984). About 15 percent (2400) of all credit unions are "associational," which includes those that are church related (Credit Union National Association 1988, p. 35).[33] Credit unions place heavy reliance on the knowledge of the character of the borrower to predict repayment of the loan. Churches have good knowledge of the character of their congregants. Therefore, churches are a natural place to house credit unions, particularly those that engage heavily in business lending.

Another role for churches is in improving access to business opportunities by better sharing information about its members. One of the most effective religious groups organized for the employment of its members is The Church of Jesus Christ of Latter Day Saints (Mormons). They operate their own welfare and employment service. A description of this can be found in their guidebooks (The Church of Jesus Christ of Latter Day Saints 1980). The basis of their employment service is a confidential survey of all adult members to find out who their employers are, if they are an employer themselves, and information on job openings where they work. Each ward (the smallest church unit) has an employment specialist who collects the information and uses it to find jobs for unemployed members. Information on job openings, unfilled in the ward, are then sent on to higher levels in the church so others can know about these openings. The employment specialist can also act as a matchmaker to link members who want to start businesses with those who already operate that type of business. In the past, the ward elders quorum would contribute money to set-up a loan fund to help members start businesses.

Alexander (1987) provides numerous examples of current efforts by black churches to directly assist in the economic life of their congregants as well as the local community. These include The Congress of National Black Churches, which is establishing a nationwide collective banking and cash management program and a master insurance agency branch of Aetna Insurance Co.; African Methodist Episcopal Church and the National Baptist Convention, which formed Leaders Energizing Neighborhood Development (LEND), which started church credit unions in six cities;[34] and The United House of Prayer for All People, which finances small businesses in the low-income housing projects it develops.

Client Resources

A major part of the financing can come from clients themselves. According to the U.S. Bureau of Census (1988, p. 90), between 60 and 75 percent of all business owners utilized no borrowed start-up capital. Most provided initial start-up capital on their own. Of those that did acquire outside sources of capital, a common source was family and friends.

As part of a capital assistance program, low-income clients should provide some of the capital themselves. The rationale is to provide for a cost of failure and to reduce the amount of outside financing. The amount of self-financing must be high enough so clients lose something significant if the business fails to insure their diligent participation. Further, too much outside loan money, that requires immediate pay-back, may burden a new enterprise with cash flow problems. However, the amount of self-financing required should not be so high that it effectively screens out people from the bottom.

Capital that is obtained from oneself, family, friends, and business associates, can be called "affinity capital."[35] Sources of affinity capital include consumption diversion, marriage, rotating credit associations, and estates.

It's difficult to obtain capital from oneself when one is poor, yet there are ways to do it. Taking an idea from Father Divine, people may be able to live in a group arrangement for a limited period of time, where food, shelter, and child care expenses are shared. Savings from group living can then be diverted to a capital fund. Another consumption diversion source is abstaining from state and church lotteries. The highest rate of lottery participation is in low-income neighborhoods, which is equivalent to a regressive tax. Instead, a community organization or a financial institution can institute a regular savings campaign that can look like a lottery. People buy tickets weekly or daily at participating outlets where payments for the tickets go into their own savings account.[36]

Marriage is an excellent source of capital for two reasons. The spouse brings to the marriage his/her social network, which can be tapped for capital, and the spouse can work in a full-time wage job providing for living expenses and capital for the business while the other spouse starts the business. A literal marriage is not necessary to do this; pair bonding can have the same effect. That is, two people can decide to be committed to each other and share resources.

A common arrangement used by Asians, Africans, and West Indians to mobilize capital is the rotating credit association. Each member of a small group would contribute a moderate amount of funds to provide a capital pool which would be lent out to one person in the group at a time. The group would meet periodically to reinforce social ties, check up on things, and place enormous social pressure not to default. There are many implementation variations of this. Light (1972) identifies the relative lack of use of these informal cooperative types of business capital mobilization arrangements as one of the reasons, in addition to discrimination, for economic backwardness of many native-born blacks. The rotating credit association would not be a practical mechanism to raise large amounts of capital for big business but it would seem useful for micro-enterprise capital formation. Rotating credit arrangements could certainly be promoted within low-income communities, perhaps through the offices of local church and community-based organizations.

Clients may need help in becoming aware of the resources that are available from family and friends. People often overlook the resources available from those who have a close social or familial tie. Sometimes it is intentional because one does don't want to be humiliated by "begging" for help. There may be ways to help clients structure arrangements with family and friends that deal with the interpersonal side of financial relationships. For example, a lender can be designated a nominal officer of the company so he or she is made to feel part of the business and an informal intermediary can be used to collect the loan so family-friend lenders do not have to be put in a position of hounding the borrower.

One way friends and relatives can help is to stipulate that burials be inexpensive and that funds from their estate be set aside for educational or entrepreneurial endeavors of the survivors. I know a wealthy entrepreneur who has set-up a venture capital fund in his will that will exist in perpetuity for his descendants. Rather than provide money that may be squandered or leave his businesses to heirs who won't operate them as well as in-place managers, he instead set-up a venture fund to assist in constructive economic pursuits. This seems a worthwhile way to assist future generations.

RESEARCH AGENDA

In researching this book, some particular pieces of missing information stand out to me. Undoubtedly, there are more missing pieces than I am presently aware of. Nonetheless, this list is suggestive. It would be helpful to obtain the following information:

1. Documentation of the interest in pursuing self-employment by low-income populations such as AFDC recipients, persons on public assistance, residents of public housing, and inmates in prison. This would require some sort of interview survey. It would be important to determine if there is a

relationship between interest in self-employment and work history, welfare rules, regulatory environment, training availability, and financing assistance. What generates interest in self-employment? What are the perceived barriers to pursuing it?

2. Descriptions of the self-employment activities that low-income/low-educated people presently participate in at a fine disaggregated level of industry and occupational detail. This would include measurements of earning levels and stability, and failure rates. In what types of businesses does self-employment lead to earning levels and stability substantially greater than wage employment?

3. Description and analysis of background and events that led low-income/low-educated people to start their businesses. Can the processes that they used to start their own businesses be emulated by programs?

4. Analysis of the growth and development of micro-enterprises started by low-income/low-educated people. What are the growth rates of their businesses, and the opportunities created or made available by the operation of their businesses? In what types of situations can micro-enterprises grow to provide jobs for others? What is the quality of those jobs? Does self-employment lead to the acquisition of human capital?

5. Legal and planning studies of local health, safety, and zoning regulations that can be waived for the low-income self-employed sector. What kind of deregulation would provide the greatest benefits to the self-employed and the least harm to others?

6. Comparative studies of regulations and policies for the micro-enterprise sector in developed countries such as Japan and West Germany. To what extent do these countries protect and encourage the micro-enterprise sector as a way to create employment for the less skilled?

7. Research techniques that can accurately pinpoint market gaps, the best low-fail micro-enterprises, and the best locations for these businesses. To what degree will the success of these businesses depend on the characteristics of the owner versus the economic environment?

8. Credit techniques that can provide micro-loans requiring little or no collateral at conventional market rates of interest. To what extent can existing credit arrangements for low-income people be modified to make them more effective? Can new types of arrangements be developed?

9. Evaluations of self-employment programs using randomly selected control groups. For some of these evaluations, waivers should be obtained from welfare agencies to freeze eligibility so incentives won't be impeded.[37]

10. Cost-effectiveness analyses comparing different approaches to economic development for low-income people. Measures of effectiveness should include net new job creation, income gains, and stability of earnings. These measures should be weighted by the degree that benefits accrue to low-income people (i.e., an income gain to a poorer person should count more than an income gain to a richer person). This should be carried out for a myriad of alternatives such as assisting existing small businesses to ex-

pand, assisting large businesses to halt their contractions, assisting the start-up of high-tech businesses, expanding existing job training programs, expanding public employment, and expanding self-employment training programs.[38] Such an exercise might reveal a best mix of job creation and poverty alleviation strategies.

SUMMARY

The following policy suggestions were made concerning creating and using supportive institutions: An advocate and information clearinghouse for micro-businesses needs to be established; producer cooperatives, solidarity groups, vertical cooperatives, and incubators are the types of organizational arrangements and institutions that can help sustain micro-businesses once they are created. Religion and/or charismatic leaders should be linked to self-employment programs. They can help one to tolerate the sacrifices involved in starting a business, provide emotional support, be a market, and provide links to mentors and sources of capital.

Sources of financing for self-employment ventures include commercial banks, credit unions, state and community micro-loan funds, venture capital matchmaking, seller-supplier-customer financing, state education budgets, Job Training Partnership Act, transfer payment diversion, private foundations, churches, and client resources.

Research is needed on the following topics: interest of low-income population in self-employment, descriptions of self-employment activities that low-income people presently participate in, determination of regulations that can be waived for the low-income self-employment sector, market research techniques to pinpoint micro-enterprise opportunities, credit provision techniques for micro-loans, evaluation of self-employment programs using random selection, and cost-effectiveness analyses comparing different approaches to fostering economic development for low-income people.

NOTES

1. There are numerous trade associations and craft guilds relating to home-based businesses (Balkin 1988c). There is a newsletter for street performers (Baird 1985), and I have heard of some ad hoc local union–type organizations for street vendors in Washington, DC, and New York. To fill a vacuum in Chicago, a network of self-employment programs was organized by myself to encourage collective advocacy for micro-enterprises (Balkin 1986).
2. The Washington, DC Board of Trade, Connecticut Ave. Association, the Apartment and Office Building Association, the Capital Hill Association of

Merchants and Professionals, the Business and Professional Association of Georgetown, the Restaurant Association, and the Chamber of Commerce have all marshalled considerable effort against street vendors in our nation's capital (Spalter-Roth and Zeitz 1985, p. 9).

3. There seems to be no conflict between big business and micro-enterprises. The interests of big business are enhanced when activities of the micro-enterprise sector leads to lower retail prices and a wider distribution of goods produced by large corporations.

4. The Department of Vocational Rehabilitation provided the most comprehensive services for self-employment, including both training and seed capital.

5. People who can't engage in earning activity directed to lift themselves out of poverty still require income support. This can be provided through transfer payments set at a level to ensure a decent quality of life. But people who can't or won't work diligently should not be inflicted upon others in an organization trying hard to generate income. The feedback of lost income for making your own business mistakes is a great teacher.

6. I call this usual type of producer cooperative a horizontal co-op because it is made up of firms producing the same good or service.

7. Given that individuals in the United States are not as communalistic as in the Third World, it may be difficult to assemble low-income people in groups of five. Perhaps for the United States, solidarity groups of three may work better. Experimentation should determine the optimal size of a solidarity group.

8. For a useful how-to-do-it book on setting up an incubator, see Small Business Administration (March, 1985).

9. This arrangement would be a more organized form of a flea market, which seems in essence to be a retail incubator.

10. The Fulton Carroll Incubator of Chicago has been encouraging inter-business linkages in their incubator. A chart of these vertical linkages is in one of their reports (Industrial Council of Northwest Chicago 1985).

11. The longevity of a movement-based business effort may also be hampered by being dependent upon a charismatic leader. If the leader dies, and no similar successor is found, the movement may whither.

12. There is race and sex discrimination in capital markets, which is a major impediment to the economic development of certain groups. This is an important issue to address for the goal of equal opportunities. Nonetheless, the lack of institutional financing may not be the major obstruction to business initiation for low-income people.

13. This does not imply that lack of training, as conventionally practiced, is the major constraint either. In conversations with some micro-business developers in Third World projects, I have learned that training is very overrated. People out in the streets or barrios know how to hustle to make a living; they are just constrained by capital. Their claim is that if just a source of noncollateral capital is provided, clients can do the rest. This is likely true for some but for not all of the U.S. low-income nascent self-employed.

14. There are many books that describe simple businesses that people with little skill and little money can start. See, for example, Feinman (1976), Revel

(1984), and Levinson (1982). Although these types of books often overstate the degree of simplicity and understate the capital requirements, they are suggestive of the types of businesses that can be considered. One job of a yet-to-be-created Micro-Business Information Clearinghouse would be to sift through these suggestions to pick the most feasible ones.

15. These figures were calculated from data in Table 14 of U.S. Bureau of the Census (1986, p. 98).

16. The Small Business Administration, under various programs, provides guarantees to commercial banks for start-up business loans. However, their application process is very cumbersome, and they generally do not deal with very small unsophisticated businesses.

17. There are approximately 400 Community Development credit unions that serve low-income communities. Most of them are members of the National Federation of Community Development Credit Unions in New York.

18. It is likely that credit unions make more small business loans than they realize, since borrowers may divert funds for household purchases into business assets or expenses.

19. The Community Reinvestment Act of 1977 involves federal agency monitoring of local financial institutions to disclose lending practices to determine how well they are meeting the local credit needs of the communities they serve and obtain deposits from. On account of this act, banks would likely be favorably disposed to provide credit for local micro-enterprise development if the cost and risk could be substantially diminished.

20. The information for this section on Vermont Job Start was obtained from a phone interview with one of their administrators and from the Corporation for Enterprise Development (1985).

21. Information was obtained from Sharon Dreyer, Iowa Department of Economic Development.

22. The CSBG program is not to be confused with the CDBG (Community Development Block Grant) program. The latter was established in the Department of Housing and Urban Development in 1974. Two objectives of CDBG are to expand economic opportunities, principally for persons of low and moderate income, and to aid in the prevention and elimination of slums and blight. Self-employment programs address both these objectives. CDBG funds are currently being used for business loan funds but the paper work is too voluminous to allow small loans for micro-enterprises. Either the regulations should be streamlined to make CBDG micro-enterprise loans feasible, or an intermediary can be used to obtain CBDG money who then will make micro-loans. See Malone (1986) and Roberts (1988).

23. Information on the Illinois CSBG micro-loan program was obtained from Gail Hedges of the Illinois Department of Commerce and Community Affairs.

24. See U.S. House of Representatives (1988) for descriptions of other micro-enterprise loan funds.

25. The cost per job created was estimated to be $4726, which is within EDA's goal of one job created for every $5000 to $10,000 of funds lent. This estimate takes into account that 25 percent of the borrowers (at a maximum) could have obtained financing elsewhere (Mt. Auburn Associates 1987).

26. The National Association of Community Development Loan Funds is in Greenfield, MA.

27. Wetzel (1983, p. 26) reports, from a survey of "angels," that the median investment size was about $20,000 and that 36 percent of past investments were less than $50,000. However, "angels" frequently pool resources with other "angels" to finance bigger ventures.

28. Wetzel (1983, p. 31) reported from his survey of "angels" that between 30 and 45 percent of his sample would accept lower rates of return for socially beneficial considerations. These included creating jobs in areas of high unemployment, developing socially useful technology, urban revitalizaton, assisting minority or female entrepreneurs, and promoting the free enterprise economy.

29. Franchisor corporations are suppliers to its franchisees, and a portion of them will finance their franchisees at least to an extent. Some will finance just the franchise fee, some the fee plus a portion of the total investment, and some the total investment. The franchisor usually sells franchises to raise capital. So it is somewhat an anomaly why a franchisor would finance the franchisee. Foster (1988) provides three reasons why a franchisor might want to do it: encouraging rapid expansion, deriving additional profits, and reinvesting surplus cash. He also provides a list of 251 franchisors who finance.

30. Self-employment training programs are available through JTPA, but no seed capital is provided. Amendments to the JTPA would be needed to allow direct financing of businesses, either through a grant or low interest loan. Further, revisions would be required concerning performance contracting. Performance would need to be clarified with respect to targeting low-income, low-skilled clients. A placement (business start-up) rate could be too low, indicating the contractor is doing a bad job assisting clients. However, the business start-up rate can also be too high, indicating "creaming."

31. I have already begun to measure the extent of self-employment activity by homeless adult men. They do engage in a variety of hustles and casual labor that can be characterized as self-employment. Preliminary findings are that it is substantial and that shelter managers think a moderate percent of their clients could own and operate a small business.

32. This was suggested by Cicero Wilson at the Wingspread Conference, Venture Capital and Job Development Strategies for the Black Community May 3–5, 1987.

33. "Associational" includes cooperatives, fraternal organizations, professional associations, trade associations, churches, and labor unions.

34. A particularly successful credit union project is at the Hartford Memorial Baptist Church in Detroit. It was started by interested congregants meeting in the church basement after a service and, among themselves, contributing $9000 to start a credit union. As part of the credit union, an economic awareness day at the church is held to encourage congregants to become entrepreneurs. Applicants for business loans are required to have a business plan and show they could not obtain financing elsewhere. Loans require collateral but they can be creative about what collateral is.

35. I heard this term from finance professor, Bismark Williams of Roosevelt University.

36. The ticket is a record of deposit and can also represent a chance to win something modest, for example, a trip to the Bahamas. Instead of states propagating the myth that people can strike it big quickly, it can be replaced

by the notion that a slow and steady build-up of capital can lead to being your own boss.

37. Care must be taken in designing control groups to separate the welfare waiver effect on income gains from the self-employment training effect.

38. An attempt at something like this was presented in Corporation for Enterprise Development (February, 1983).

10

Job Creation Through Encouragement of Self-Employment

INTRODUCTION

When clients of a self-employment training program start businesses, program staff feel a great sense of satisfaction and accomplishment because positive results are plainly visible. The attainment of work with good earnings by low-income, low-educated, out-of-work individuals is a very worthy accomplishment, in itself, regardless of whether total employment in the economy has increased. Were any jobs created? The answer seems clearly "yes," because individuals who were not working before are now working. Further, some of them have hired labor. From the point of view of society, however, the answer is not clear in aggregate terms. One issue concerns what these people would have been doing in absence of the program. This is an issue of *impact*. Pessimistically, if they had been working in a wage job or started their business anyhow, then no additional jobs were really created by the efforts of the program. The same number of jobs would exist with or without the program. This aspect of program job creation is discussed in the next chapter.

Another issue concerns *displacement*. Even if the program does have impact, sales and jobs may have been lost elsewhere in the economy due to expansion in the number of businesses created by the program.[1] This can be industry specific: for example, a new peanut stand causes an existing peanut stand to go out of business, which in turn causes the old peanut stand owner to be unemployed. Alternatively, displacement can be diffuse: for example, consumers who spend more income on peanuts, due to the new peanut stand, now spend less on custom-printed T-shirts and movies. The displacement issue, however, is not unique to self-employment development but is a problem for all manpower development and business assistance programs.

The displacement problem can be avoided, or largely avoided, if demand in the economy is expanding at a rate sufficient that an increase in expenditures on goods in one sector does not force a reduction of demand elsewhere in the economy. If some displacement should occur, it is only very temporary until a new job or new business is obtained. This is the arena of macro-economics and aggregate demand.

Economic notions about how one could expect self-employment programs to result in net job creation, is explored. Following that is a suggested model to estimate the amount of job creation from self-employment development policy.

JOB REDISTRIBUTION

Even if some displacement does occur, job training for low-income/low-educated people is still a worthwhile strategy because jobs and income are being redistributed to the bottom of the income distribution, reducing income inequality. If displacement does occur, it is likely to be less than 100 percent. More jobs will be newly created than are lost; net new job creation will occur. A reason to expect this is the differences in the sales/labor ratio between micro-enterprises and larger businesses. If every dollar gained in sales to a low-level micro-enterprise is offset by a dollar lost in sales to some larger more sophisticated business, net new jobs will be created because micro-enterprises are more labor intensive than larger businesses. A dollar in sales supports more jobs in micro-enterprises than a dollar in sales for larger businesses. The amount of any job loss will be reduced further by the degree that the economy is expanding.

POSSIBLE MACRO-ECONOMIC EXPANSIONARY EFFECTS OF ENCOURAGING SELF-EMPLOYMENT

The following macro-economic effects are presented to show the types of phenomena that may accompany the simultaneous expansion of the self-employment sector so that net new job creation can be expected. Some of these mechanisms may not hold; nor do all need to hold to expect net job creation.

Profit Wedge

This is similar to the tax wedge concept of supply-side economics (Hailstones 1982). The employer's cost for a worker is greater than the wage received by the worker. In the supply-side case, this is due to taxes. If payroll taxes were reduced, for example, the employer cost of hiring a worker would decrease. Therefore, firms would want to hire more labor. At the same time, workers' real wages have gone up, causing an increase in labor supplied. The expected effect is an increase in employment, gross national product, and economic growth.

In the profit wedge concept, the labor market is conceived of a bit differently. There is a demand for the services of labor, directly, by consumers. In this market the cost of services to consumers is greater than the income received by labor due to the profits and organizing expenses of the firm. The firm is performing an intermediary (i.e., go-between) function. If labor disintermediates by selling their services directly to consumers (self-employment), the cost to consumers decreases, and the income received by labor increases.[2] Both have the complementary effect of increasing employment, gross national product, and economic growth. In other words, eliminating the middleman expands the economy: net new jobs will be created.[3]

Improving the Phillips Curve

The Phillips Curve is a portrayal of an inverse relationship between inflation and unemployment.[4] When unemployment becomes very low, the rate of inflation is expected to increase. This inhibits the ability of expansionary forces to reduce unemployment further because it raises the possibility of increasing inflation. However, if increases in production can come from expansion of resources rather than bidding up prices of existing resources, the economy can expand smoothly without increases in inflation. This encourages macro-economic expansion. Self-employment programs that target people with distant ties to the labor force, bringing them into the labor force, provide such a circumstance.

Increased Capital Formation

Self-employment encouragement increases capital formation. The act of starting a business involves capital formation, which is called investment. On the supply side an increase in investment expands productive capacity and improves productivity. In the Keynesian framework, an increase in investment also expands aggregate demand through a multiplier process. Both effects are complementary to expanding real output and employment.

Reducing Access Cost—Increasing Spending

A proliferation of micro-businesses makes it more convenient to make purchases and thus, easier to spend income. Search costs for goods and services are reduced. In the Keynesian macro-economic framework, this increases the propensity to consume, which increases aggregate demand. In the monetarist framework this leads to increases in the velocity of circulation of money which increases aggregate demand.

Complementary to the Keynesian effect above is the further increase in the propensity to consume due to increasing incomes for low-income people. Poor people have higher propensities to consume than rich people. To the extent that poor people's gain in income is greater than rich people's losses (if any), from a self-employment encouragement policy, the overall propensity to consume increases. This then effectuates an expansion in aggregate demand.

A MODEL FOR ESTIMATING THE AMOUNT OF JOB CREATION BY SELF-EMPLOYMENT PROGRAMS FOR LOW-INCOME PEOPLE

The intent here, as well as in the next chapter, is to outline some issues one should consider when making claims about the job creation aspect of a self-employment program. A program operator does not actually need to perform analyses like the ones described. A preliminary model was developed by Balkin (1986) to show variables, relationships, and parameters that might be used to infer net new job creation from an expansion in self-employment programs. That model is briefly described here.

The model portrays the linkages involved for a transformation of a target population to a pool of applicants, to program slots, to new businesses, to surviving enterprises, to newly created jobs, and, finally to net job creation. Depending on the degree of interest in the target population, a pool of potential participants is generated. This is the demand for program slots. How much of this demand will be filled depends on available funding. Given some amount of program slots, a certain percent of initial participants will drop out of the initial training phase. Some of the remaining graduates start businesses, and some will initially fail. Some of the survivors will remain a one-person operation, and some will grow, adding employees. From the process so far we have observed newly created businesses and jobs, but at the same time, some other businesses may have failed or experienced a contraction due to the new businesses entering the economy. After this last effect is taken into account, the amount of net job creation can be determined.

Estimating Net Job Creation

For demonstration purposes, a preliminary estimation for a large-scale self-employment training effort was made using a set of as-

Table 10.1
Maximum and Minimum Estimates of Net Job Creation

# of net jobs created		Assumptions
Displacement		
0	50%	
MAX 7,151,288	3,575,644	50% of target population are interested, full funding, 10% dropout rate, 25% failure rate, 50% growth rate.
MIN 794,588	397,294	10% of target population are interested, full funding, 25% dropout rate, 25% failure rate, 0% growth rate.

sumptions about the values of the various parameter rates in the model. The target population was chosen to be persons 15 years and older who have income below poverty level and are jobless. This amounted to 14 million people in 1984.

There are six key parameter rates: percent of target population interested in self-employment, funding rate, dropout rate, failure rate, enterprise growth rate, and displacement rate.[5] A range of estimates was provided by considering optimistic and pessimistic values of the parameters based on what is known from available literature.

Estimates of Net Job Creation

A set of estimates of job creation was generated. Twenty-four different estimates were obtained by using all the different combinations of parameter values. Table 10.1 presents only the maximum and minimum nonzero estimates, showing the sensitivity of the estimates to different assumptions of displacement rates.[6] Estimates of job creation range from a high of about 7 million additional net new jobs to a low of about 400,000. Cost projections were also made.[7] The entire program effort would cost, at a maximum, approximately 20 billion dollars. Full implementation would occur, of course, over a span of several years and cost would be spread accordingly. It would also be expected that the initial parameter rates would improve over time. Using the calculation for the maximum number of net new jobs of about 7 million, the cost per net new job created would be $2765. The cost for successfully placing a low-income person in business would be $3111.[8] This is similar to the cost per adult client entering employment, averaged over the first 21 months of the existence of JTPA, which was $3319 (U.S. Department of Labor 1985). The minimum total cost is about 3.5 billion dollars. Of course, in such a case, a much smaller number of clients is served.

All cost calculations are based on an assumed $3000 cost of a fully used program slot. Of course, it could easily be true that a self-employment program such as I propose could cost much more or much less. Further, it is insufficient to judge this program approach on cost estimates such as these alone: A full blown cost/benefit or advantages/ disadvantages analysis is required.[9] The budgetary impact of these self-employment programs is likely to be much smaller than these cost calculations. One can expect reductions of people in welfare and an increase in newly paid taxes as well as a reduction in criminal offense rates. These benefits could offset part or all of the program costs.[10] There is also the main benefit to consider—additions to gross national product represented by the increased earnings from the newly created jobs.

One should also ponder the possibility that no new training programs are needed to assist low-income people into self-employment activity. A policy shift that removed impediments to self-employment could go a long way to helping people create jobs by themselves.[11] The training program approach to help low-income people create jobs should be considered as only one type of assistance strategy. By comparing the costs and benefits of different approaches, an optimal strategy mix might be determinable.

SUMMARY

Reasons were suggested why assisting low-income people into self-employment is expansionary, leading to net job creation. These are the principles of differences in sales/labor ratios, the profit wedge, shifting the Phillips Curve, reducing access cost, and increasing business investment. A preliminary model was presented with hypothetical parameter values to estimate amounts of net job creation by promoting self-employment training programs. For demonstration, a set of 24 estimates was obtained. The maximum number of net new jobs to be created was estimated to be approximately 7 million at a cost of about

20 billion dollars or $2800 per net job created. The minimum number of net new jobs to be created was zero, assuming a 100 percent displacement rate. The minimum nonzero number of net new jobs to be created was about 400,000 at a cost of about 3.5 billion dollars or $9000 per net job created. The government budget impact could be much smaller than these cost calculations if one considered welfare diversion, client contributions, decreases in the number of people on welfare, reductions in the use of social services, decline in crime, and the increase in newly paid taxes.

NOTES

1. Thompson (1986, p. 23), in a Schumpeterian vein (1934), views entrepreneurs as creating progress but not necessarily employment. "Inventors and innovators, by definition, create change and thereby disrupt the established order; they quite literally destroy industries, occupations, and skills with new products and processes."

2. This is easiest to envision in the service sector. However, it may also be applicable in the manufacturing sector either for simply produced goods or for goods where specialization in production processes can be emulated by subcontracting networks. A new self-employed person may have to provide some of the functions that the employer firm previously provided. That is good because it results in more work and improved development for the self-employed person.

3. Self-employment rather than wage employment implies risks, and organizational and marketing costs, formerly borne by the firm, are now being incurred by the individual. If the employer does this much more efficiently, self-employment income might be lower than wage employment income.

4. For more information about the Phillips Curve, consult any introductory college economics text.

5. For simplicity, I have assumed that no clients would have started businesses without the program: "deadweight" is zero. Including a "deadweight" rate would reduce the number of jobs created.

6. An assumption of a 100 percent displacement rate would imply, of course, zero net new jobs created. Therefore, in the Table 10.1, I have provided estimates using only the assumption of either a 50 percent or zero displacement rate.

7. Costs of unemployment and stress to displaced workers were not included in the calculations. Also, the cost estimates do not imply what incremental government expenditure would be. Resources could be diverted from other programs, and clients might be able to contribute some of the resources. Also not included were government savings that would result from welfare reduction and increased tax payments.

8. Cost per net new job created is smaller than cost per placement because additional jobs are created by some new businesses hiring employees.

9. For examples of cost-benefit analyses that can be applied to self-em-

ployment programs in the United States, see Cortes et al. (1987); Kilby and D'Zmura (1985); Lassen (1984); Johnson and Thomas (1984); and Kemper et al. (1981).

10. It should not be expected that successful participants of self-employment programs all go off welfare. It can be expected, though, that welfare payments will be reduced for most participants. Many of these new businesses may not generate sufficient income for clients to immediately leave welfare completely. This is particularly true for Medicaid benefits which should be continued.

11. Sometimes this issue is referred to as choosing policies that are narrow and deep (e.g., training progams for a select few) versus a broad and shallow approach (e.g., removing regulatory and legal barriers). What we may need, perhaps, are policies that are broad and deep.

11

Evaluation for Self-Employment Programs

INTRODUCTION

A striking feature of almost all the U.S. programs was the lack of a rigorous evaluation effort. Program operators were sincerely concerned that their clients actually start a business, but there was generally insufficient consideration given to the articulation of program goals; follow-up was seldom performed or performed adequately; and control groups were not utilized. If programs are to seek subsidization and expand, they should demonstrate or at least argue persuasively that they benefit low-income people and that their resources are used in a worthwhile way.

THINKING ABOUT IMPACT

Impact is defined as the outcome caused by the program—the effects occurring to clients and society that would not occur in the absence of the program or operationally, the performance of the program compared to a control group. Evaluation is difficult, time consuming, and expensive. In trying to develop ways for assisting low-income people to start their own small businesses, it is natural and perhaps prudent that evaluation concerns are ignored. Implementation comes before evaluation. When initiating a new program, mistakes are going to be made. Only after the process is thoroughly worked out and defects eliminated should one engage in a rigorous impact evaluation.[1]

At this time, a major objective of self-employment policy should be to develop tested program formats that can be replicated so large numbers of low-income people can be helped. A necessary condition for knowing whether a program ought to be replicated is knowing the impact it has.

Banker's Viewpoint

Since many of the existing programs have some element of loan assistance connected to them, a banker's view of outcome generally prevails. However, this is different from a public policy view of impact. In the banker's view, reducing loan repayment risk is paramount, and success is defined as the loan being repaid. The more this happens, the better the program. Evaluations, in this mindset, focus on loan repayment rates. Bankers do not consider what would happen to the business if they did not make the loan.

The public policy view is different. In that view, the issue is how many businesses and jobs can be generated and how much can income be increased, which would not occur otherwise. The public policy view is also concerned with business profitability and growth but the focus is for the set of businesses that would not be profitable or as profitable on their own. Its aim is to use scarce resources to affect society in beneficial ways that wouldn't occur otherwise. The banker, in contrast, prefers providing services to those businesses with the highest rates of profit, regardless of whether those businesses need the help of the banker. For example, if a program loans money to entrepreneurs and many businesses are started, but those businesses would have been initiated anyway without that assistance, no impact occurs. The intervention accomplishes little: Perhaps it has made things more convenient for the entrepreneurs, enabled them to reduce some of their costs, and reduced the time it took to initiate their businesses. However, two basic questions need to be addressed: Are these the effects that were intended, and why should this particular segment of society receive subsidized assistance? If the target group is upper-income people, it is difficult to provide a satisfactory answer.

Assisting People at the Bottom: A Numerical Example

When poor people start small businesses, it seems likely that the outcomes may be different and the above two questions are easier to answer. It is likely that fewer businesses would be started by a program assisting poor entrepreneurs rather than rich entrepreneurs, though more businesses would be started than would have occurred in the absence of the program. This should be the intention of the program: It seems worthwhile as a principle of equity (helping the poor), as a principle of efficiency (employing idle resources and increasing business activity), and as a principle of public finance (reducing the welfare

Table 11.1
Hypothetical Table of Business Start-up Rates

Well-off		Poor	
in program	control	in program	control
WE	WC	LE	LC
90	90	40	10

rolls, and picking high return public investments). A numerical example may be helpful. Consider four groups interested in becoming self-employed, each of one hundred people:

Group WE: Well-off Experimental group. These are people who are well-off in terms of income, wealth, or education and who are provided assistance to start a business.

Group WC: the Well-off Control group. These are exactly identical to the group above except that they do not receive any assistance.

Group LE: the Low-income Experimental group. These are poor with low levels of formal education and who are provided assistance to start a business.

Group LC: the Low-income Control group. These are exactly identical to Group LE except that they do not receive any assistance.

Table 11.1 shows some possible results on business start-ups. If we were just to observe the start-up rates of those groups active in programs (WE and LE), we would observe that the program offering assistance to upper class individuals, WE, is more "successful" than the program serving poor individuals, LE. Ninety start-ups for the WE group is better than 40 start-ups for the LE group.

Now consider impact to be outcome *above* that which would occur in absence of the program (experimental outcome minus control outcome).[2] The impact of the upper-income program (start-up rate of WE minus start-up rate of WC) is *less* than the impact of the program serving poor individuals (start-up rate of LE minus start-up rate of LC). Zero (90 minus 90) is less than 30 (40 minus 10). The program for poor people, in this example, has greater impact. Thirty additional start-ups are better than none. Bankers, though, would rather lend to businesses in program WE. One could argue that the firms of the well-off entrepreneurs are creating many jobs in addition to their own, but in the example above, those would have occurred without any program.

Consider another case. A program for well-off entrepreneurs may have some impact, in terms of start-up rates, even though it is a smaller impact than for the poor. The program for well-off entrepreneurs may benefit society more because those fewer but more sophisticated firms caused by the intervention are generating more jobs—the trickle down effect. However, one then has to determine what kinds of jobs they are and the types of individuals they are for. Then this should be compared to the types of jobs generated by programs for low-income self-employed people.[3]

The numerical example above was simplified. There are many methodological issues to consider before one can get to a table such as Table 11.1. Principal among them is choice and measurement of effectiveness indicators.

MEASURES OF EFFECTIVENESS

It is important to consider what the goals of the program are and to distinguish between ultimate goals and intermediate process outcomes. Intermediate process outcomes are those things that the program accomplishes that provide an input to produce something else. For example, a business start-up is an intermediate process outcome where it may or may not lead to an enhanced earnings stream. Most of the programs I have studied have just concerned themselves with intermediate outcomes. This is understandable because they are easier to measure. Intermediate outcomes that are often measured are the program completion rate and the number of businesses initiated as a percent of clients completing the program (or as a percent of program participants).[4] It is useful to measure these intermediate outcomes because they are key elements in the process of achieving goals, but they should not be confused with ultimate goals: They are the means, not the ends.

An important goal is enhancing lifetime earning streams. Based on present skills, age, health, race, and class, the income to be earned over the remainder of a life is fairly predictable—that is a lifetime earnings stream. A goal of a training program is to improve the level and stability of that earnings stream for the client-owner and his/her employees, if any.[5] Intermediate outcomes that enhance earnings are desirable. Therefore, it is important to check if an intermediate outcome does enhance earnings. For example, acquiring business skills is an intermediate outcome, not an ultimate goal. If one wants to focus on this outcome (e.g., learning accounting principles) in an evaluation, there should be some demonstration that this is somehow linked to ultimate goals. Does the acquisition of business skills improve earning ability?

In addition to earning stream goals, there are personal client goals and externality goals. Personal goals relate to the internal psyche of clients and the well-being of their families.[6] These could concern self-esteem and family stability. For example, helping individuals start businesses may result in no additional earnings but it improves self-esteem because personal independence is increased, and it strengthens family cohesion because parents and children spend more time together. That benefit may be attributable to the program, but it has to be measured, and checked for two things. First, does the effect operate as expected? Pessimistically, it is possible that clients fail at businesses, lowering their self-esteem and making their families less stable, or they succeed in their business but it wrecks their personal and family life. Secondly, compared to a control group, do these effects occur with greater frequency? It is possible that members of a control group, who were more likely to remain in wage jobs or remain on welfare, have greater improvement in self-esteem and family stability than the ones assisted in business. If a beneficial effect is claimed for the program, one should demonstrate that it exists in greater amounts with program clients compared to a control group or at least make an argument why it would occur less in a hypothetical control group.

Externality goals refer to effects that accrue to society as a by-product of the program. These goals include reducing criminal offense rates, reducing the use of public social services, and enhancing community economic development. No self-employment training program I have observed considered reduction in participation in criminal activities as a dimension of effectiveness. This would be a measure of effectiveness that is particularly relevant for programs that target low-income people. The savings to society for reducing crime can be large; so this is an effect that can translate into a large monetary benefit attributable to the program.[7]

One could also expect that those coming out of a self-employment program with improved earnings and a sense of greater control over their lives use welfare and its ancillary services less. This permits a reduction in taxes or allows government expenditures to be used elsewhere. Other benefits accruing to the community that are not captured by clients are in the realm of community economic development. These benefits include improved access to goods and services, stimulating sales to firms supplying the new self-employed, lower prices to consumers, and demonstration effects encouraging other low-income people to start businesses and engage in economic self-help. These benefits do not have to be translated into monetary equivalent to provide useful decision-making information. But if these are to be claimed as benefits attributable to the program, it should be demonstrated—or argued—that they exist in greater amounts emanating from the program than from a control group.

FOLLOW-UP

There are some intermediate outcomes that can be measured during the program, for example, program completion rates. Measurement of other outcomes requires post-program follow-up. A business start-up, in most of the programs studied, did not occur immediately after program completion. It often took weeks or months to generate the first customers. Even if follow-up occurs three to six months after the program, we still don't know how many of the businesses survive in the long run. Most small business failures don't occur the first year of operation. The new owners still have capital and enthusiasm, and firm growth is slow enough that they are not beset by severe expansion problems. It seems a two-year follow-up should be a minimum. Little is known about the life cycle process of small businesses that low-income people own.[8] Therefore, the longer the follow-up, the better it is. Follow-up personal interviews or mail surveys should try to measure the economic activities of the clients, whether they started a business or not, and should continue tracking clients even if their businesses fail. Earnings may be enhanced by the skills learned and networks acquired in the process of starting and operating a business. These secondary learning effects should be considered benefits attributable to the program if they occur.

It is important to also do follow-up on a control group to check their small business and other economic outcomes. It is the comparison of program clients to the control group that determines impact. In addition, follow-up should not occur at just one point in time in the far future, but should occur periodically (e.g., every three or six months) until the end of the evaluation. A system would need to be developed to ensure clients' and controls' participation in these periodic surveys. One approach is to pay them to keep in touch. Interviews, while more expensive, are preferable to mail surveys because many low-income people have problems reading and writing.

CONTROL GROUPS

The idea of a control group is to represent what would have occurred to clients in the self-employment program if that program did not exist. In picking a control group, one should try to ensure that it is as nearly identical as possible to the experimental group, except of course that the controls do not participate in the program. The best way to do this is to select both experimental and control groups from a common pool of program applicants randomly.[9] There are other ways of picking a control group, but all pose threats to validity (Campbell & Stanley 1963). Nonetheless, use of any control group is better than none, especially when one has some notion of the biases involved. Examples of nonrandomly picked control groups are applicants to the program who were rejected; people who wanted to apply to the program but couldn't because they lived too far away; and participants in a non-business-oriented training program.[10] Further, one could also use aggregate statistics for various disadvantaged groups as a type of benchmark control. One could, for example, compare the percent of unemployed people living in poverty who obtained jobs in the last year to the percent of program enrollees who started businesses or found jobs.

Thinking about these issues is sometimes foreign to program managers. They want to select clients most likely to start a business successfully rather than because they want to achieve program impact. Therefore they may think little about what alternatively would happen to clients.

ON DOING AN EVALUATION

There are other evaluation issues to deal with besides the ones mentioned above.[11] My sense is that either one should try a very stripped-down version of evaluation at low cost or implement a very tight, sophisticated, though expensive, design. The alternative is to consider carefully whether any extra sophistication warrants the added expense. Even if maximum evaluation effort is not feasible, it helps to understand good evaluation. It can pose thoughtful questions to program managers like, "is my success rate due to choosing extra bright clients who would have succeeded on their own without the program?"

It may be too early to implement sophisticated evaluation for most self-employment programs. Perhaps, the emphasis now can be to develop a myriad of programs to find those that seem promising. "Promising" is easier to measure than impact on earnings. Criteria of "promising" should include that the program be capable of processing many people, be potentially replicable, serve individuals who have low levels of education and income, and cause some business start-ups to occur.[12] Further, many programs serve too few clients to provide large enough sample sizes to attain a reasonable degree of statistical accuracy.

SUMMARY

For self-employment training to expand as part of the manpower training mix and a poverty alleviation strategy, better evaluaton efforts will have to be made. Issues related to evaluation were discussed that concerned whether the program makes a difference compared to what would have occurred otherwise; not viewing the program intent as trying to pick sure winners; distinguishing between intermediate outcomes and ultimate goals, stressing the importance of postprogram follow-up; and encouraging the use of control groups. Sophisticated and expensive evaluation is worthwhile to do on a limited basis, but even without it, simply considering the methodological issues of evaluating self-employment training can stir thinking about the philosophical basis of programs and improve their operation.

NOTES

1. However, one should conduct a "process" evaluation early on, just to determine whether the operation of the program and the flow of clients through its various elements are in some sense satisfactory. This is done prior to testing for impact.

2. In the evaluations of the British Enterprise Allowance Scheme, the amount of business starts that would occur in absence of the program is referred to as "deadweight." Evaluators obtained estimates of deadweight by asking program participants who started their businesses whether they would have started without the program.

3. When local economic developers attract high-tech firms, a typical outcome is that job slots are created either for highly paid well-educated professionals or low-paid service workers. Self-employment may be a better deal for low-educated residents than high-tech industry low-paid service wage jobs.

4. Sometimes the "percent of people completing the program who have started a business *or found jobs*" is also used. This last outcome measure should be more thoroughly considered. Even though the focus is on self-employment, an outcome of obtaining a good wage job (or obtaining more formal education) that otherwise would not have occurred is a "success" also. Another intermediate outcome often used is the clients' opinion about how they liked the program. This can be useful in terms of finding out what parts of the program were perceived to be the most helpful and what was missing. However, far too much reliance has been placed on this as a complete evaluation. When I evaluated ex-offender job programs, I found that clients typically said they liked the program and found it worthwhile even though no jobs were obtained.

5. Effects to earning streams, from manpower training progams, are usually estimated by extrapolating (with decay) post-program earning improvements over the remaining work life of clients.

6. Freedland (1987) takes the view that earning gains should be the focus for judging success of micro-enterprise development programs and that "psychological benefits should be derived through other means."

7. In the evaluation of the Supported Work Demonstration Project, benefits per ex-addict participant, for just the outcome of reduced criminal arrests, amounted to $5000. Ignoring this outcome would have led to the program not passing the cost/benefit test for this target group (Kemper et al. 1981).

8. A classic on this topic is Mayer and Goldstein (1961). More studies of that type are needed.

9. This technique is referred to as a classical experiment. It too suffers from drawbacks but is generally considered the best way to measure progam impacts. For a discussion on the strengths and weaknesses of classical experiment manpower program evaluation design, see Spiegelman (1988) and Burtless and Orr (1987).

10. There are ways to correct for the selection bias that can occur when using nonequivalent comparison groups (Heckman & Hotz 1988).

11. Considerable research has been conducted on evaluating manpower and training programs. We should look to the techniques developed there to guide the evaluation of small business development programs. For examples, see Borus (1972); Perry et al. (1975); Borus (1979); Manpower Demonstration Research Corporation (1980); and Long et al. (1981). There are research organizations that specialize in manpower evaluation. In addition, many universities have economics, labor, and urban research centers attached to them that have the capability of assisting self-employment programs to conduct evaluations. Another source of assistance is from organizations that conduct and evaluate self-employment programs in the Third World. One group would be the 25 private development organizations that formed the Small Enterprise Evaluation Project (Buzzard & Edgcomb 1987).

12. I have argued elsewhere (Balkin 1988) that business starts, though important, are neither a necessary nor a sufficient condition for the success of a self-employment training program.

Bibliography

Abdelsamad, M. and Kindling, A. 1978. "Why Small Businesses Fail." *S.A.M. Advanced Management Journal,* Spring, pp. 24–32.

Abt Associates, Inc. 1988. *Proposal to Evaluate A Demonstration of Alternative Uses of Unemployment Insurance to Provide Self-Employment Assistance.* Cambridge, MA.

Aldrich, H. and Zimmer, C. 1986. "Entrepreneurship through Social Networks." In R. Smilor and D. Sexton, eds., *The Art and Science of Entrepreneurship.* New York: Ballinger, pp. 3–23.

Alexander, B. 1987. "The Black Church and Community Empowerment." In R. Woodson, ed., *On the Road to Economic Freedom.* Washington, DC: Regnery Gateway.

Allen, D. 1987. *Enterprise Allowance Scheme Evaluation: First Eighteen-Months National Survey.* Moorfoot, England: Manpower Services Commission.

Allen, D. and Hunn, A. 1985. "An Evaluation of the Enterprise Allowance Scheme." *Employment Gazette,* August, pp. 313–317.

Anderson, B. 1979. "Minorities and Work: The Challenge for the Next Decade." In C. Kerr and J. Rosow, eds., *Work in America: The Decade Ahead.* New York: Van Nostrand.

Anderson, C. and Lehman, K. 1986. *A Guide to the Possibilities and Pitfalls of Starting a Business as a Low Income Parent.* Minneapolis, MN: Cooperative Community Development Program of the Hubert H. Humphrey Institute of Public Affairs.

Armington, C. and Odle, M. 1982. "Small Business—How Many Jobs?" *Brookings Review,* Winter, pp. 14–17.

Aronson, R. 1985. *Self-employment and the Male-Female Earnings Differential: A Prospectus.* Cornell University, New York State School of Industrial and Labor Relations.

———. 1987. *The Relative Earnings of the Non-Farm Self-Employed: An Exploratory Analysis.* Cornell University, New York State School of Industrial and Labor Relations.

Arthur Young and Company. 1982. Evaluation of Business Starts Among Graduates and Rejected Applicants in the HETADI Training Project. Sponsored by the CETA Program of the City and County of Honolulu. Honolulu, HI: Hawaii Entrepreneurship Training and Development Institute.

Ashe, J. 1985a. *The Pisces II Experience: Local Efforts in Micro-Enterprise Development,* Washington, DC: AID.

———, ed. 1985b. *The Pisces II Experience: Case Studies from the Dominican Republic, Costa Rica, Kenya, and Egypt,* Vol. 2. Washington, DC: AID, December.

———. 1987. "Micro-Enterprises: A Suggested Strategy for Business Development." *Resources for Community-Based Economic Development.* November, pp. 1–4.

Bailey, R., ed. 1971. *Black Business Enterprise: Historical and Contemporary Perspectives.* New York: Basic Books.

Bailey, T. R. 1987. *Immigrants and Native Workers: Contrasts and Competition.* Boulder, CO: Westview Press.

Baird, S. 1985. Chicago Update. *Street Performers Newsletter* (Cambridge, MA). August.

Balkin, S. 1986. *Self-Employment for Low Income People: A Report to the National Commission on Jobs and Small Business.* Springfield, VA: National Technical Information Service.

———. 1987a. "Self-Employment for Low Income People: A Real Option." *The Entrepreneurial Economy,* March, pp. 2–4.

———. 1987b. "Self-Employment: A Review of the Literature and Job Creation Policies for Low Income People." Paper presented at the Annual Meetings of the Midwest Economics Association, March.

———. 1987c. *Directory of the Chicago Self-Employment Network.* Roosevelt University, Department of Economics.

———. 1988a. "Networks, Mentors, and Entrepreneurs: A Reply to Carsrud, et al." Unpublished paper. Roosevelt University, Department of Economics.

———. 1988b. "Self-Employment Assistance Programs in the United States Targeted to Low Income Disadvantaged People." *Proceedings of the Annual Meetings of the Industrial Relations Research Association.* May.

———. 1988c. *Home Based Businesses as Potential Self-Employment Opportunities.* Working Papers in Economics and Political Economy. Chicago, IL: Roosevelt University.

———. 1988d. *Franchises as Potential Self-Employment Opportunities.* Working Papers in Economics and Political Economy. Chicago, IL: Roosevelt University.

———. 1988e. *CETA Entrepreneurial Programs.* Working Papers in Economics and Political Economy. Chicago, IL: Roosevelt University.

Balkin, S. and Czechowski, D. E. 1986. *Survey of CETA Entrepreneurial Programs: Supplement Report to the National Commission on Jobs and*

Small Business. Springfield, VA: National Technical Information Service.

Bane, M. J. and Jargowsky, P. A. 1987. "Urban Poverty and the Underclass: Basic Questions." Paper prepared for the APPAM Research Conference, Washington, DC.

Bangser, M., Healy, J. and Ivry, R. 1985. *Welfare Grant Diversion: Early Observations from Programs in Six States.* New York: Manpower Demonstration Research Corporation.

Barclay, A. H., et al. 1979. *The Development Impact of Private Voluntary Organizations: Kenya and Niger.* Washington, DC: DAI (Development Alternatives, Inc.).

Bates, T. 1981. "Black Entrepreneurship and Government Programs." *Journal of Contemporary Studies,* Fall, pp. 59–70.

———. 1984/1985. "Urban Economic Transformations and Minority Business Opportunity." *The Review of Black Political Economy,* Winter, pp. 21–36.

———. 1985a. "Impact of Preferential Procurement Policies on Minority-Owned Businesses." *The Review of Black Political Economy,* Summer, pp. 51–65.

———. 1985b. "Entrepreneur Human Capital Endowments and Minority Business Viability." *The Journal of Human Resources,* Fall, pp. 540–554.

———. 1986. "Characteristics of Minorities Who Are Entering Self-Employment." *The Review of Black Political Economy,* Fall, pp. 31–49.

Bauman, K. J. 1987. *Expanding Self-Employment Opportunities in the Great Lakes Region.* Madison, WI: Great Lakes Commission Economic Analysis and Policy Task Force.

———. 1988. "Characteristics of the Low Income Self-Employed." *Industrial Relations Research Association Proceedings: December, 1987.* pp. 339–345.

Bearse, P. J. 1984. "An Econometric Analysis of Black Entrepreneurship." *Review of Black Political Economy,* Spring, pp. 111–134.

Becker, E. H. 1984. "Self-Employed Workers: An Update to 1983." *Monthly Labor Review,* July, pp. 14–18.

Bendick, M. and Egan, M. L. 1987a. "Look Who's Becoming an Entrepreneur." *Across the Board.* January, pp. 52–54.

———. 1987b. "Transfer Payment Diversion for Small Business Development." *Industrial and Labor Relations Review,* July, pp. 528–542.

Berlin, G. 1986. "Job Creation and Business Development: An Overview." In H. Rosen, ed., *Job Creation: U.S. and European Perspectives.* Washington, DC: The National Council on Employment Policy.

Bernick, M. 1987. *Urban Illusions: New Approaches to Inner City Unemployment.* New York: Praeger.

Better Business Bureau. 1983. *Tips on Work-at-Home Schemes.* Arlington, VA: Council of Better Business Bureaus, Inc.

Birch, D. L. 1979. *The Job Generation Process.* Center for Neighborhood and Regional Change. Massachusetts Institute of Technology.

———. 1987. *Job Creation in America: How Our Smallest Companies Put the Most People to Work.* New York: The Free Press.

Birley, S. 1985. "The Role of Networks in the Entrepreneurial Process." *Journal of Business Venturing,* Winter, pp. 107–117.

Blau, D. M. 1987. "A Time Series Analysis of Self-Employment in the United States." *Journal of Political Economy,* June, pp. 445–467.

Blaustein, A. I. and Faux, G. 1972. *The Star-Spangled Hustle: White Power and Black Capitalism.* Garden City, NY: Doubleday.

Bluestone, B. 1969. "The Political Economy of Black Capitalism." In D. Gordon, ed., *Problems in Political Economy: An Urban Perspective.* Lexington, MA: D. C. Heath and Co., 1971, pp. 138–146.

Bonacich, E. 1973. "A Theory of Middleman Minorities." *American Sociological Review,* October, pp. 585–594.

———. 1987. "Making It in America: A Social Evaluation of the Ethics of Immigrant Entrepreneurship." *Sociological Perspectives,* October, pp. 446–466.

Bonacich, E. and Modell, J. 1980. *The Economic Basis of Ethnic Solidarity: Small Business in the Japanese American Community.* Berkeley: University of California Press.

Borjas, G. J. 1985. "The Self-Employment of Immigrants." Discussion Paper No. 783-85. Madison, WI: Institute for Research on Poverty–University of Wisconsin, October.

———. 1986. "The Self-Employment Experience of Immigrants." *The Journal of Human Resources,* Fall, pp. 485–506.

Borus, M., ed. 1972. *Evaluating the Impact of Manpower Programs.* Lexington, MA: Lexington Books, 1972.

———. 1979. *Measuring the Impact of Employment-Related Social Programs.* Kalamazoo, MI: W. E. Upjohn Institute for Employment Research.

Brimmer, A. F. 1969. "Small Business and Economic Development in the Negro Community—Statement Before the U.S. House of Representatives Select Committee on Small Business." In R. Bailey, ed., *Black Business Enterprise: Historical and Contemporary Perspectives.* New York: Basic Books, pp. 164–172.

Brock, W. A. and Evans, D. S. 1986. *The Economics of Small Business: Their Role and Regulation in the U.S. Economy.* New York: Holmes and Meier.

Brockhaus, R. and Horwitz, P. 1985. "The Psychology of the Entrepreneur." In D. Sexton and R. Smilor, eds., *The Art and Science of Entrepreneurship.* Cambridge, MA: Ballinger.

Bromley, R., ed. 1985. *Planning for Small Enterprises in Third World Cities.* Oxford, England: Pergamon Press.

Brotz, H. 1964. *The Black Jews of Harlem.* Glencoe, IL: Free Press.

Browne, R. S. 1985. "Book Review: The Black Power Imperative." *The Review of Black Political Economy,* Summer, pp. 101–103.

Bruns, L. 1986. "The Story of Lady Slipper Designs." In B. Brabec, ed. *Craft Marketing Success Secrets.* Naperville, IL: Barbara Brabec Productions, pp. 69–70.

Burks, I. 1984. *Director's Planning Guide—Minority Business Enterprise Project.* Washington, DC: American Association of Community and Junior Colleges, September.

Burtless, G. 1984. "On Manpower Policies for the Disadvantaged." *The Brookings Review,* Fall, pp. 18–22.

Burtless, G. and Orr, L. L. 1987. "Are Classical Experiments Needed for Manpower Policy?" *The Journal of Human Resources,* Vol. 21, no. 4, pp. 606–639.

Burton-Snell, K. 1988. *Resources and Barriers to Self-employment: An Examination of State Government.* Lansing, MI: Governor's Office of Job Training.

Business Week. 1985. "The Forgotten Americans: Minority Unemployment and What to Do about It." September 2, pp. 50–55.

Buzzard, S. and Edgcomb, E., eds. 1987. *Monitoring and Evaluating Small Business Projects: A Step by Step Guide for Private Development Organizations.* New York: PACT (Private Agencies Collaborating Together).

Campbell, D. and Stanley, J. 1963. *Experimental and Quasi-Experimental Designs for Research.* Boston: Houghton Mifflin Co.

Cantillon, R. 1755. Essai sur la Nature du Commerce en Générale (ed. H. Higgs) London: Macmillan (1931).

Carland, J. W., Hoy, F., Boulton, W. and Carland, J.A.C. 1984. "Differentiating Entrepreneurs from Small Business Owners: A Conceptualization." *Academy of Management Review,* Vol. 9, pp. 354–359.

Carson, C. S. 1984. "The Underground Economy: An Introduction." *Survey of Current Business,* May, pp. 21–37.

Carsrud, A., Gaglio, C., and Olm, K. 1987. "Entrepreneurs—Mentors, Networks, and Successful New Venture Development: An Exploratory Study." *American Journal of Small Business,* Fall, 1987, pp. 13–18.

Carstensen, C. 1985. "The Appropriateness of Entrepreneurial Training in Wisconsin's Employment and Training System." Employment and Training Policy Paper No. 3. Madison, WI: State of Wisconsin Department of Industry, Labor and Human Relations.

Casson, M. 1982. *The Entrepreneur: An Economic Theory.* Totowa, NJ: Barnes and Noble Books.

Castle, D. J. 1985. "Psychological and Sociological Benefits of Participation in Lady Slipper Designs Cottage Industry Program." Report to the Board of Directors of Lady Slipper Designs.

Chen, Gavin, et al. 1982. "Minority Business Today: Problems and Their Causes." Research Division, Minority Business Development Agency, U.S. Department of Commerce, Washington, DC: January.

Chock, P. 1981. "The Greek-American Small Businessman: A Cultural Analysis." *Journal of Anthropological Research,* Spring, pp. 46–60.

Christopher, G. 1986. *Illinois Public Aid and Policy Barriers and Disincentives to the Self-Employment Initiative of the AFDC Recipient.* Chicago, IL: Women's Self-Employment Project.

Chung, Joseph S. 1979. "Small Ethnic Business as a Form of Disguised Unemployment and Cheap Labor." In *Civil Rights Issues of Asians and Pacific Americans: Myths and Realities.* Washington, DC: U.S. Commission on Civil Rights, May 8-9, pp. 508-517.

The Church of Jesus Christ of Latter-day Saints. 1980a. *Church Employment System Guidebook.* Salt Lake City, Utah.

———. 1980b. *Welfare Services Resources Handbook.* Salt Lake City, Utah.

Cobas, J. 1987. "On the Study of Ethnic Enterprise: Unresolved Issues." *Sociological Perspectives,* October, pp. 467–472.

Collins, O. and Moore, D. 1970. *The Organization Makers: A Study of Independent Entrepreneurs.* New York: Meridith.

Corey, L. 1966. "The Middle Class." In Bendix and Lipset, eds., *Class Status and Power,* 2d ed. Glencoe, IL: Free Press, pp. 371–380.

Cornuelle, R. 1983. *Healing America: What Can Be Done about the Continuing Economic Crisis.* New York: G. P. Putnam's Sons.

Corporation for Enterprise Development. 1983. Entrepreneurial Expansion: The Best Way to Create Jobs? *The Entrepreneurial Economy* February, 1983, pp. 5–6.

———. 1984. *Entrepreneurial Training: State Enterprise Development Implementation Packet#6.* Washington, DC.

———. 1985a. No Seeds, No Trees: A Profile of Seed Capital Funds, Washington, DC.

———. 1985b. The Self-Employment Opportunity Act of 1985: New Hope for the Unemployed, Washington, DC.

———. 1986. *The Entrepreneurial Economy* 4 (June), entire issue.

Cortes, M., Berry, A., and Ishaq, A. 1987. *Success in Small and Medium-Scale Enterprises: The Evidence from Columbia.* Washington, DC: The World Bank.

Credit Union National Association. 1988. "Credit Union Profile: Services Offered and Operating Characteristics, as of December 1987." Madison, WI: Credit Union National Association.

Crimmins, J. and Keil, M. 1983. *Enterprise in the Nonprofit Sector.* Washington, DC: Partners for Liveable Places.

Cronon, E. D. 1955. *Black Moses: The Story of Marcus Garvey and the Universal Negro Improvement Association.* Madison, WI: University of Wisconsin Press.

Cross, T. L. 1970. *Black Capitalism: Strategy for Business in the Ghetto.* New York: Atheneum.

Cruden, R. 1969. *The Negro in Reconstruction.* Englewood Cliffs, NJ: Prentice-Hall.

Curry, L. P. 1981. *The Free Black in Urban America, 1800-1850: The Shadow of the Dream.* Chicago: University of Chicago Press.

Czuchna, A. 1986. "Seniors Learn the Greenhouse Business." *Michigan Farmer,* February 15, pp. 32–33.

Davidson, J. 1987. "Melting Pot Boils as Influx of Asian Merchants into Black Neighborhoods Is Greeted Grimly." *The Wall Street Journal,* July 31, p. 32.

Davies, R. 1978. *The Informal Sector: A Solution to Unemployment.* (In the 'From Rhodesia to Zimbabwe' Booklet Series). London: Catholic Institute for International Relations, 1978.

Davis, E. F., et al. 1975. "Establishment of a Minority Small Business Training Program: In Retrospect." *Michigan State University Business Topics,* Spring, pp. 64–72.

Davis, F. G. 1972. *The Economics of Black Community Development.* Chicago: Markham.

Dow, L. 1977. "High Weeds in Detroit: The Irregular Economy Among a Network of Appalachian Migrants." *Urban Anthropology*, Vol. 16, pp. 111–128.

Du Bois, W.E.B. 1903. *The Souls of Black Folk*. Chicago: A. C. McClung.

Eastwood, C. 1983. "Chicago Street Vendors: Informal Sector Economics and Political Realities." Paper presented at the Annual Meetings of the American Anthropological Association, Chicago, IL, November.

———. 1988. *Municipal Regulation of Street Vendors: The Chicago Case*. Ph.D. dissertation, University of Illinois–Chicago.

Equity Policy Center. 1984. "Street Foods as Source of Income for Women." Washington, DC.

Essien-Udom, E.U. 1962. *Black Nationalism: A Search for an Ideology in America*. Chicago: University of Chicago Press.

Evans, D. S. and Leighton, L. S. 1987. Self-Employment Selection and Earnings over the Life Cycle. Washington, DC: U.S. Small Business Administration, Office of Advocacy.

Evanson, E. 1984. "Employment Programs for the Poor: Government in the Labor Market." *FOCUS*, Fall, pp. 1–7.

Fain, T. S. 1980. "Self-Employed Americans: Their Number Has Increased." *Monthly Labor Review*, November, pp. 3–8.

Farnsworth, C. 1988. "Micro-loans to the Third World." *New York Times*. February 21. Sec. 3, p. 1.

Fass, S. 1986. "Innovations in the Struggle for Self-Reliance: The Hmong Experience in the United States." *International Migration Review*, Vol. 20, no. 2, pp. 351–376.

Feedback-ILE. 1985. Expanding the Opportunity to Produce, No. 1, April, pp. 3–5.

Feinman, J. 1976. *100 Surefire Businesses You Can Start with Little or No Investment*. Chicago: Playboy Press.

Feit, R. 1987a. "Expanding Entrepreneurial Opportunity: An Alternative Route to Self-Sufficiency." Background Paper for the Corporation for Enterprise Development, Washington, DC

———. 1987b. *Resource List (Selected)*. Washington, DC: Corporation for Enterprise Development.

Ferman, L. A. 1985. "Participation in the Irregular Economy. "Paper presented at the National Meetings of the American Sociological Association, August.

Ferman, L., Henry, S. and Hoyman, M., eds. 1987. *The Informal Economy*, an issue of *The Annals*. September.

Fleming, W. L. 1970. *The Freedmen's Saving Bank*. Westport, CT: Negro Universities Press, reprinted from a 1927 edition.

Foley, E. 1972. "A Small Business Program for the Ghetto." In Vatter. H. G. and Palm, T., eds., *The Economics of Black America*. New York: Harcourt Brace Jovanovich, pp. 245–248.

Folques, D. 1984. *L'Aide aux Chomeurs Createurs D'Enterprise en 1983*, pp. 49–52.

Fonstad, C., et al. 1982. *The Smallest Businesses of the Poor: An Annotated Bibliography*. Cambridge, MA: ACCION International/ASITEC.

Foreman-Peck, J. 1985. "Seedcorn or Chaff? New Firm Formation and Performance of the Interwar Economy." *The Economic History Review,* August, pp. 402-422.

Fortune. 1970. "Black Capitalism in the Muslim Style," January, p. 44.

Foster, D. L. 1988. *Franchising for Free: Owning Your Own Business Without Investing Your Own Cash.* New York: John Wiley and Sons, Inc.

Franklin, J. Hope. 1961. *Reconstruction after the Civil War.* Chicago: University of Chicago Press.

Fratoe, F. 1986. "A Sociological Analysis of Minority Business." *The Review of Black Political Economy,* Fall, pp. 5–29.

Frazier, E. 1957. *Black Bourgeoisie: The Rise of a New Middle Class in the United States.* New York: The Free Press.

Fredland, J. E. and Little, R. 1981. "Self-Employed Workers: Returns to Education and Training. *Economics of Education Review,* Summer, pp. 315–337.

———. 1985. "Psychic Income and Self-Employment." *Journal of Private Enterprise,* Fall, pp. 121–126.

Freedland, M. 1987. "Micro-Business: Another View." *Resources: For Community Based Economic Development,* November, p. 2.

Friedman, R. E. 1986. "Expanding the Vision of the Entrepreneurial Economy." *The Entrepreneurial Economy,* 4 (December/January), pp. 2–3.

———. 1987. *A Hand-Up, Not a Handout: An Introduction to Transfer Payment Investment Policy and Practice.* Washington, DC: Corporation for Enterprise Development.

———. 1988a. Testimony before the Select Committee on Hunger. U.S. House of Representatives, Self-Employment for the Poor: The Potential of Micro-Enterprise Credit Programs, April 20.

———. 1988b. *The Safety Net as Ladder: Transfer Payments and Economic Development.* Washington, DC: The Council of State Policy and Planning Agencies.

Friedman, R. E. and Jones M. 1985. "Pay the Unemployed to Create Jobs." *New York Times,* September 8, Sec. F, p. 2.

Friedman, R. E. and Schmitt, A. 1979. *Job Creation Through Enterprise Development: CETA and the Development of Local Private–Public Enterprises.* Washington, DC: Corporation for Enterprise Development.

Fuchs, V. R. 1982. Self-employment and Labor Force Participation of Older Males. *The Journal of Human Resources,* Summer, pp. 339–357.

Fuglesang, A. and Chandler, D. 1986. *Participation as Process—What we can learn from Grameen Bank Bangladesh.* Oslo, Norway: Norwegian Ministry of Development Corporation.

Gallo, C. 1983. "The Construction Industry in New York City: Immigrants and Black Entrepreneurs." Working paper, New York: Conservation of Human Resources, Columbia University.

Gartner, W. B. 1988. "Who Is an Entrepreneur? Is the Wrong Question." *American Journal of Small Business,* Spring, pp. 11–32.

Garvin, W. J. 1973. "Fostering Minority Business Ownership." In D. Carson, ed., *The Vital Majority: Small Business in the American Economy.* Washington, DC: US Government Printing Office.

Geertz, C. 1963. *Peddlers and Princes.* Chicago: University of Chicago Press.

Gershuny, J. I. 1979. "The Informal Economy: Its Role in Post-Industrial Society." *Futures,* pp. 3–15.

Ghai, D. 1984. *An Evaluation of the Impact of the Grameen Bank Project.* Dkaha, Bangladesh: Grameen Bank, March.

Gibb, A. and Ritchie, J. 1982. "Understanding the Process of Starting Small Businesses." *European Small Business Journal,* Vol. 1, pp. 26–45.

Goetz, B. 1973. "Management of Risk in Small New Enterprises." *S.A.M. Advanced Management Journal,* January, pp. 21–27.

Goldmark, S. and Rosengard, J. 1983. "Credit to Indonesian Entrepreneurs: An Assessment of the Badan Kredit Kecamatan Program." Report prepared for the U.S. Agency for International Development. Washington, DC: Development Alternatives, Inc., May.

Goldscheider, C. and Kobrin, F. E. 1980. "Ethnic Continuity and the Process of Self-Employment." *Ethnicity,* Vol. 7, pp. 256–278.

Gould, L. C. 1969. "Juvenile Entrepreneurs." *American Journal of Sociology,* May, pp. 710–719.

Gould, S. and Lyman, J. 1986. *Report of the National Strategy Session on Women's Self-Employment.* Washington, DC: Corporation for Enterprise Development.

———. 1987. "A Working Guide to Women's Self-Employment." *The Entrepreneurial Economy,* (March), pp. 5–14.

Granovetter, M. 1985. "Economic Action and Social Structure: The Problem of Embeddedness." *American Journal of Sociology,* November, pp. 481–510.

Gratteau, H. and Lipinski, A. 1986. "Clout Throttles Cab Riders." *Chicago Tribune,* May 25, Sec. 1, p. 1.

Grayson, P. 1983. "Male and Female Operated Non-Farm Proprietorships, 1980." *Statistics of Income Bulletin,* Spring, pp. 9–20.

Greenberg, J., et al. 1980. "The Itinerant Street Vendor: A Form of Nonstore Retailing." *Journal of Retailing,* Summer, pp. 66–80.

Gropper, R. C. 1975. *Gypsies in the City.* Princeton, NJ: Darwin Press.

Gutmann, P. 1978. "Are the Unemployed, Unemployed?" *Financial Analysts Journal,* September/October.

Haber, S. E., Lamas, E. J., and Lichtenstein, J. H. 1986. "Estimates of Business Ownership from the Survey of Income and Participation." Unpublished paper. George Washington University.

———. 1987. "On Their Own: The Self-employed and Others in Private Business." *Monthly Labor Review.* May, pp. 17–23.

Hagen, E. E. 1962. *On the Theory of Social Change.* Homewood, IL: Dorsey Press.

Hailstones, T. J. 1982. *A Guide to Supply Side Economics.* Richmond, VA: Robert Dame Inc.

Halkett, J., et al. 1985. The Cooperative Approach to Crafts, Cooperative Information Report 33. Washington, DC: U.S. Department of Agriculture, Agricultural Cooperative Service.

Handy, J. W. 1988. "Discussion on Panel: Self-Employment as a Source of Job

Creation for Low Income People." *Industrial Relations Research Association Proceedings: December, 1987,* pp. 349–345.

Hansen, J. 1979. "The Real Black Economy." *New Society,* September 13, pp. 553–554.

Harper, M. 1984. *Entrepreneurship for the Poor.* London: ITT Publications and the German Agency for Technical Cooperation.

Hart, K. 1973. "Informal Income Opportunities and Urban Employment in Ghana." *Journal of Modern African Studies,* Vol. 2, pp. 61–89.

Hatch, C. R. 1987. "Learning from Italy's Industrial Renaissance." *The Entrepreneurial Economy,* July/August, pp. 4–10.

Hawaii Entrepreneurship Training and Development Institute. 1985. *Overview of HETADI's Entrepreneurship Training Programs.* Honolulu, HI: Hawaii Entrepreneurship Training and Development Institute.

Heckman, J. J. and Hotz, V. J. 1987. "Are Classical Experiments Necessary for Evaluating the Impact of Manpower Training Programs?" *Proceedings of the Fortieth Annual Meeting of the Industrial Relations Research Association,* pp. 268–291.

Heinze, R. G. and Olk, T. 1982. "Development of the Informal Economy: A Strategy for Resolving the Crisis of the Welfare State." *Futures,* June, pp. 189–204.

Henze, L., Nye N. and Schramm, R. 1988. *Roundtable Workshop for Business Development and Self-Employment Loan Funds Serving Low Income People: Summary Report.* Report to the Ford Foundation. Medford, MA: Center for Management and Community Development, Tufts University.

Henze, L., Nye, N., Schramm, R. and Hoekman, S. 1988. *Workshop for Funders of Business Development and Self-Employment Loan Funds: Proceedings.* Report to the Ford Foundation. Medford, MA: Center for Management and Community Development, Tufts University.

The Hill Rag. 1985. "Vending Law Changes," August 16, pp. 19–20.

Himebaugh, E. 1982. "Making Job Makers." *Herald Times,* January 24, Sec. D, p. 1.

Hossain, M. 1986. *Credit for Alleviation of Rural Poverty: The Experience of Grameen Bank in Bangladesh.* Working paper No. 4, Grameen Bank Evaluation Project. Dhaka, Bangladesh: Bangladesh Institute of Development Studies.

Hostetler, J. A. 1980. *Amish Society,* 3d Ed. Baltimore: Johns Hopkins University Press.

Howe, I. 1976. *World of Our Fathers.* New York: Simon and Schuster.

Hunt, R. 1985. *Private Voluntary Organizations and the Promotion of Small-Scale Enterprise.* AID Evaluation Special Study No. 22. Washington, DC: U.S. Agency for International Development, July.

Hurh, W. M. and Kim, K. C. 1986. "The Success Image of Asian Americans: Its Validity, Practical and Theoretical Implications." Paper presented at the Annual Meeting of American Sociological Association, New York, September.

Illinois Department of Commerce and Community Affairs. 1987. *Organizing*

Self-Employment Programs: A Guide for Development Organizations. Springfield, IL: State of Illinois.

Illinois Department of Commerce and Community Affairs. 1987. *Self-Employment Training Programs: Case Studies.* Springfield, IL.

Industrial Council of Northwest Chicago. 1985. *Development Plans of the Kinzie Industrial Corridor and the Fulton Carrol Center: A New Business Development Strategy.* Chicago.

Informisep. 1984. *United Kingdom: Evaluation of the Pilot Enterprise Allowance Scheme.* December, pp. 10–13.

Institute for Research on Poverty. 1985. "Antipoverty Policy: Past and Future." *FOCUS,* Summer, pp. 1–25.

Iowa Department of Economic Development. 1988. *Iowa's Self-Employment Investment Demonstration (SEID) Pilot Project.* Information Report. Des Moines, IA.

Jackall, R. and Leven, H. M., eds. 1984. *Worker Cooperatives in America.* Berkeley, CA: University of California Press.

Jane Addams Center. 1987. *Home Day Care Provider Training Questionnaire Results,* Fall.

———. 1988. *Child Care Initiatives Newsletter,* Spring.

Joe, T 1982. *Profiles of Families in Poverty: Effects of the FY 1983 Budget Proposals on the Poor.* Washington, DC: The Center for the Study of Social Policy.

Joe, T. and Eckels, T. 1981. "Enterprise Development as an Employment Strategy for Welfare Recipients." Conference Background Paper no. 16. Washington, DC: Corporation for Enterprise Development.

Johnson, P. and Rodger, J. 1983. *Self-Employment among Redundant Employees: A Report of a Research Study.* Moorfoot, Sheffield, England: Manpower Services Commission.

Johnson, P. S. and Thomas, R. B. 1984. "Government Policies Towards Business Formation: An Economic Appraisal of a Training Scheme." *Scottish Journal of Political Economy,* June, pp. 131–146.

Jones, M. 1985. *Transfer Payment Investment Policy: Letting Them Have Their Boots and Bootstraps Too.* Washington, DC: Corporation for Enterprise Development.

Kahn, H. C. 1964. *Business and Professional Income Under the Personal Income Tax.* Princeton, NJ: Princeton University Press.

Kain, J. and Persky, J. 1969. "Alternatives to the Gilded Ghetto." In J. Kain, ed., *Race and Poverty: The Economics of Discrimination.* Englewood, NJ: Prentice Hall.

Kaladonis, G. 1988. "Debunking the Eleventh Commandment: Small Businesses Do Not Create 82 Percent of All New Jobs." *Chicago Enterprise,* May, pp. 11–13.

Kanahele, G. S. 1981. "Entrepreneurship as a Development Tool." In Friedman and Schweke, eds., *Expanding the Opportunity to Produce: Revitalizing the American Economy Through New Enterprise Development.* Washington, DC: The Corporation for Enterprise Development.

Katz, W. L., ed. 1968. *The Atlanta University Publications.* New York: Arno Press.

Keim, A. N. ed. 1975. *Compulsory Education and the Amish: The Right Not to be Modern*. Boston: Beacon Press.

Kemper, P., et al. 1981. *The Supported Work Evaluation: Final Benefit-Cost Analysis: Vol. 5 of the Final Report*. New York: Manpower Demonstration Research Corporation.

Kent, C., Sexton, D., and Conrad, S. 1981. *Critical Lifetime Experiences of Entrepreneurs: A Preliminary Analysis*. Waco, TX: Baylor University Center for Private Enterprise and Entrepreneurship.

Kephart, W. M. 1987. *Extraordinary Groups: An Examination of Unconventional Lifestyles*, 3d Ed. New York: St. Martin's Press.

Kern, C. S. 1984. *Home Businesses: Small Business Bibliography Number 2*. Washington, DC: U.S. Small Business Administration, U.S. Government Printing Office.

Kierulff, H. E. 1975. "Can Entrepreneurs Be Developed?" *Michigan State University Business Topics*, Winter, pp. 39–44.

Kilby, P. 1979. "Evaluating Technical Assistance." *World Development*, Vol. 7, pp. 309–323.

Kilby, P. and D'Zmura, D. 1985. *Searching for Benefits: Aid Special Study No. 28*. Washington, DC: U.S. Agency for International Development.

Kim, C. K. and Hurh, W. M. 1983. "Korean Americans and the 'Success' Image: A Critique." *Amerasia*, Vol. 10, no. 2, pp. 3–21.

———. 1985. "Ethnic Resurces Utilization of Korean Immigrant Entrepreneurs in the Chicago Minority Area." *International Migration Review*, Spring, pp. 82–111.

Kirzner, I. M. 1973. *Competition and Entrepreneurship*. Chicago: University of Chicago Press.

Kleiman, C. 1985. "Loan Fund Aids Businesswomen." *Chicago Tribune*, January 21.

Knight, F. H. 1921. *Risk, Uncertainty and Profit*. Chicago: University of Chicago Press.

Kwong, P. 1987. *The New Chinatown*. New York: Hill and Wang.

Laban, D. N. and Lentz, B. F. 1985. *The Roots of Success: Why Children Follow in their Parents' Career Footsteps*. New York, NY: Praeger.

Laffer, A. 1979. *Economics of the Tax Revolt*. New York: Harcourt Brace and Jovanovich.

Lassen, C. 1984. *A Systems Approach for the Design and Evaluation of PVO Small Enterprise Development Projects: Report of a PVO Working Group*. Washington, D.C.: Partnership for Productivity/International.

Lazear, E. P. and Moore, R. L. 1984. "Incentives, Productivity, and Labor Contracts." *Quarterly Journal of Economics*, May, pp. 275–296.

Leff, N. H. 1979. "Entrepreneurship and Economic Development: The Problem Revisited." *Journal of Economic Literature*, March, pp. 46–64.

Leibenstein, H. 1978. *General X-efficiency Theory and Economic Development*. New York: Oxford University Press.

Lenski, G. 1963. *The Religious Factor: A Sociological Inquiry*. Garden City, New York: Doubleday and Co.

Levinson, J. C. 1982. *555 Ways to Earn Extra Money*. New York: Holt, Rinehart and Winston.

Levitan, S. A. 1969. "Community Self-determination and Entrepreneurship: Their Promises and Limitations." *Poverty and Human Resources Abstracts,* Vol. 4, no. 1, pp. 16–24.

Levitan, S. A. and Johnson, C. M. 1984. *Beyond the Safety Net.* Cambridge, MA: Ballinger.

Levitan, S. A. and Gallo, F. 1988. *A Second Chance: Training for Jobs.* Kalamazoo, MI: W. E. Upjohn Institute of Employment Research.

Lieberson, S. 1980. *A Piece of the Pie: Black and White Immigrants since 1880.* Berkeley, CA: University of California Press.

Light, I. 1972. *Ethnic Enterprise in America: Business and Welfare Among Chinese, Japanese, and Blacks.* Berkeley: University of California Press.

———. 1984. "Immigrant and Ethnic Enterprise in North America." *Ethnic and Racial Studies,* April, pp. 195-216.

Light, I. and Bonacich, E. 1988. *Immigrant Entrepreneurs: Koreans in Los Angeles, 1965-1982.* Berkeley: University of California Press.

Lincoln, C. E. 1973. *The Black Muslims in America.* Boston: Beacon Press (rev. ed.).

Lipset, S. and Bendix, R. 1954. "Social Mobility and Occupational Career Patterns." *American Journal of Sociology,* January, pp. 366–374.

Long, D., Mallar, C., and Thornton, C. 1981. "Evaluating the Benefits and Costs of the Job Corp." *Journal of Policy Analysis and Management.* Fall, pp. 55–76.

Long, J. E. 1982. "The Income Tax and Self-Employment." *National Tax Journal,* Vol. 35, no. 1, pp. 31–42.

Lovell-Troy, L. 1980. "Clan Structure, and Economic Activity: The Case of Greeks in Small Business Enterprise." In S. Cummings, ed., *Self-Help in Urban America: Patterns of Minority Business Enterprise.* New York: Kennikat Press, pp. 58–85.

———. 1981. "Ethnic Occupational Structures: Greeks in the Pizza Business." *Ethnicity,* March, pp. 82–95.

Lucas, R. E. 1978. "On the Size Distribution of Business Firms." *Bell Journal of Economics,* Autumn, pp. 508–523.

Lunding, F. S., Clements, C. E., and Peskins, D. S. 1978. "Everyone Who Makes It Has a Mentor." *Harvard Business Review,* July–August, pp. 89–95.

MacMillan, I. C. 1983. "The Politics of New Venture Management." *Harvard Business Review,* Nov.–Dec., pp. 8–16.

Magdol, E. 1977. *A Right to the Land: Essays on the Freedman's Community.* Westport, CT: Greenwood Press.

Maier, M. 1985. "Is Small Beautiful? Few Jobs, Poor Conditions in Small Firms." *Dollars and Sense.* January/February, pp. 12–14.

Malone, L. 1986. *Business Loans and the Small Cities Community Development Block Grant: A Summary and Analysis.* Washington, DC: Council of State Community Affairs Agencies.

Mangum, S. L. and Keyton, J. 1986. *A Review of the JTPA Title III Entrepreneurial Training Pilot Programs.* Final Report. Ohio Bureau of Employment Services, December.

Mangum, S. L. and Tansky, J. 1988. "Self-Employment Training as an Intervention Strategy for Displaced or Disadvantaged Workers." *Industrial*

Relations Research Association Proceedings: December, 1987, pp. 346–355.

Manpower Demonstration Research Corp. 1980. *Summary and Findings of the National Supported Work Demonstration.* Cambridge, MA: Ballinger Publishing Co.

Markle, W. D. 1982. *Impact of the Chicago Building Code on Small Businesses.* Chicago: Center for Urban Economic Development, University of Illinois at Chicago.

Maryland Department of Economic and Community Development. 1986. *Financing Overview for Business.*

Maryland Small Business Development Financing Authority. 1986. *Information Brochure—Equity Participation Investment Program in Franchising,* November.

Mayer, H. and Goldstein, S. 1961. *The First Two Years: Problems of Small Firm Survival and Growth.* Washington, DC: Small Business Administration.

McClelland, D. C. 1961. *The Achieving Society.* Princeton, NJ: D. Van Nostrand Co.

McClelland, D. C. and Winter, D. 1969. *Motivating Economic Achievement.* New York: The Free Press.

McDermott, M. J. 1986. "Maryland Targets the 'Disadvantaged.' " *Franchise,* May/June, pp. 42–45.

McGee, T. C. and Young, Y. M. 1977. *Hawkers in Southeast Asian Cities: Planning for the Bazaar Economy.* Ottawa: International Development Research Center.

Meyer, D. B. 1980. *The Positive Thinkers: Religion as Pop Psychology from Mary Baker Eddy to Oral Roberts.* New York: Pantheon Books.

Michaelson, S. 1979. "Community Based Economic Development in Urban Areas." In B. Chinitz, ed., *Central City Economic Development.* Cambridge, MA: Abt Books.

Mier, R. and Wiewel, W. 1983. "Business Activities of Not-for-Profit Organizations." *American Planning Association Journal,* Summer, pp. 316–325.

Mills, C. W. 1951. *White Collar.* New York: Oxford University Press.

Model, S. 1985. "A Comparative Perspective on the Ethnic Enclave: Blacks, Italians, and Jews in New York City." *International Migration Review,* Spring, pp. 65–81.

Moffit, R. 1986. Work Incentives in the AFDC System: An Analysis of the 1981 Reforms. *American Economic Review,* May, pp. 219–223.

Mohorovic, T., ed. 1987. *Business Failure Record.* New York: Dun and Bradstreet.

Moody, J. C. and Fite, G. C. 1984. *The Credit Union Movement: Origins and Development 1850 to 1980.* Dubuque, IA: Kendall/Hunt Publishing Co.

Moser, C.O.N. 1978. "Informal Sector or Petty Commodity Production: Dualism or Dependence in Urban Development." *World Development,* Vol. 6, no. 9/10, pp. 1041–1064.

Mt. Auburn Associates. 1987. *Factors Influencing the Performance of the U.S. Economic Development Administration Sponsored Revolving Loan Funds.* Washington, DC: U.S. Economic Development Administration.

Myrdal, G. 1944. *An American Dilemma: The Negro Problem and American Democracy.* New York: Harper and Brace.

The National Economic Development and Law Center. 1986. *Economic Development Strategies for Low Income Women: A Training Manual.* Berkeley, CA, February.

Nelson, R. E., ed. 1986. *Entrepreneurship and Self-Employment Training.* Manila, Philippines: Asian Development Bank and International Labor Organization.

Noer, H. 1985. *Business Failure Record 1982–1983.* New York: Dun and Bradstreet Economic Analysis Department.

Nye, J. 1985. *Small Business Management Training Tools Directory.* Washington, DC: American Association of Community and Junior Colleges and the Small Business Administration.

Oakes, V. H. 1970. *The Negro Adventure in General Business.* Westport, CT: The Negro University Press.

Obrinsky, M. 1983. *Profit Theory and Capitalism.* Philadelphia: University of Pennsylvania Press.

O'Connell, M. 1986. "Learning from the Third World—New Model of Financing Self-Employment." *The Neighborhood Works,* July–August, pp. 1, 3–4.

OECD. 1986. Self-Employment in OECD Countries. *OECD Employment Outlook,* September, pp. 43–65.

Ofari, E. 1970. *The Myth of Black Capitalism.* New York: Monthly Review Press.

Osthaus, C. R. 1976. *Freedmen, Philanthropy, and Fraud: A History of the Freedman's Bank.* Urbana, IL: University of Illinois Press.

Palmer, J., ed. 1978. *Creating Jobs: Public Employment Programs and Wage Subsidies.* Washington, DC: The Brookings Institution.

Pandey, J. and Tewary, N.B. 1979. "Locus of Control and Achievement Values of Entrepreneurs." *Journal of Occupational Psychology,* pp. 107–111.

Park, T. 1981. "Reconciliation of Personal Income with IRS Taxable Income." *Survey of Current Business,* November.

Perry, C., et al. 1975. *The Impact of Government Manpower Programs.* Philadelphia, PA: The Wharton School Industrial Research Unit, University of Pennsylvania.

Phillips, B. 1984. *Job Generation.* Washington, DC: U.S. Small Business Administration. Office of the Chief Counsel for Advocacy, June.

Piore, M. J. 1971. The Dual Labor Market: Theory and Implications. In David Gordon, ed., *Problems in Political Economy: An Urban Perspective.* Lexington, MA: D. C. Heath and Co., pp. 90–101.

Piore, M. J. and Sabel, C. F. 1984. *The Second Industrial Divide: Possibilities for Prosperity.* New York: Basic Books.

Plattner, S. 1976. "The Economics of Peddling." In Stuart Plattner, ed., *Formal Methods in Economic Anthropology.* Washington, DC: American Anthropological Association, pp. 55–76.

Pomer, M. 1986. "Labor Market Structure, Intragenerational Mobility and Discrimination: Black Male Advancement out of Low-paying Occupations, 1962–1973." Unpublished paper. University of California at Santa Cruz, February.

Portes, A. 1987. "The Social Origins of the Cuban Enclave Economy of Miami." *Sociological Perspectives,* October, pp. 340–372.

Portes, A. and Bach, R. L. 1985. *Latin Journey: Cuban and Mexican Immigrants in the United States.* Berkeley: University of California Press.

Portes, A., Dewey J. Castells, M., and Benton, L., eds. 1988, *The Informal Economy: Studies in Advanced and Less Developed Countries.* Baltimore: Johns Hopkins University.

Portes, A. and Sassen-Koob, S. 1987. "Making It Underground: Comparative Material on the Informal Sector in Western Market Economies." *American Journal of Sociology,* July, pp. 30–61.

Pryde, P. 1987. "Investing in People: A New Approach to Job Creation." In R. Woodson, ed., *On the Road to Economic Freedom.* Washington, DC: Regnery Gateway.

Puls, B. 1987. *State Small Business Entrepreneurial Assistance for the Low Income, Unemployed and Underemployed.* Draft Report. National Conference of State Legislature, September.

———. 1988. *From Unemployed to Self-Employed: A Program Analysis.* Denver, CO: National Conference of State Legislatures.

Purnick, J. 1983. "Koch Vetoes a Plan He Proposed to Limit New York Food Peddlers." *New York Times,* July 23, p. 1.

Quinn, J. F. 1980. "Labor-Force Participation Patterns of Older Self-Employed Workers." *Social Security Bulletin,* April, pp. 17–28.

Raab, S. 1986. "Many Stores Cited for Tax Evasion." *New York Times,* November 2, p. 16.

Revel, C. 1984. *168 More Businesses Anyone Can Start and Make a Lot of Money.* New York: Bantam.

Reynolds, L. 1985. "Unemployment Insurance for Startup Capital?" *In Business,* July–August, pp. 38–39.

Rial, C. and Howell, C. 1986. *Final Report on PRI Financial Intermediaries.* Report to the Ford Foundation, Program Related Investments (PRI). New York.

Ricketts, E. R. and Sawhill, I. V. 1986. "Defining and Measuring the Underclass." Discussion paper. Washington, DC: The Urban Institute.

Roberts, B. 1988. *State CDBG Loan Assistance to Start-up Firms: A Summary and Analysis.* Washington, DC: Council of State Community Affairs Agencies.

Roberts, P. C. 1984. *The Supply Side Revolution.* Cambridge, MA: Harvard University Press.

Roche, G. R. 1979. "Much Ado about Mentors." *Harvard Business Review,* January–February, pp. 14–28.

The Roper Organization. 1987. *The American Dream: A National Survey by the Wall Street Journal.* Princeton, NJ: Dow Jones and Company, Inc.

Rosenberg, S. 1981. "Occupational Mobility and Short Cycles." In F. Wilkinson, ed., *Dynamics of Labor Market Segmentation,* pp. 229–240.

Rosentraub, M. and Taebel, D. 1980. "Jewish Enterprise in Transition: From Collective Self-Help to Orthodox Capitalism." In S. Cummings, ed., *Self-Help in Urban America: Patterns of Minority Business Enterprise.* New York: Kennikat Press, pp. 191–214.

Rotter, J. B. 1966. "Generalized Expectations for Internal Versus External Control for Reinforcement." *Psychological Monographs,* Vol. 80, no. 1, pp. 1–27.

Rozen, M. 1984. "New Networks of Immigrant Enterpreneurs." *New York Times,* September 30, Sec. F, p. 15.

Rugg, C. 1988. "Seed Capital Program Gives Low Income Residents Chance at Entrepreneurship." *Mott Exchange,* Summer, pp. 1–7.

Salo, M. T. 1985. "The Gypsy Niche in North America: Some Ecological Perspectives on the Exploitation of Social Environments." Unpublished paper.

Samuelson, D. S. 1986. *Inner City Economic Development Strategies and New Enterprise Partnerships.* Samuelson Associates, Chicago.

Sanders, J. M. and Nee, V. 1987. "Limits of Ethnic Solidarity in the Enclave Economy." *American Sociological Review,* December, pp. 745–773.

Sarachek, B. 1980. "Jewish American Entrepreneurs." *Journal of Economic History,* June, pp. 359–372.

Scase, R. and Goffee, R. 1980. *The Real World of the Small Business Owner.* London: Croom Helm.

Schell, D. W. and Davig, W. 1981. "The Community Infrastructure of Entrepreneurship: A Sociopolitical Analysis." *Frontiers of Entrepreneurship Research.* Wellesley, MA: Center for Entrepreneurial Studies, Babson College.

Schumpeter, J.A. 1934. *The Theory of Economic Development* Cambridge, MA: Harvard University Press.

Schweider, E. and Schweider, D. 1978. *A Peculiar People: Iowa's Old Order Amish.* Ames: Iowa State University Press.

Scott, E. J. and Stowe, L. B. 1918. *Booker T. Washington: Builder of a Civilization.* New York: Doubleday, Page and Co.

Sekera, J. 1982. *Entrepreneurship Training and Commercial Banks: The 'Be Your Own Boss' " Program—A Case Study.* Corporation for Enterprise Development, Washington, DC.

———. 1983. *Women and Enterprise, Part II.* Washington, DC: American Enterprise Institute.

Sethuraman, S. V. 1976. "The Urban Informal Sector: Concept, Measurement and Policy." *International Labour Review,* July–August, pp. 69–81.

Sexton, D. L. and Bowman, N. 1985. "The Entrepreneur: A Capable Executive and More." *Journal of Business Venturing,* Winter, pp. 129–140.

Shapero, A. 1975. "The Displaced, Uncomfortable Entrepreneur." *Psychology Today,* November, pp. 83–88.

———. 1979. *The Role of Entrepreneurship in Economic Development at the Less-Than-National Level.* Columbus, OH: Ohio State University Faculty of Management Sciences.

———. 1981. "The Role of Entrepreneurship in Economic Development at the Less-Than-National Levels." In Friedman and Schweke, eds., *Expanding the Opportunity to Produce: Revitalizing the American Economy Through New Enterprise Development.* Washington, DC: The Corporation for Enterprise Development.

Shapero, A. and Sokol, L. 1982. "Social Dimensions of Entrepreneurship." In

Kent, Sexton, and Vesper, eds., *Encyclopedia of Entrepreneurship*. Englewood Cliffs, NJ: Prentice-Hall.

Shapiro, G., Hazeltine, F., and Rowe, M. 1978. "Moving Up: Role Models, Mentors, and the Patron System." *Sloan Management Review,* Vol. 19, pp. 51–58.

Shorebank Corporation. 1986. "Good Faith Fund: A Microenterprise Seed Capital Fund Design and Operating Projections." Supplemental Report: Southern Development Bancorporation, an Arkansas Development Bank Holding Company Model. September.

Simon, C. P. and Witte, A. D. 1982. *Beating the System: The Underground Economy*. Boston: Auburn House, 1982.

Smith, J. D., Moyer, T. and Trzcinski, E. 1982. *The Measurement of Selected Income Flows in Informal Markets*. Survey Research Center, University of Michigan.

Smith, J. D. 1987. "Measuring the Informal Economy." In L. Ferman, H. Stuart, and M. Hoyman, eds., *The Informal Economy,* an issue of *The Annals*. September, pp. 83–99.

Solomon, G. 1986. *National Survey of Entrepreneurial Education*, 3d ed. Washington, DC: U.S. Small Business Administration.

South, N. 1982. "The Informal Economy and Local Labour Markets." In J. Laite, ed., *Bibliographical Reports on Local Labour Markets and the Informal Economy*. London: Social Science Research Council.

Sowell, T. 1975. *Race and Economics*. New York: Longman.

Spalter-Roth, R. M. and Zeitz, E. 1985. "Street Vending in Washington, D.C.: Reassessing the Regulation of a 'Public Nuisance.'" Occasional Paper no. 3. Washington, DC Center for Washington Area Studies, The George Washington University.

Spiegelman, R., presider. 1988. "Are Social Experiments a Useful Policy Technique?" Panel session of four papers by G. Burtless, B. Barnow, O. Ashenfelter, J. Heckman, and V. Holtz in *Proceedings of the Fortieth Annual Meetings of the Industrial Relations Research Association,* pp. 268–302.

Star, A. D. 1979. "The Status and Opportunities for Minorities, Women, Aged, and Other Special Interest Groups in Small Business." In A. Cooper and W. Dunkelberg, eds., *The Regional Environment for Small Business Entrepreneurship, Region V*. A Report to the Small Business Administration.

———. 1981. "The Proliferation of Quasi-Businesses." *Journal of Small Business Management,* January, pp. 56–61.

Star, A. D. and Massel, M. 1981. "Survival Rates for Retailers." *Journal of Retailing,* Summer, pp. 87–99.

Stearns, K. 1985a. "Assisting Informal-Sector Microenterprises in Developing Countries." *The Entrepreneurial Economy,* November, 1985, pp. 7–13.

———. 1985b. Assisting Informal-Sector Microenterprises in Developing Countries. Ithaca, NY: Cornell University, Department of Agricultural Economics.

Steinbach, C. 1985a. "Eight Lessons from Europe." *The Entrepreneurial Economy,* January, pp. 4–14.

————. 1985b. "Europeans Are Giving Unemployed an Opportunity to Become Entrepreneurs." *National Journal,* March 9, pp. 527–529.

Stevens, R. L. 1984. "Measuring Minority Business Formation and Failure." *The Review of Black Political Economy,* Spring, pp. 71–84.

Stuart, M. S. 1940. *An Economic Detour: A History of Insurance in the Lives of American Negroes.* College Park, MD: McGrath Publishing Co.

Swain, F. S. 1988. Testimony before the House Select Committee on Hunger: Self-Employment for the Poor: The Potential of Micro-Credit Programs. Washington, DC, April 20.

Sway, M. 1984. "Economic Adaptability: The Case of the Gypsies." *Urban Life,* April, pp. 83–98.

Swayne, C. and Tucker, W. 1973. *The Effective Entrepreneur.* Morristown, NJ: General Learning Press.

Taggart, R. 1981. *A Fisherman's Guide: An Assessment of Training and Remediation Strategies.* Kalamazoo, MI: W. E. Upjohn Institute of Employment Research.

————. 1982. *Hardship: The Welfare Consequences of Labor Market Problems.* Kalamazoo, MI: W. E. Upjohn Institute for Employment Research.

Taub, R. P. 1988. *Community Capitalism: Banking Strategies and Economic Development.* Boston, MA: Harvard Business School Press.

Tawney, R. H. 1926. *Religion and the Rise of Capitalism.* New York: Harcourt, Brace and Co.

Temali, M. and Campbell, C. 1984. *Business Incubator Profiles.* Minneapolis, MN: Hubert Humphrey School of Public Policy.

Tendler, Judith. 1987. "What Ever Happened to Poverty Alleviation?" A Report Prepared for a Review of Ford Foundation Programs on Livelihood, Employment, and Income Generation. New York.

Thompson, Wilbur. 1986. "Cities in Transition." *Annals,* November, pp. 18–34.

Time. 1979. Peddling Pays: Sidewalk Hustlers Multiply. January 22, p. 78.

Toby, Jackson, 1969. *Ex-Offenders as Small Businessmen: Opportunities and Obstacles.* Final Report to the U.S. Department of Labor—Office of Manpower Research (Grant #91-32-68-74).

Todaro, M. 1985. "The Urban Informal Sector." In M. Todaro, *Economic Development in the Third World,* 3d ed. New York: Longman.

Transatlantic Perspectives. 1978. "The New Entrepreneurs of Europe." Spring–Summer.

Trinia, A. R., Welsch, H. T., and Young, E. C. 1984. "Information Search Patterns among Hispanic Entrepreneurs." *Journal of Small Business Management,* October, pp. 39–45.

U.S. Dept. of Commerce. 1986. *Women and Business Ownership: An Annotated Bibliography.* Washington, DC: U.S. Government Printing Office.

U.S. Dept. of Commerce, Bureau of the Census. 1980. *1977 Survey of Minority-Owned Business Enterprises.* Washington, DC: U.S. Government Printing Office.

————. 1985. *1982 Survey of Minority Owned Business Enterprises—Black.* Washington, DC: U.S. Government Printing Office.

————. 1985. *Money Income and Poverty Status of Families: 1984* (Series P-

60), Advance Data, Current Population Reports. Washington, DC: U.S. Government Printing Office.

———. 1987. *1982 Characteristics of Business Owners*. Washington, DC: U.S. Government Printing Office.

U.S. Department of Labor. 1985. *JTPA Fact Sheet*. Washington, DC.

U.S. House of Representatives. 1988. *Access and Availability of Credit to the Poor in Developing Countries and the United States*. Staff Report of the Select Committee on Hunger. Washington, DC: U.S. Government Printing Office.

U.S. Internal Revenue Service. 1979. *Estimates of Income Unreported on Individual Income Tax Returns*. U.S. Government Printing Office. Washington, DC: U.S. Government Printing Office.

U.S. Senate, Committee on Small Business. 1984. *Handbook for Small Business: A Survey of Small Business Programs of the Federal Government*. Washington, DC: U.S. Government Printing Office.

U.S. Small Business Administration. 1985. *Small Business Incubators: New Directions in Economic Development: A Handbook for Community Leaders*. Washington, DC.

———. 1985. *The Recent Growth of Women-Owned Businesses*. Washington, DC: U.S. Small Business Administration, Office of Advocacy, March.

———. 1985. *The State of Small Business*. Washington, DC: U.S. Government Printing Office, May.

———. 1986. *The State of Small Business,* Washington, DC: U.S. Government Printing Office.

———. 1988. *Capital Formation in the States*. Washington, DC: Office of Advocacy, U.S. Small Business Administration.

Useem, M. 1980. "Corporations and Corporate Elite." *Annual Review of Sociology,* Vol. 6, pp. 44–77.

Uzzell, D. J. 1980. "Mixed Strategies and the Informal Sector: Three Faces of Reserve Labor." *Human Organization,* Vol. 34, no. 1, pp. 40–49.

Venable, A. S. 1972. *Building Black Business: An Analysis and a Plan*. New York: Earl G. Graves Publishing.

Viner, J. 1978. *Religious Thought and Economic Society,* ed. by J. Melitz and D. Winch. Durham, NC: Duke University Press.

Waldinger, R. 1986. *Through the Eye of a Needle: Immigrant Enterprise in New York's Garment Trades*. New York: New York University Press.

Walker, J. E. K. 1986. "Racism, Slavery and Free Enterprise: Black Entrepreneurship in the United States Before the Civil War." *Business History Review,* Autumn, pp. 343–382.

Washington, B. T. 1901. *Up from Slavery*. New York: Bantam Books.

Weber, M. 1920. *The Protestant Ethic and the Spirit of Capitalism*. Translated by Talcott Parsons. London, 1930.

Weisbrot, R. 1983. *Father Divine*. Boston: Beacon Press.

Weisser, M. 1986. *A Brotherhood of Memory: Jewish Landsmannshaften in the New World*. New York: Basic Books.

Wetzel, W. E., Jr. 1983. "Angels and Informal Risk Capital." *Sloan Management Review,* Summer, pp. 23–34.

———. 1984. "Venture Capital Network, Inc.: An Experiment in Capital Formation." Paper presented at the Entrepreneurship Research Conference, Georgia Institute of Technology, April 24–25.

Wial, H. J. 1988. *The Transition from Secondary to Primary Employment: Jobs and Workers in Ethnic Neighborhoods*, Ph.D. dissertation. Department of Economics, Massachusetts Institute of Technology.

Wilkerson, I. 1987. "Growth of the Very Poor Is Focus of New Studies." *New York Times,* December 20, p. 15.

Williams, T. and DeLusia, V. 1987. *Venture Capital and Job Development Strategies for the Black Community: A Report on a Policy Forum.* Minneapolis, MN: Hubert H. Humphrey Institute of Public Affairs.

Wilson, K. L. and Martin, W. A. 1982. "Ethnic Enclaves: A Comparison of the Cuban and Black Economies in Miami." *American Journal of Sociology,* July, pp. 135–160.

Wilson, K. L. and Portes, A. 1980. "Immigrant Enclaves: An Analysis of Labor Market Experiences of Cubans in Miami." *American Journal of Sociology,* September, pp. 295–319.

Wilson, M. 1986. "Funder's Network on Women's Economic Development." Ms. Foundation for Women, Inc. Memo.

Wilson, W. J. 1987. *The Truly Disadvantaged: The Inner City, the Underclass, and Public Policy.* Chicago: University of Chicago Press.

Wollard, D. A. 1973. "Small Business Administration Loan Programs." In D. Carson, ed., *The Vital Majority: Small Business in the American Economy.* Washington, DC: U.S. Government Printing Office.

Women's Economic Development Corporation. 1985a. "Celebrating Two Years." *The WEDCO Newsletter,* Fall, p. 1.

Women's Economic Development Corporation. 1985b. "Early lessons from WEDCO Experience." Memo.

Women's Economic Development Corporation. 1985c. "The Business of Small Business." St. Paul, MN: Women's Economic Development Corporation.

Wong, C. C. 1977. "Black and Chinese Grocery Stores in Los Angeles' Black Ghetto." *Urban Life.* January, pp. 439–464.

Woodson, R. L., ed. 1987. *On the Road to Economic Freedom: An Agenda for Black Progress.* Washington, DC: Regnery Gateway.

Wyllie, I. 1954. *The Self-Made Man in America: The Myth of Rags to Riches.* New Brunswick, NJ: Rutgers University Press.

X, M. and Haley, A 1964. *The Autobiography of Malcolm X.* New York: Grace Press.

Yancy, R. J. 1974. *Federal Government Policy and Black Business Enterprise.* Cambridge, MA: Ballinger.

Young, K. Y. 1983. "Family Labor, Sacrifice and Competition: The Case of Korean Owned Fruit and Vegetable Stores in New York City." *Amerasia Journal,* Fall/Winter, pp. 53–71.

Young, K. Y. and Stontz, A.H.L. 1985. "Is Hard Work the Key to Success? A Socioeconomic Analysis of Immigrant Enterprise." Working paper at Center for Applied Research, Pace University, March.

Yunus, M. 1982. *Grameen Bank Project in Bangladesh—A Poverty Focused Rural Development Programme.* Dhaka, Bangladesh: Grameen Bank.

———. 1984. *On Reaching the Poor.* Dhaka, Bangladesh: Grameen Bank.

———. 1987. *Obstacles to Participation in Economic Activity.* Dhaka, Bangladesh: Grameen Bank.

Zeldes, L. A. 1986. "Home Work: It May Be Illegal but Its Popularity Is Booming." *Lincoln Park—Lakeview Booster,* May 7, pp. 1 and 8.

Zey, M. G. 1984. *The Mentor Connection.* Homewood, IL: Dow Jones–Irwin.

Zimmer, C. and Aldrich, H. 1987. "Resource Mobilization Through Ethnic Networks." *Sociological Perspectives,* October, pp. 422–445.

Index

OECD. *See* Organization for Economic Cooperation and Development

Ofari, E., 79, 221

Office of Economic Opportunity, 88

Office of Minority Business Enterprise. *See* Minority Business Development Agency

official vs. unofficial self-employment, 4

Older Americans Act, 137

Omnibus Budget and Reconciliation Act of 1987, 139

Organization for Economic Cooperation and Development (OECD), 48, 109, 221

Osthaus, C. R., 73, 86, 221

Pakistanis, 55

Park, T., 32, 221

People Organized and Working for Economic Rebirth (POWER), 80

perception of credibility, 20, 21

Perry, C., 205, 221

personal goals, 200–201

personality characteristics of the entrepreneur, 16–17

Phillips Curve, 191, 195

Piore, M. J., 9, 221

PISCES Project. *See* Program for Investment in the Small Capital Enterprise Sector

policies for expanding low-income people's participation in self-employment: create supportive institutions, 163–69; develop programs, 150–59; do nothing, 143–44; focus of policies, 143; remove government impediments, 145–50

Pomer, M., 44, 50, 221

Portes, A., 54, 66, 67, 221; with Bach, R. L., 66, 221; with Dewey, J., Castells, M., and Benton, L., 160–61, 221–22; with Sasseen-Koob, 160, 161, 222

poverty alleviation strategies, 10, 83, 183, 203

poverty population, 35

POWER plan. *See* People Organized and Working for Economic Rebirth

PREP, 178

private and voluntary organizations, (PVOs), 177–78

private foundations, 177–78

PRODEME. *See* Program for Development of Micro-Enterprises

producer cooperatives, 10, 165, 166–67, 184

program design, 150–59

Program for Development of Micro-Enterprises (PRODEME), 94–97; micro-enterprise component, 95–96, 96–97; soldiarity groups, 95, 96

Program for Investment in the Small Capital Enterprise Sector, (PISCES), 93–94, 166; characteristics of successful projects, 97; demonstration projects, 93–94; demonstration projects in Dominican Republic, 94–97

Project C.U.R.E., 124–25, 138

promising, 203

Protestant work ethic, 24, 61, 63, 68, 73, 100, 104

Pryde, P., 174, 222

psychological theories of the entrepreneur, 16–17

Puerto Ricans, 52

Puls, Barbara, 136, 222

Quinn, J. F., 36, 222

Rabb, S., 161, 222

Randolph Sheppard Vending Program for the Blind, 154

Reconstruction Finance Corporation, 82

refugee economic adjustment, 68

registration of business, 147

relative satisfaction, 55, 56

religion and charismatic leadership, 168–69, 184; Father Divine, 76–

ABOUT THE AUTHOR

STEVEN BALKIN received his Ph.D. from Wayne State University, specializing in the field of Urban Economics. He taught for nine years in the Department of Criminal Justice at the University of Illinois at Chicago, performing research on issues related to illegal entrepreneurship. He has published on a wide variety of criminal justice topics. Currently he is Associate Professor at Roosevelt University in the Department of Economics. His research interests are poverty and economic development, focusing on issues relating to self-employment and microenterprises.